Deleuze and Music

D1614459

Deleuze and Music

Edited by Ian Buchanan
and Marcel Swiboda

Edinburgh University Press

© The contributors, 2004

Edinburgh University Press Ltd
22 George Square, Edinburgh

Reprinted, 2006

Typeset in 10.5 on 13 Sabon
by Hewer Text Ltd, Edinburgh, and
printed and bound in Great Britain by
Antony Rowe Ltd, Chippenham, Wilts

A CIP record for this book is
available from the British Library

ISBN 0 7486 1891 0 (hardback)
ISBN 0 7486 1869 4 (paperback)

The right of the contributors
to be identified as authors of this work
has been asserted in accordance with
the Copyright, Designs and Patents Act 1988.

Contents

Introduction: Deleuze and Music   1
    Ian Buchanan

1 Studies in Applied Nomadology:
    Jazz Improvisation and Post-Capitalist Markets   20
        Eugene Holland

2 Is Pop Music?   36
    Greg Hainge

3 Deleuze, Adorno, and the Composition of Musical Multiplicity   54
    Nick Nesbitt

4 Affect and Individuation in Popular Electronic Music   76
    Drew Hemment

5 Violence in Three Shades of Metal: Death, Doom and Black   95
    Ronald Bogue

6 Becoming-Music: The Rhizomatic Moment of Improvisation   118
    Jeremy Gilbert

7 Rhythm: Assemblage and Event   140
    Phil Turetsky

8 What I Hear is Thinking Too:
    The Deleuze Tribute Recordings   159
        Timothy S. Murphy

9 Music and the Socio-Historical Real: Rhythm, Series
    and Critique in Deleuze and O. Revault d'Allonnes   176
        Jean-Godefroy Bidima

10 Cosmic Strategies: The Electric Experiments of Miles Davis   196
     Marcel Swiboda

    Notes on Contributors   217
    Index   221

For Sebastian James Buchanan, and Monica and Joseph Swiboda

With thanks to Jackie Jones, Tanya Buchanan, Barbara Engh, Martin McQuillan, Will Rea, Simon O'Sullivan, Ola Stahl, Joanne Crawford, Kurt Hirtler and Tom Syson for their help and support.

Introduction

Deleuze and Music

Ian Buchanan

> In no way do we believe in a fine-arts system; we believe in very diverse
> problems whose solutions are found in heterogeneous arts.
>
> Deleuze and Guattari, *A Thousand Plateaus*

Context

If, as some Deleuzians like to think, *A Thousand Plateaus* is a contemporary version of that fabled key to all mythologies the poor misguided Mr Casaubon spent his life toiling over without ever finishing, then it is a key that is itself in need of a key. Its terminology is abstruse and difficult to engage with and the presentation of its argument so long and convoluted it tends to get lost in the exfoliation of the concepts themselves. Deleuze's citation of Leibniz's lament that just when he thought he'd reached safe harbour he found himself to be still all at sea has a prophetic quality for readers of his own work because it describes exactly how many readers are left feeling by their first encounter with *A Thousand Plateaus*.[1] Yet if you read the conclusion carefully it is clear that the actual architecture of the argument is quite simple and the concepts you really need to understand few in number. This is the gambit of the pages to follow which endeavour to make Deleuze and Guattari's work useable without succumbing to the contemporary compulsion to make it 'user friendly'. In particular, what I aim to do is give the 'new' reader of Deleuze and Guattari enough conceptual know-how to get through the chapter on the refrain, which as this volume testifies several times over is one of the most important and interesting pieces of work ever done on music. I will have succeeded if the reader is able to grasp that while music is a problem of the refrain according to Deleuze and Guattari, the refrain itself is neither the beginning of music nor in itself musical, but the properly anti-musical content of music (Deleuze and Guattari 1987: 300–1).

Deleuze and Guattari say that you can read the chapters of *A Thousand Plateaus* in any order you like, all except the conclusion which they say should be read at the end. The conclusion comprises concepts and the rules of their use stripped of supporting argument, or rather it is the concepts and rules of use operating in a world already understood from a Deleuzian point of view so there is no need of supporting argument. It is comparable in this respect to a scientific treatise. As they point out in *What is Philosophy?*, the difference between science and other discourses is that once an idea has been tested and proven it can then be accepted and used without further need for revision or explanation, that is, we don't need to prove Boyle's Law to use it. If Freud insisted until the end of his life that psychoanalysis was a science it was for this reason; thus Lacan and after him Žižek are entirely correct to insist in their turn that a dogmatic reading of Freud is the only proper way to read him. This doesn't mean it cannot be falsified, nor proven incorrect, only that one must take it as a whole. You cannot accept this part of Freud, his concept of the unconscious, say, and reject another part, like the oedipal complex, because the two are inextricably linked. The former is literally unthinkable without the latter.

For scholars habituated to the idea that Deleuze and Guattari are anarchic nomads for whom anything goes, it must be difficult to imagine either Deleuze or Guattari saying that one should approach their work in this apparently reverential way, even though Deleuze himself is adamant that one should treat other philosophers this way. Yet in spite of their protestations to the contrary, there is no other way: what they present is precisely a system of thought for understanding and engaging with the whole world. They might shy away from speaking of universals or truths but they have no problem putting forward concrete rules, and they have no difficulty saying this is how things really work. Having said that, one must take care not to over-emphasise the science elements in their work at the expense of the other discourses they draw on, especially history and archaeology. The point I'm making is that no single discourse, indeed no single component of their work, may be pulled out and used as an optic through which to view the whole. One must grasp the whole first, all at once, and use that to understand the concepts. That still leaves us with the question of how to read Deleuze and Guattari 'as a whole'.

The answer does not lie as many seem to think in exhaustively sifting through their frequently arcane footnotes and case studies, nor in delving into the sources of these footnotes and the abstruse knowledge that inspired them. Reading up on botany will not bring us any nearer to an understanding of the concept of the rhizome. Studying particle physics will not enhance our grasp of their concept of flows. These are false trails sprung from a failure to grasp that the rhizome in botany is always already a concept and not a thing. It is the botanist's way of articulating the functioning of the plant. If one is to draw inspiration from this source, then it has to be through an examination of the relation between the concept of rhizome and the thing it surveys, especially the way the former decodes the latter and abstracts a transportable 'key'. But this will not bear much fruit because it decontextualises the concept and thereby makes it difficult to see what it is exactly that Deleuze and Guattari do with it. It is this kind of detached reading of Deleuze and Guattari that has prompted readers of secondary texts on their work to think it is all just so much mumbo jumbo. By itself, the rhizome is not an especially interesting concept. Its formulation relies on the simultaneous and mutual presupposition of (at least) five other critical concepts and in their absence it does indeed appear eccentric.

Reading Deleuze and Guattari as a whole means reading their conceptual edifice all at once. This, as Žižek has explained with respect to Lacan and Freud, is what a dogmatic reading actually amounts to. Of course, cutting a swathe through the complex presentation of these concepts is not always so easy a task. It is for this reason that writing users' guides to their work has turned into a veritable cottage-industry in the years since their deaths. My first recommendation, which will no doubt strike many as barbarous, is that readers should simply flip to the concrete rules and abstract machines plateau of *A Thousand Plateaus* and try to get their head around that first. Thus prepared they can voyage into the text forewarned and thus forearmed as to which bits and pieces of it they should pay the closest attention to. My second recommendation is that one take seriously Deleuze and Guattari's suggestion that *A Thousand Plateaus* can be read as one listens to a record – each section implies, and replies to, the one that preceded it and for that very reason functions as a seed or crystal engendering the next. To put it another way, it matters little where you start because wherever it is you do begin you are going to have to backtrack a bit and – at the same time – skip ahead in order to make sense of it all.[2]

So, what are the essential concepts? The conclusion to *A Thousand Plateaus* specifies six: strata and stratification, assemblages, rhizome, plane of consistency (body without organs), deterritorialisation, abstract machines (Diagram and Phylum). All the other concepts put forward by Deleuze and Guattari are thus to be regarded as subsets of these six. Moreover, these six concepts, which as I've emphasised already are all intricately inter-linked, are sufficient to describe the way the world works in its entirety, from its subatomic bases to its furthest-flung cosmic reaches. Before we can explore them in more detail, they first of all need to be contextualised in what may provisionally be termed the schizoanalytic system. In *What is Philosophy?* Deleuze and Guattari say that the purpose of philosophy is to invent new concepts. If we inquire why philosophy should want to do that, or more generally why such a discourse should be of interest or indeed use to humankind then the answer would be it helps us to overcome the baleful condition of a life determined by inadequate ideas. It is not the novelty of the concepts that is crucial, but whether or not they manage to penetrate the thick veil of phantoms, phantasms, superstitions and opinions generated by the manifold sad passions shrouding daily life. Inadequate ideas are ideas ignorant of causes. In contrast, adequate ideas are those that have a sound understanding of the true cause of things.

Deleuze's entire philosophy is dedicated to the mission of overcoming inadequate ideas.[3] That is why, in spite of its admittedly abstract appearance it is nonetheless appropriate to describe it as a practical philosophy. This is the sense, too, in which is appropriate to describe it as an experimental philosophy. It is here that the contrast with dialectics, a contrast Deleuze and Guattari frequently (but by no means straightforwardly) foreground themselves, proves instrumental to an understanding of the whole.[4] Dialectics is a theory of synthesis, it supposes that the world is in its first flush chaotic, a teeming multitude of random atoms pinging off each other with no discernible order or purpose, the proverbial night when all cows are black. As soon as the mind grasps these atoms it introduces order – it negates this state of negativity and produces a view of things that can be affirmed. The problem Deleuze and Guattari have with this position is that it supposes that the end point, understanding, is radically different from the starting point, chaos, without being able to explain how one kind of substance can be transformed into another. For Deleuze and Guattari, chaos is not a starting point, it is an end point – it literally spells the end of things – we never fully escape. Theirs is not a theory of synthesis as such because for them everything is always already connected. How could it not be? We cannot imagine something that is truly disconnected because in the very process of imagining it we proceed by way of connections. What varies then is the modality of things – our concepts, our thoughts, indeed being itself, can be more or less chaotic, more or less ordered, but never completely chaotic or completely ordered. This is why their philosophy is a philosophy of immanence: one is always in the middle of things.

Deleuze's book on Spinoza, *Expressionism in Philosophy*, is for this reason an essential key to unlocking his work. There he maps out in detail the philosophy of connections which careful readers of *A Thousand Plateaus* will see underpins that work as well as its ethical and conceptual basis. Readers who get confused about whether Deleuze and Guattari are pro-drugs or anti-drugs, for or against this or that sexual perversion, should be more attentive to this element of the work's composition because it is evident that Deleuze and Guattari do maintain a clear line on what is ethical.[5] Theirs is not an ethics that decides in advance how one ought to proceed, nor does it exercise either a power of judgement or selection; it is, rather, a creative, or experimental ethics, which is always on the look-out for the way forward. As Badiou correctly says, Deleuze's philosophy entails an ethics of life, but this does not mean as he erroneously concludes that it is secretly a philosophy of death. Badiou thinks philosophy must proceed from difference – life and death – whereas Deleuze takes the view that philosophy and indeed life is difference itself (as an ongoing process of differentiating) (Badiou 2000: 12–15). Difference is not something we uncover like a lost sock under the bed, it is what we produce through the act of living itself. If Deleuze is sometimes described as a vitalist, and if he doesn't himself reject this term altogether, it is because he is prepared to say that even the inorganic can have life insofar as it engenders difference.

Concepts

If we keep in mind the purpose of schizoanalysis, namely to overcome inadequate ideas, we will have much less difficulty in working out the nature and function of the concepts it has produced. Following Spinoza, Deleuze and Guattari identify two types of connections – those that lead to composition and those that result in decomposition. For convenience, they refer to the former as 'connections' and the later as 'conjugations'. But they insist there is no such thing as a pure connection, so a theory of connections is more accurately described as a theory of mixture or coexistence. The therapeutic implication one must draw from this is that one can only reduce the number of conjugations by actively increasing the connections, but one cannot escape conjugating powers altogether. This is why they describe the drug addict's body without organs as bad, or botched: in the depths of his or her stupefaction, the addict no longer knows how to make connections. Paranoia grips them and they retreat into their narcotic-induced Plato's cave. What I termed their ethics has no other formulation than this: increase the power of connection and thereby decrease the power of conjugation. Get drunk on water so as to keep alive the power of connection. This is schizoanalysis in a nutshell. With this in hand, we can now turn to six concepts I said we need to get a handle on to understand Deleuze and Guattari properly.

1. stratification
2. assemblages
3. rhizome
4. plane of consistency
5. deterritorialisation
6. abstract machines

Stratification produces strata, of which there are three kinds – physicochemical, organic, anthropomorphic (or alloplastic). Human history is largely confined to the third stratum, but it is shaped by its relation to the other two. Strata are in effect the bedrock of all existence, they are literally the 'stuff' of existence. Outside strata neither forms nor substances, organisation nor development, content nor expression, exist. It is a chaotic, disarticulated realm not even supported by the minimal connection of rhythms. Life cannot obtain there. So while destratification is constantly courted for its liberating effects, one must nevertheless proceed with caution because moving too quickly can result in profound psychosocial disconnection, autism, catatonia, even death; in fear of these eventualities, one can also swing back towards even more rigorous forms of stratification such as fascism. But if one does not destratify, at least a little, one winds up stultified, hide-bound, a postmodern version of the 'organisation man'. Striking a balance between these two outcomes is the basic day-to-day task we must all take up in the course of our lives.

The image Deleuze and Guattari give of a stratum is instructive. Rather than the expected picture of a visibly layered slice of rock torn from the pages of a geology textbook, they instead indicate a lobster. More particularly, as the frontispiece to the chapter emphasises, it is the creature's literally gigantic pincers that catches their imagination. So although they speak of strata in terms of layers, the defining picture we should keep in mind is that of a pair of pincers because Deleuze and Guattari quite precisely define strata as double articulations – that is, articulations that not only travel in pairs, but are in fact double in themselves. Seemingly prosaically, they also describe strata as judgements of God, or little death sentences, but as we'll see in a moment these descriptions are apt indeed. Although the distinction between the two articulations is real, it is also arbitrary inasmuch as the actual order of the articulations remains fully reversible. It makes no sense – or, rather, it is sheerly a matter of perspective – to determine which articulation comes first because the process is not stepped.

One articulation does not lead to the next, rather the two occur at the same time in a relationship of mutual presupposition. In other words, one cannot retroactively construct a moment that is prior to articulation; that is why Deleuze and Guattari constantly insist everything takes place in the middle. If we ask what an act or event consists of, we are forced, they say, to discriminate between actions and passions affecting bodies and those acts which impact not on the body as such, but on its incorporeal attributes. Deleuze and Guattari use the example of a judge's sentence which transforms the accused into a convict:

> In effect, what takes place beforehand (the crime of which someone is accused), and what takes place after (the carrying out of the penalty) are actions-passions affecting bodies (the body of property, the body of the victim, the body of the convict, the body of the prison); but the transformation of the accused into a convict is a pure instantaneous act or incorporeal attribute that is the expressed of the judge's sentence. (Deleuze and Guattari 1987: 80–1)

On their view, form organises matter into a succession of compartmentalised and hierarchised 'substances' or 'formed matters' or what, in a different critical language is called 'content'. But, this is content viewed from the double perspective of selection and succession: not a given, content is chosen, and always in a specific order – man before woman, white before black, self before or other, and so forth. The order itself has no intrinsic meaning, but once in place it acquires a meaning. Like sedimentary rock caught in the grips of the earth itself, this content is transformed into a stable and functional form which is then actualised in everyday life, producing new sets of contents.

Judith Butler might have saved herself many of the conceptual agonies she suffers in trying to think through the 'materiality of the body' (as she puts it) if only she was not so prejudiced against Deleuze and Guattari (Butler 1993). Her own work shows that gender cannot be thought except as a double articulation, but she introduces an unnecessary complication (or obfuscation, depending on your perspective) in the form of identification. As the example of the judge's sentence makes obvious, the convict does not need to identify with his new status for that status to impact on his existence. He is a convict regardless of his fantasies to the contrary, and his body will be subjected to the actions-passions associated with that state of being whether he acknowledges his changed symbolic status or not. By the same token, the power of gender as an expressed resides in the fact that it does not matter if one chooses not to identify oneself as either 'man' or 'woman', those attributes will still impact on your existence because they are the form for which your body is the content. The apparent facticity of the body – the penis, the vagina, and so forth – are, as Butler rightly argues, always already caught in the pincers of cultural determinations, so that one can never say 'sex' is ungendered; and yet, 'sex' (as a set of bodily facts) clearly does function as a kind of bedrock or presupposition for gender that gives it a relative autonomy. It is the mutually reinforcing quality of the sex/gender divide that Deleuze and Guattari mean by stratification or double articulation. One cannot escape this deadlock because the terms of the debate are in themselves a trap, or double bind, that draws one ever deeper into its clutches the more one tries to 'deconstruct' it.

If gender is a cultural construct, what is to prevent whatever succeeds it from also being one? As Deleuze put it in *Difference and Repetition*, what we need to realise is that the real problem philosophy must confront is not the difference between forms of thought, but the seemingly unavoidable fact that thought must have a form. One could surely say the same about gender. The essential problem isn't how one defines gender – or, how accommodating of 'difference' it can be made to be – but the seemingly inescapable fact that we must have *a* gender. But we should not conclude from this, as Butler rightly highlights, that one can simply set aside gender by upholding sex as its genderless opposite. Sex is content to gender's form. As such, it is just as much a 'formed matter' as gender, albeit of a different order. The body is gendered (gender steals our body) because gender exists, because that is what gender does, it genders; but gender itself exists because other discursive regimes such as the 'family' require a system of differentiation in order to function (Deleuze and Guattari 1987: 276). In other words, gender exists because from the point of view of another stratum there are bodies standing in need of regulation. So gender is a stratum, but it is always already the substratum of another stratum, which in turn is the substratum of still another stratum.

The essential question we have to answer concerning strata, Deleuze and Guattari say, is what accounts, simultaneously, for their unity and diversity? For strata do have a unity of composition, but this does not prevent them from varying quite considerably from one stage of their existence to the next. To explain this we need to look more carefully at the relations between individual strata and indeed within strata. For in spite of the static-seeming terminology, strata are anything but inert. Doubtless this is why Deleuze and Guattari prefer the image of a snapping pair of pincers to layers of rock sitting on top of one another as stately and passively as the dead in their sarcophagi. But as vivid as this picture is, it does not help us to think through a problem such as the one sketched above, namely the interrelation of powerful discursive regimes like sex and gender. Having made the crucial point that strata are forms of articulation that select matter and form it into substances (first articulation) and then encode it in such a way that it can serve as the basis of further articulations that can use it without either defining it or explaining it (second articulation), Deleuze and Guattari go on to explain that each stratum in fact comprises of four distinct articulations, or what they call milieus: (1) an exterior milieu of materials; (2) an interior milieu of composing elements; (3) an intermediary milieu of membranes or limits; and (4) an annexed or associated milieu.

If we take the example of the seed and the crystalline stratum, we see that the interior and exterior milieu are both interior to the stratum. The difference between them is relative, a matter of organisation, because for the crystal to form the seed must interiorise the solution in which it is suspended, but at the same time assert its exteriority so as to prickle the solution into settling around it. It must become like the solution, that is, crystalline, and at the same time remain different enough to provoke the response, that is, crystallisation. Similarly, the solution itself has to relax its interior organisation sufficiently to allow a new form of organisation to develop and overtake it. This is why Deleuze and Guattari always insist that all becoming is double – it can only take place when, as in this example, there is an aptitude, as they put it, for a switch from one form of organisation to another. In every encounter, the distinction that needs to be made isn't between inside and outside, interior and exterior, but between the different types of organisation – the crystalline and the crystal. But this is all sounding very scientific and abstract. In the chapter of the Wolf-Man, we are presented with the same theoretical problem, but here milieus are referred to by their other name, or rather their technical name: multiplicities. Here, then, is a classic instance where an oscillatory reading strategy pays dividends – by looking back at the earlier chapter we can clarify the present concern, and, at the same time, shed light on what until now has appeared not a little mysterious.

What does it mean to love somebody, they ask.

> It is always to seize that person in a mass, extract him or her from a group, however small, in which he or she participates, whether it be through the family only or through something else, then to find that person's own packs, the multiplicities he or she encloses within himself or herself which may be of an entirely different nature. To join them to mine, to make them

penetrate mine, and for me to penetrate the other person's. (Deleuze and Guattari 1987: 35)

When we first meet the other, they, like us, are an undifferentiated – or, rather, an indiscernible – particle in a larger mass (society, the family), so the first thing we need to do is identify their exterior milieu (that which sets them apart – a laugh or smile, they way they hold their head), which is not their public face so much as their private face in public. But then we have to break through that facade to find their interior milieu. What does that little smile conceal? At the same time, we have to open ourselves to them, communicate, so that our respective multiplicities may intermingle and form a new multiplicity. The exterior milieus may be many and varied, however, and quite frequently they get in the way of what might perhaps have been a harmonious mixing.

> For Kafka, Felice is inseparable from a certain social machine, and, as a representative of the firm that manufactures them, from parlograph machines; how could she not belong to that organisation in the eyes of Kafka, a man fascinated by commerce and bureaucracy? But at the same time, Felice's teeth, her big carnivorous teeth, send her racing down other lines, into the molecular multiplicities of a becoming-dog, a becoming-jackal . . . (Deleuze and Guattari 1987: 36)

Between the different types of multiplicity, molar (exterior milieu) and molecular (interior milieu) there are intermediary milieus – or epistrata – that function like membranes, regulating the exchanges between the milieu and the resulting transformations in organisation.

These internal exchanges tell us how the stratum functions, but not yet how it lives. To really begin to 'breathe' the stratum needs to capture new energy sources – that is what the associated milieus are, 'sources of energy different from alimentary materials' (Deleuze and Guattari 1987: 51). Capture requires the perception of susceptible materials, that is, the sensing of materials the stratum can incorporate into itself, and the corresponding ability to undertake that incorporation.

> The development of the associated milieus culminates in the animal worlds described by von Uexküll, with all their active, perceptive, and energetic characteristics. The unforgettable associated world of the Tick, defined by its gravitational energy of falling, its olfactory characteristic of perceiving sweat, and its active characteristic of latching on. (Deleuze and Guattari 1987: 51)

All confrontations with the other take place in the space between this outer ring of the associated milieu, or the parastratum, and the exterior limit in its constantly modified form, or the epistratum. The implication of this last sentence is that the exterior limit is itself a multiplicity, not a rigid cable-like perimeter. And it is here that we learn of the origin of the concept of the line of flight, one of Deleuze and Guattari's more nebulous terms.

> Since the associated milieu always confronts a milieu of exteriority with which the animal is engaged and in which it takes necessary risks, a *line of flight* must be preserved to enable the animal to regain its associated milieu when danger appears . . . A second kind of line of flight arises when the associated milieu is rocked by blows from the exterior forcing the animal to abandon it and strike up an association with new portions of exteriority, this time leaning on its interior milieus like fragile crutches. (Deleuze and Guattari 1987: 55)

In other words, the strata are very far from static, unchanging lumps of rock – they are dynamic, complex, articulated formations, restlessly pushing against internal and external limits.

Strata are the bedrock of existence, which is why I have dwelled on them at such length, but there is more to existence than sheer respiration, more even that the instinctive fight or flight perception-responses of animals. Thus we turn to one of Deleuze and Guattari's more complex concepts. Sitting over the top of, but also suffusing it, is the assemblage which as Deleuze and Guattari put it, is the unconscious in person (Deleuze and Guattari 1987: 36). It is tempting to treat strata, now, as the life of instincts which the assemblage then manages, but strata are not to be confused with instincts or drives and the assemblage does not belong to a different order of being from the strata. To think otherwise would be to return us to Freud. Assemblages operate within strata, but they operate in 'zones where milieus become decoded: they begin by extracting a *territory* from the milieus' (Deleuze and Guattari 1987: 502). Decoded does not mean deciphered, rather it literally means the code has been detached from a milieu and made available for an alternative use. Think of costume design. If you want to dress like a bee, you can create a costume that is a facsimile of a bee, or you can attach a couple of yellow and black ribbons to your skirt and perhaps put some antennae-like things in your hair and thereby call to mind a certain beeishness. The first strategy is mimetic and the result is usually laughable because it calls to mind nothing so much as a someone in a costume; the second strategy, by contrast, is expressive, and usually more successful because it calls to mind not someone in a costume, but what Deleuze and Guattari would call a 'becoming-bee'.[6] This strategy works by showing that the bee's essential characteristics are not intrinsic as such, but extrinsic and detachable, and that man's fixed exterior is permeable. As such, Deleuze and Guattari give the suggestive name 'assemblage converter' to these decoded fragments (Deleuze and Guattari 1987: 325).

Few words are more closely associated with the work of Deleuze and Guattari than 'rhizome', but for this very reason it has been accorded an overly luminous status. Bad readers of their work make it their practice to uncover what might be called the rhizome within: internet dating, it is claimed, is rhizomic because it is (allegedly) all about making unexpected connections; likewise window-shopping in a large mall is rhizomic, for pretty much the same reason. For Deleuze and Guattari, however, the rhizome is a monitory example of the ineradicable ambivalence of all practices because, as they put it, 'rhizome lines oscillate between tree lines that segment and even stratify them, and lines of flight or rupture that carry them away' (Deleuze and Guattari 1987: 506). The rhizome is the kind of matrix (for the want of a better word) one forms if one is able to proceed by way of connections; the arborescent is the kind of matrix one forms if one is only able to proceed by way of conjugations. Reality, though, as I've stressed already, is generally an unstable admixture of the two. But we're still missing something essential here because the picture that is emerging is that of a binary between two states of being: rhizomic and arborescent. This is not at all what Deleuze and Guattari have in mind. Part of the problem, of course, is that the term itself through its apparent debt to botany introduces a profoundly mystifying sense of indirection.

As we pass from the assemblage to the rhizome we shift our concerns from the plane of organisation to the plane of consistency. And as we'll see, it is the term 'consistency' that presses itself forward more and more as the linchpin in our understanding of the whole. We can perhaps clarify the difference between these two planes by turning our attention to the body without organs, the plane of consistency's other name.[7] The body without organs is not a notion or concept, strictly speaking, but a practice or set of practices. 'You never reach the body without organs, you can't reach it, you are forever attaining it, it is a limit' (Deleuze and Guattari 1987: 150). The Body without Organs is the absolute limit of stratification. This is what Artaud is referring to when he says he wants to have done with judgement of god: strata. It is helpful at this point to ask why should Deleuze and Guattari want to introduce still another 'concept', what problem does it engage? Evolution: it is the constant besetting problem of all Deleuze and Guattari's work. 'It is difficult to elucidate the system of the strata without seeming to introduce a kind of cosmic or even spiritual evolution from one to the other, as if they were arranged in stages and ascended degrees of perfection' (Deleuze and Guattari 1987: 69). The problem, in other words, is how to explain the transformation of the strata without having to suppose some grand all-too-Hegelian Becoming?[8] The answer, not unexpectedly, is in the thinking-through of the nature of the relation between the strata and the body without organs.

Stratification is a thickening of the surface of the body without organs. Moreover, it is secondary, not primary: 'absolute deterritorialisation is there from the beginning, and the strata are spin-offs, thickenings on a plane of consistency that is everywhere, always primary and always immanent.. In other words, 'we cannot content ourselves with a dualism or summary opposition between the strata and the destratified plane of consistency' (Deleuze and Guattari 1987: 70). Thickening is a change in consistency – think of the way cream can be thickened into butter. It implies a propensity in the substance itself, rather than the introduction of a foreign agent. Thickening is thus a properly immanent process. In talking about the plane of consistency, then, we must take care not to emphasise the plane at the expense of consistency, since the plane is itself the effect of consistency.[9] Consistency, meanwhile, is the effect of the types of relations a particular substance embodies and the changes to these that ensue when they enter into relations with other substances. If you freeze milk, for instance, it becomes a solid precisely because the particles that compose it have slowed down to such an extent that the intermediary relations between them have changed nature, once fluid connections become rigid conjugations. Frozen milk is stratification taken to its death-like extreme, while thawed milk is the body without organs, the point being that each state is inherent in the other, not merely as a potential that may or may not be realised, but as what it is right now: frozen milk is milk that has been slowed down and thawed milk is milk that has been accelerated.

As the above examples illustrate, it is appropriate in many respects to describe Deleuze and Guattari's thinking as a philosophy of limits. They theorise several kinds of limit, but two are especially important: the relative limit and the absolute limit. Consider the question: how many people are there in a crowd? If we start with just one person, then obviously we don't have a crowd. But if we have 100, then perhaps we do. This is, of course a question of consistency. What is the precise point between these two numbers, 1 and 100, when one can say with confidence that a crowd has formed? By the same token, if the number were to increase from 100 to 101, would we have more of a crowd? The line separating the small group and the crowd is the line of deterritorialisation

– the absolute limit which if crossed brings about generalised transformation. As such, the multiplicity of whatever size, small group or crowd, has a definite border (Deleuze and Guattari 1987: 245).

Deterritorialisation is primary – stratification is secondary. This being so, it is actually misleading to speak of *de*territorialisation as a process that takes away the territory from some previously existing entity. By the same token, *re*territorialisation cannot be a process of restoring a territory to an entity that has been deprived of one without implying that deterritorialisation is in fact a process of *de*territorialisation. In one of the least noticed sentences in the whole of the Deleuzian corpus, we are told in very precise terms that reterritorialisation is a compensation and substitute for deterritorialisation: 'Anything can serve as a reterritorialisation, in other words, "stand for" the lost territory; one can reterritorialise on a being, an object, an apparatus or system . . .' (Deleuze and Guattari 1987: 508; ellipsis in original). Lacan's notion of the phallus is doubtless the grandest of all reterritorialisations: it compensates our 'lack' and 'stands for' an impossible plenitude.

> Reterritorialisation must not be confused with a return to a primitive or older territoriality: it necessarily implies a set of artifices by which one element, itself deterritorialised, serves as a new territoriality for another, which has lost its territoriality as well. (Deleuze and Guattari 1987: 174)

At last, then, we come to the abstract machine. The abstract machine operates in concrete assemblages. Its operation is defined by deterritorialisation – it opens the assemblage to new forms: it is what enables the assemblage to become other than it is. It is not intrinsically 'good' however, since just as it can open assemblages it can close them as well. It is an amphibious as well as an ambivalent operator, able to function equally well on the plane of consistency and the stratum.

> The abstract machine exists enveloped in each stratum, whose Ecumenon or unity of composition it defines, and developed on the plane of consistency, whose destratification it performs (the Planomenon). Thus when the assemblages fit together the variables of a stratum as a function of its unity, they also bring about a specific effectuation of the abstract machine as it exists outside the strata. (Deleuze and Guattari 1987: 73)

It might be more helpful if we come at this from a different direction and ask: How does it work? Deleuze and Guattari devote one whole chapter to answering this question by discussing one type of abstract machine – the face – which because of its neurotic character tends to make the concept seem as though it refers to symptom formation rather than an affirmative aspect of the unconscious. Their point, though, is that the assemblage is susceptible to seizure from the outside. Sometimes it takes the form of a neurosis, at others a revelation, and at still others a liberation. Abstract machines are our means of making and changing the sense of our circumstances.[10] If the assemblage is the body of the world, then the abstract machine is its expression.

> Love is an intermingling of bodies that can be represented by a heart with an arrow through it, by a union of souls, etc., but the declaration 'I love you' expresses a noncorporeal attribute of bodies, the lover's as well as that of the loved one. (Deleuze and Guattari 1987: 81)

Whether I have provided sufficient explanation for the six concepts I claim define the Deleuzian universe will be found out, I suppose, in the next section as I use them to unpack (in a deliberately preparatory way) just what I think Deleuze and Guattari mean to say about music. My aim here is simply to initiate a conversation the rest of the volume will continue, each author providing a different and at times conflicting perspective on essentially the same set of problems motivating me here: What do Deleuze and Guattari think music is? Can we use their understanding of it to enhance our own? Is it cogent? Does it work?

Music

To begin with, Deleuze and Guattari define music as a problem of content and expression.

> What does music deal with, what is the content indissociable from sound expression? It is hard to say, but it is something: *a* child dies, a child plays, a woman is born, a woman dies, a bird arrives, a bird flies off. We wish to say that these are not accidental themes in music (even if it is possible to multiply examples), much less imitative exercises; they are something essential. (Deleuze and Guattari 1987: 299)

Why is music so often concerned with death – death of a child, death of a mother and so on? Because, Deleuze and Guattari reason, of 'the "danger" inherent in any line that escapes, in any line of flight or creative deterritorialisation: the danger of veering toward destruction, toward abolition' (Deleuze and Guattari 1987: 299). Death, as the moment when we confront the point where the line of flight meets the line of abolition, is a necessary dimension of music, or the sound assemblage. Music doesn't awaken a death instinct, that isn't why it gives us a taste for death; it confronts death, stares it in the face. This is why the refrain is the content proper to music: the refrain is our means of erecting, hastily if needs be, a portable territory that can secure us in troubled situations. We whistle in the dark to keep the phantoms of our mind's imagining at bay; we sing as we march off to war to give us not merely courage but an intimation of immortality; we hum as we work to lighten our burden. In every case, our music-making is expressive inasmuch as it serves to construct a territory. That territory defends against the anxieties, fears, pressures we feel; it doesn't do away with them, of course, but it gives them a different form.

The refrain is the block of content proper to music, but it should not be mistaken for the origin of music. 'The refrain is rather a means of preventing music, warding it off, or forgoing it' (Deleuze and Guattari 1987: 300). That said, without the refrain music would not exist, 'because music takes up the refrain, lays hold of it as a content in a form of expression, because it forms a block with it and takes it somewhere else' (Deleuze and Guattari 1987: 300). Music as should now be apparent is a double articulation: on the one hand, it brings together a block of content (the refrain) and a form of expression (becoming) – it is this latter idea which causes the most problems because it is difficult to speak about 'becoming' without lapsing into a discourse of transmogrification or some other teratological sub-branch of evolutionary theory. But if it doesn't refer to a process of mutation, then what does it refer to? And, more importantly, I suppose, how does it help us to understand music? We can approach these questions in a very practical manner – as I've said above, Deleuze and Guattari's philosophy is foremost a practical philosophy. What sound do horses' hooves make? They clip-clop down a cobbled lane as the milkman returns home after a tiring night's work, or they thunder across the turf in a race against time and perhaps even death: the sound, in other words, is always already something else, a homecoming, a race or a rescue. And even as one writes 'thundering hooves' one is already thinking of kettledrums. Thus in conjuring up the horse, the musician does not try to imitate the clip-clop or thundering of hooves, he or she writes music that calls to mind a homecoming or a rescue. This is why becoming is double: the sound of the horse is the sound of homecoming while homecoming is the sound of clip-clopping hooves on a cobbled street.[11]

Music lays hold of the refrain, but doesn't extinguish it. This is why we are always lapsing back into its grips – we remember the chorus of pop songs, we hum their riffs and we dance to rhythms blissfully ignorant of the words that accompany them.[12] By the same token, since 'its force of deterritorialisation is the strongest, it also effects the most massive of reterritorialisations, the most numbing, the most redundant' (Deleuze and Guattari 1987: 348). This is its potential fascism: we rally to war to the sound of trumpets. So what is a refrain? It is a crystal.

> It acts upon that which surrounds it, sound or light, extracting from it various vibrations, or decompositions, projections or transformations. The refrain also has a catalytic function: not only to increase the speed of the exchanges and reactions in that which surrounds it, but also to assure indirect inter-actions between elements of devoid of so-called natural affinity, and thereby to form organised masses. (Deleuze and Guattari 1987: 348)

I haven't tried to be exhaustive. There is of course much more to be said about what Deleuze and Guattari have to say about music, not to mention the half-dozen concepts I have foregrounded. My hope is that what I have set out here will, in its own way, function like a crystal and bring about the crystallisation of still more concepts.

References

Badiou, A. (2000), *Deleuze: The Clamor of Being*, trans. L. Burchill, Minneapolis: University of Minnesota Press.

Buchanan, I. (2000), *Deleuzism: A Metacommentary*, Edinburgh: Edinburgh University Press.

Buchanan, I. (2002), 'Deleuze and Hitchcock: Schizoanalysis and *The Birds*', *Strategies: Journal of Theory, Culture and Politics*, 15 (1): 105–18.

Butler, J. (1993), *Bodies that Matter: On the Discursive Limits of Sex*, London: Routledge.

Deleuze, G. and Guattari, F. (1987), *A Thousand Plateaus: Capitalism and Schizophrenia*, trans. B. Massumi, Minneapolis: University of Minnesota Press.

Deleuze, G. (1990), *Expressionism in Philosophy: Spinoza*, trans. M. Joughin, New York: Zone Books.

Deleuze, G. (1994) *Difference and Repetition*, trans. P. Patton, New York: Columbia University Press.

Deleuze, G. and Guattari, F. (1994), *What is Philosophy?* New York: Columbia University Press.

Stivale, C. (1998), *The Two-Fold Thought of Deleuze and Guattari: Intersections and Animations*, London: The Guildford Press.

Williams, J. (2003), *Gilles Deleuze's* Difference and Repetition: *A Critical Introduction and Guide*, Edinburgh: Edinburgh University Press.

Žižek, S. (2004), *Organs without Bodies: On Deleuze and Consequences*, London: Routledge.

Notes

1. The trouble starts when one uses this feeling as the basis for reading Deleuze and Guattari, as Stivale (1998) does, because what ensues cannot but be an empty gesture by virtue of the fact it reterritorialises on memory. Its gambit is that of the photograph not the diagram.

2. I must admit, though, this is perhaps an old-fashioned or outmoded way of listening to a record (itself an utterly outmoded piece of technology). For instance, I don't know if today's listeners of Britney Spears or Justin Timberlake listen to their CDs with the slightest concern for its gestalt. Maybe the gestalt mode of listening passed with the concept album of the prog' rock era? Of course, if one follows Adorno in thinking that listening today has become thoroughly deconcentrated, it may be asking too much to think we listen to the whole song. Certainly, as I have argued elsewhere (Buchanan 2000), there is reason to think it is only the chorus that is really listened to nowadays. At any rate, it should be clear that what I am proposing is an interactive mode of reading that doesn't restrict itself to a linear working through of the text.

   That said, I would want to distinguish what I am saying from Brian Massumi's uptake of this idea in his foreword to A *Thousand Plateaus* because whereas he uses it to suggest that one may pick and choose which parts of the whole one utilises, my suggestion is the opposite: we should read it in an interactive fashion so as to grasp the whole.

3. For a detailed explanation of this point, see Buchanan 2000: 30–2.

4. In *Difference and Repetition*, perhaps mischievously, Deleuze describes his goal as developing a 'superior dialectics'. I have long held, though, that this remark needs to be taken seriously as indicating that Deleuze's precise goal was to reinvent dialectics. Thus projects like Zizek's (2004) which try to show Deleuze is dialectical in the old-fashioned sense are to be regarded as 'revisionist' in precisely the sense Žižek would understand that term, namely a deliberate and ideologi-cally-driven attempt to rewrite the master's texts. More interesting, then, is Williams (2003) project, which tries to show just what Deleuze's 'superior dialectics' would look like.

5. 'Drugs are too unwieldy to grasp the imperceptible and becomings-imperceptible; drug users believed that drugs would grant them the plane, when in fact the plane must distil its own drugs, remaining master of speeds and proximities' (Deleuze and Guattari 1987: 286).

6. 'There is a territory precisely when milieu components cease to be directional, becoming dimensional instead, when they cease to be functional to become expressive' (Deleuze and Guattari 1987: 315).

7. Žižek (2004) thinks the opposite of the body without organs is something he refers to as organs without bodies, but this just shows how inattentive a reader of Deleuze and Guattari he is because the idea of organs without bodies is a nonsense in the Deleuzian system. As such, Žižek's intervention is not a useful estrangement of Deleuze's work, but a glib obfuscation that tends to confirm Deleuze's view that a philosopher must be allowed to ask his own questions and formulate her own problems.

8. I have always felt, and here Deleuze's use of the term 'stages' is a clue, that Hegel is a codeword in Deleuze's vernacular for Stalin, or more generally for any view of the future that considers it both desirable and possible to programme it, regardless of human cost. I think this is the light against which one has to read Deleuze's sometimes Fourieresque emphasis on spontaneity. For Deleuze, Hegel stands for a future proofed against contingency, and that as far he is concerned is genuinely monstrous. Those commentators (Badiou and Žižek, in particular) who have argued that Deleuze's Hegel is a caricature are correct, as far as that goes, but they need to take it a step further and ask what allegorical purpose that caricature serves. It is in order to answer these types of questions that we urgently need a good biography of Deleuze.

9. Deleuze and Guattari 1987: 270.

10. In a different place, I have tried to show how the notion of the abstract machine can be used to 'analyse' a text in a manner comparable to psychoanalysis. See Buchanan 2002.
11. 'When Hitchcock does birds, he does not reproduce bird calls, he produces an electronic sound like a field of intensities or a wave of vibrations, a continuous variation, like a terrible threat welling up inside us' (Deleuze and Guattari 1987: 305).
12. For me, the striking instance of this is the white Australian reception of Yothu Yindi's 'Treaty' and Midnight Oil's 'Beds are Burning' – you'd never know these were songs about land rights from the way they were embraced by essentially the same people who voted for, or at least expressed a certain sympathy for, Pauline Hanson's One Nation.

Chapter 1

Studies in Applied Nomadology: Jazz Improvisation and Post-Capitalist Markets

Eugene Holland

What follows is best understood as a kind of thought-experiment: 'To think is to experiment', Deleuze and Guattari maintain. Furthermore, this thought-experiment has a utopian strain, involving an intractable refusal of the present; it is the utopian impulse that 'links philosophy with its own epoch', Deleuze and Guattari insist, for 'it is with utopia that philosophy becomes political and takes the criticism of its own time to the highest point'.[1] The question to be raised is therefore, where today might utopian thinking imagine that the best chances lie for the improvement of human life, or at least for some 'resistance to death, to servitude, to the intolerable, to shame and to the present' (Deleuze and Guattari 1994: 110)? Here, the concept I want to experiment with is 'nomadism', a concept created by Deleuze and Guattari in the 'Treatise on Nomadology' plateau of *A Thousand Plateaus* (Deleuze and Guattari 1987: 351–423).

Despite the familiar connotations of the term, it is important not simply to equate the concept of nomadism in Deleuze and Guattari with nomadic peoples. This is not to say that nomadism has nothing whatsoever to do with nomadic peoples, for it does.[2] But it cannot be limited to or by that single reference. For the terms of *A Thousand Plateaus* don't operate in the usual way: rather than designate a single determinate phenomenon, they create a meshwork of selective references, both internal (that is, to other concepts) and external (to other phenomena).[3] Following the principle of internal variation from *Difference and Repetition* (Deleuze 1994), different 'versions' of the concept of nomadism co-exist in *A Thousand Plateaus*, and no attempt is made to align them on a single uniform essence, to settle the differences among them. Variation through differential repetition of the 'same' concept – or of 'different' concepts with the same name – is considered fruitful, enriching.[4] So in order to explicate some less well-known aspects of the Deleuzo-Guattarian concept of nomadism, I will differentiate the concept both internally and externally, by examining not principally nomadic peoples, but nomad science, nomad music, and the nomadic market.[5]

The Greek term *nomos* is crucial to the 'Treatise on Nomadology' where Deleuze and Guattari discuss nomadism most directly and extensively. But the Greek term itself can be internally differentiated, by considering it in relation to a series of distinct concepts from which it is most often distinguished in Greek philosophy: *physis*, *logos*, and *polis*.[6] As distinguished from *polis*, *nomos* refers to space outside of city walls (originally pasture-land), a space not subject to the laws and mode of organisation of the state (or city-state).[7] It is the distinction between *polis* and *nomos* that generates the sense of nomadism as a way of occupying space that is characteristic of nomadic peoples.[8] Notice that in this context, *nomos* does not refer directly to a form of social organisation, which is my main interest here. Indeed, as estimable as nomadism may appear as a way of occupying space, nomadic peoples' social relations themselves are often far from ideal.

Far more often in Greek philosophy, *nomos* is distinguished from *physis*. In this context, it refers to the domain of human culture as distinct from that of nature. If we were to formulate a speculative topography, we could situate the realm of *nomos* between the unruly realm of nature or wilderness (*physis*), on one hand, and the enclosed and regulated space of the city or the state (*polis*), on the other. But such a formulation remains too spatialised to do justice to the third sense of *nomos*, which is the one I want to focus on here, where *nomos* is distinguished from *logos*. This latter, to be sure, can be related directly to the space of the city: *logos* refers to the law of the State, as well as more generally to reason and discourse. In this context, *nomos* might translate as 'custom' or even 'rule-of-thumb', as distinct from 'law'. I am reminded here of John Holt's dictum that (unlike a city- or nation-state) 'a community follows more rules than it knows'.[9] Customary rules (*nomos*) govern group behaviour without being deliberately founded as legislation or explicitly represented to it in the form of law (*logos*).

At this point, our speculative topography either breaks down completely, or must be radically extended to map the dialectic of enlightenment and the conquest of nature by Western reason and science: for the term 'law' is henceforth taken to apply not only to the city and the organisation of social relations, but to nature and the functioning of matter, energy, and life. Customary rules-of-thumb are unlike either the laws made to govern the behaviour of social subjects or the laws discovered to govern the behaviour of natural objects. Indeed, the very etymology of 'rule-of-thumb' nicely expresses the difference between *nomos* as an embodied mode of measurement and an approximate form of knowledge or practice, on one hand, and *logos* as a formal system of abstract measurement, exact observation, logical theorisation, and empirical verification, on the other.[10] The *nomos/logos* distinction thus underlies the opposition Deleuze and Guattari propose between minor or nomad science and what they call royal or state science (Deleuze and Guattari 1987: 446 and passim).

Royal versus nomad science

Much could be said about these two 'versions' of science. For our purposes, two points are essential. One is the difference between the principles of 'following' and 'reproducing' that characterise the two kinds of science; the other involves the social consequences that follow from them.

Royal science proceeds by extracting invariant ('universal') laws from the variations of matter, in line with the binary opposition of form and matter: matter is essentially variable, but 'obeys' formal laws that are universal. Reproducing the results of a successful experiment is crucial to establishing the veracity and universality of the hypothesised law that the experiment was designed to test. Nomad science, by contrast, proceeds not by extracting a constant but by following the variations or 'singularities' of matter. Its operations are better mapped by the four-fold Hjelmslevian distinction between content and expression, each of which involves form and substance, rather than the binary opposition of form and matter.[11]

Let's take, as an illustration, a piece of wood. Royal science will want it milled to established specifications – as a 2 by 4, for instance – so it can be used in building construction whose designs are based on the availability of lumber conforming to certain predictable 'constants' (size, regularity of grain, strength, surface appearance, and so on). Any knots that occur are considered mere imperfections, and may indeed lower the quality rating of the piece of wood as construction lumber, or preclude its use altogether. A sculptor, serving here as nomad scientist, will assess the piece of wood very differently. For the sculptor, knots and grain irregularities appear as singularities, features that inhere in the wood-matter as its unique form of content. And in the sculptor's hands, each singularity can become a substance of expression: a knot may become the eye of a fish; a grain pattern may become the waves of the sea. Or something else entirely: the content/expression relation here is one of contingency, not necessity. The material singularity of the piece of wood thereby comes to embody in the sculptor's hands what Deleuze and Guattari in *What is Philosophy?* call a *sensation* (Deleuze and Guattari 1994: 163ff.). In the sensations embodied in works of art, content and form, the raw material and artistic composition, become indiscernible; it becomes impossible to determine whether the wood grain itself suggests ocean waves, or whether ocean waves make us see the wood grain in this way: 'the plane of the material (the wood grain) ascends irresistibly and invades the plane of composition of the sensations themselves (the work of art) to the point of being part of them or indiscernible from them' (Deleuze and Guattari 1994: 166).[12] Instead of a pre-given form being unilaterally imposed on completely indeterminate or inert matter, artistic sensations arise in-between, in what Hjelmslev calls the 'reciprocal determination of expression and content'.

This illustration may appear to be far from scientific, but there are fields within science – of which we are becoming increasingly aware, although some were known to the Greeks – where singularities of this kind rather than constants abound. Fluid dynamics is perhaps the best known of these fields: it is impossible to predict exactly where an accelerating liquid will swerve, or even to which side an eddy will form; there are no laws for these phenomena.[13] Royal science was in fact constituted in part by the rejection of fluid dynamics (which were considered a special case, an exception to the laws of nature) in favour of solids; but even here, gravitational dynamics are only rigorously predictable between two bodies: the effects of gravity on three or more bodies of roughly equal mass in close proximity become as unpredictable as a liquid whorl.

Here we are broaching the fields of so-called chaos theory and non-linear mathematics, which lie well beyond the scope of this essay.[14] A more familiar illustration of nomad science, however, is available in evolutionary biology. Crucially, revolutionary science cannot predict evolution or reproduce it experimentally; what it does instead is follow its development. (It is no less a science for this.) To put the point another way, there are no universal laws governing evolution, only patterns of what has happened. Even the original notion of 'survival of the fittest' has given way more recently to the notion of 'survival of the sufficiently fit':[15] not only is random mutation (by definition) not predictable or reproducible, but neither is the interaction of a mutation with its environment. Rewind and rerun evolution 100 times, as the scientific wisdom now has it, and even if you could reproduce the same mutations, you would get up to 100 different results (Kauffman 1995). Evolution is thus a matter of what Deleuze and Guattari call 'itineration' rather than 'iteration' or reproduction according to universal law: it traces a path that can be followed, but not predicted (Deleuze and Guattari 1987: 460).

Turning to the social consequences of the distinction between royal and nomad science, Deleuze and Guattari insist that 'nomad science doesn't lead science in the direction of power, or even of autonomous development' (Deleuze and Guattari 1987: 462; translation modified). And this difference involves among other things the relations of sciences to work: 'royal science entertains different relations to work than nomadic science' (Deleuze and Guattari 1987: 456). Useful here is the distinction (for which Deleuze and Guattari don't themselves use these terms) between the technical division of labour and the social division of labour. The technical division of labour arises from the level of complexity of tasks, skills, and knowledges involved in a given process of production; but it does not in itself entail any hierarchy of status or power among specialists participating in the process. The social division of labour, by contrast, although it often overlaps a technical division of labour, involves distinctions of prestige or power that have nothing intrinsically to do with the skills exercised or level of participation in the process. Most notable is the social division of intellectual and manual labour, which is an essential feature of royal science, according to Deleuze and Guattari:

> [R]oyal science operates a 'disqualification' of manual labour, a 'deskilling' . . . Without conferring on 'intellectuals' any real, autonomous power, royal science nonetheless empowers them relatively by withdrawing all autonomy and power from labourers (formerly artisans) who now do nothing more than reproduce or execute the plans formulated by the 'intellectuals' (technocrats/managers). (Deleuze and Guattari 1987: 456)

Due to the power of royal science to extract abstract concepts from the concrete operations of productive practice, conception and execution become distinct activities, and each gets assigned to a distinct status group (Deleuze and Guattari 1987: 463). Bacon's programme for the development of science illustrates this process perfectly: he charges agents of the Royal Academy with the task of visiting local workshops to extract whatever knowledges were in practice there, and then bringing them back to the academy where they would be elaborated into formal scientific knowledge, only to be eventually re-applied to the production process in the form of technology, thereby liquidating the autonomy of the workers and subjecting them to managerial control (Bacon 2000).

It is significant that this is not a directly or obviously political form of control: it stems instead from a form of the division of labour which, howsoever 'natural' or necessary it has come to seem as the gap between

conception and execution has widened with the ever-increasing application of technology, nonetheless operates normatively to subordinate
manual to intellectual labour. As Deleuze and Guattari insist, 'if the
State always tends to repress minor and nomad sciences . . . it's not
because they lack accuracy or precision, . . . but because they entail a
division of labour opposed to that of State norms' (Deleuze and Guattari
1987: 456). To the (royal) conception of science that sees universal laws
as distinct from yet applicable to inert matter corresponds a conception of
society as being composed of inert subjects susceptible and indeed bound
to the application of universal laws by the state. From which Deleuze and
Guattari will conclude that *the manner in which a science, or a conception of science, contributes to the organization of the social field, and
in particular [the way in which it] induces a certain division of labour (e.g.
intellectual/manual or social/technical) forms an intrinsic part of that
science itself* (Deleuze and Guattari 1987: 456–7; emphasis added). I
want to argue the same thing about jazz and classical music: the manner
in which each contributes to the organisation of the social field is intrinsic
to its value relative to the other. At the same time, we will see that
improvisational jazz foregrounds processes of 'itinerative following'
rather than 'iterative reproducing,' just as nomad science does.

Jazz as nomad music

Jazz is not the only instance in the field of play – playing music, playing
sports, playing games – that can be characterised as nomadic.[16] Deleuze
and Guattari themselves expound on the formal differences between go
and chess: the one involves a multiplicity of interchangeable pieces
operating in an open or 'smooth' space, the other a hierarchy of distinct
pieces operating in a closed and 'striated' space.[17] A similar argument can
be made regarding the formal differences between soccer and (North
American) football (Holland 1987; Holland 1999). The playing field in
soccer, for one thing, while not nearly as open a space as a go board (the
soccer field has goals, after all), is considerably less striated than the
football field, which in addition to having goals (of two kinds), is so
striated that every yard-line is marked! The degree of distinction and
hierarchy among soccer players is also considerably less than among
football players. Soccer players (particularly the goalie) are not as
interchangeable as go pieces, but offensive and defensive players and
activities alternate roles far more fluidly in soccer than in football, which
stops the action and substitutes entire teams in changing from offence to
defence and back. In soccer, offensive players play defence and defensive

players play offence (and score goals) far more routinely than in football, where such role-changes are exceptional and very short-lived (never lasting more than one play in a row). Soccer teams also exhibit almost no internal hierarchy, whereas football teams are rigidly hierarchised, with linesmen doing the grunt-work (the manual labour, as it were) and quarterbacks calling the plays (the 'intellectual labour'). (In some cases it is the coach rather than the quarterback who calls the plays; in soccer, coaches play a far smaller role, especially during game-time.) In a sense, football evidences a clear social division of labour along with an extensive technical division of labour; soccer has a much less pronounced technical division of labour, and no social division of labour to speak of.

Returning now to the field of music, I want to argue that jazz resembles soccer more closely than football; and that football – ironically enough, given their difference in prestige-value – resembles classical music more closely than jazz. In order to do so, I will draw on an anthropological–historical study of the evolution of music in Western society by Jacques Attali (1985). Two general points, however, should already be clear from what we have said about the way Deleuze and Guattari characterise nomadism and nomad science. For one thing, improvisational jazz repudiates 'reproducing' in favour of following or indeed creating. Whereas a classical symphony orchestra merely reproduces in performance what the composer has already created and written down in the score, jazz bands intentionally depart from what is already known in order to improvise and create something new.[18] Even when working from a chord-chart, for example, jazz improvisation is far more itinerative than iterative: solos vary in length, there is no set order as to who takes one when, a clever soloist can change keys or tempo unexpectedly and challenge the others to follow his or her lead, and so on.

And this brings us to the second point: in jazz improvisation, there is no need for a band-leader (even if soloists sometimes serve such a function temporarily, and get the band to follow them in a spontaneous key- or tempo-change), whereas classical symphony orchestras always have a conductor as well as a composer. Elias Canetti, in *Crowds and Power*, provides a succinct analysis of the orchestra conductor. Like Deleuze and Guattari, Canetti is interested as much (or more) in *the manner in which a symphony orchestra performance contributes to the organisation of the social field* as he is in the music actually produced:

> Someone who knew nothing about power could discover all of its attributes, one after another, by careful observation of a conductor. The reason why this has never been done is obvious: the music the

conductor evokes is thought to be the only thing that counts . . . the idea
of his activity having another, non-musical meaning never enters his head.
(Canetti 1962: 394)

Canetti goes on to describe this non-musical aspect of the conductor's
role in terms that make its pertinence to social organisation patently clear:
the conductor 'has the power of life and death over the voices of the
instruments'; 'their diversity stands for the diversity of mankind [sic]'; 'the
voices of the instruments are opinions and convictions on which [the
conductor] keeps a close watch'; 'he is omniscient, for, while they have
only their part in front of them, he has the whole score'; 'he is the living
embodiment of law'; 'the code of laws is in his hand, in the form of the
score' (Canetti 1962: 395–96). The conductor wields this kind of absolute
power not just over the orchestra, but over the audience, too:

> The immobility of the audience is as much part of the conductor's design
> as the obedience of the orchestra. They are under a compulsion to keep
> still. [. . .] The presence of the players disturbs no-one; indeed they are
> scarcely noticed. Then the conductor appears and everyone becomes still.
> [. . .] While he is conducting no-one may move, and as soon as he finishes
> they must applaud. (Canetti 1962: 395)

Most important for our purposes, however, is the nature of the
compact between conductor and orchestra members themselves: he holds
symbolic life-or-death power over their voices; without him, they are
nothing: 'the willingness of [orchestra] members to obey him makes it
possible for the conductor to transform them into a unit, which he then
embodies' (Canetti 1962: 395). As in football, the classical symphony
orchestra requires a *transcendent instance of command* in the figure of the
conductor to guarantee coordination, whereas coordination arises more
spontaneously and in a manner *immanent* to the group activity in soccer
and in jazz. Football and classical music, in other words, entail a social
division of labour whereby some merely execute discrete parts of what
others (coaches and composers, quarterbacks and conductors) conceive
and command; coaches develop elaborate compendia of plays (sometimes
stretching to hundreds of pages) of which players are then called upon to
execute their individual parts under the direction of the quarterback, in
much the same way that orchestra members execute their parts of the
musical score under the direction of the conductor.[19] There's almost none
of that to speak of in soccer and improvisational jazz. Now Attali is useful
in pursuing this line of argument because, like Deleuze and Guattari with
respect to forms of science, he deems forms of music to have social
consequences. For Attali, in other words, the manner in which a form of

music contributes to the organisation of the social field – and in particular, the way in which it induces a certain division of labour (intellectual
vs manual) – forms an intrinsic part of that music itself.

Attali takes music to be not just a reflection but what he calls a *herald* of
modes of social organisation, and this is because music provides society
with the most efficient manner of generating structure out of differences.
All societies require and are indeed based on the structuration of differences, most notably differences among people and/or social roles. Distinctive of music is that it structures differences in *sound*, perhaps the
easiest material on which to impose form, and thereby transforms noise
into music. Music in general is thus for Attali even more than for Canetti
an archetypical exercise of power, and hence a key to understanding
social organisation. What's more, because of the ease with which music
structures differences in sound, Attali considers it to be *prophetic*: music
announces forms of social organisation before they are achieved in other,
more resistant modes of materiality, that is, in social relations themselves.
Thus as Attali puts it, the orchestral music of Mozart and Bach –
including 'the manner in which [it] contributes to the organization of
the social field,' that is, with the mediation of a transcendent leader and
the subordination of players' activity to his command – embodies the
bourgeois dream of a harmonious yet hierarchically-structured social
totality 'better than and prior to the whole of nineteenth-century political
theory' (Attali 1985: 5–6).

Based on these premises, Attali's analysis of the evolution of musico-
social relations traverses four stages, of which the latter two are most
crucial here.[20] In the first stage (pre-modern society), music accompanies
ritual sacrifice, and its social function is to make people forget – to make
them forget the violence entailed in structuring differences to found and
maintain social order.[21] In the second stage (early modern society), which
Attali calls *the age of representation*, music's social function is not to
make people forget, but to make them believe – to make them believe in
the intrinsic harmony of the social order under the command of a leader.
In the third stage (capitalist society), music functions not to make people
forget or believe, but to silence them, and to make them listen silently and
endlessly to music designed to distract their attention or stimulate their
appetites. In this third stage, which Attali calls the *era of repetition*, music
has been commodified: the elevator and grocery-store music of Muzak;
top-40 hit-parades and the record industry in general.

Attali's fourth stage, which he calls *composition*, is partly an extra-
polation from observable trends, and partly, I think, an ideal cure for all
that's wrong with the earlier stages (especially stages two and three).

Whereas the stage of representation was linked with the technology of printing (of musical scores), and repetition was linked with technologies of sound-recording (records, cassettes, CDs, mini-disks, mp3 and so on), Attali links composition with the recent upsurge in the invention of new musical instruments themselves (particularly electronic instruments), as well as with the ongoing invention of new musical genres or codes.[22] Even more important, composition involves a reappropriation of music by ordinary people, and a novel merging of the roles of producer and consumer: rather than slavishly reproduce other people's music from a score, or passively listen to reproductions of it in silence, people in the era of composition will themselves produce and enjoy their own music. The era of composition will thus put an end to social alienation in music, which Attali defines as performing in accordance with a programme or code established in advance and by someone else; instead, message and code are to be invented and performed simultaneously in a process of continual creation where the process itself counts for more than any finished product.

Needless to say, Attali's characterisation of 'composition' bears strong resemblances to jazz improvisation, and he himself acknowledges the resemblances. For one thing, improvisational jazz is the musical genre where the musical 'message' does not pre-exist on a score or a recording, but is invented every time anew. (Of course, jazz improvisation can be recorded, but live jazz is considered the only true form by most aficionados.[23]) Moreover, jazz is not only inventive, it is also quintessentially collective and democratic: it is never just a matter of inventing one's own message-and-code, but inventing in such a way that one's message communicates and intersects fruitfully with others – other members of the band, other bands, people in the audience – without the need for a fixed code (such as a score) or a leader. Jazz, in other words, involves sharing the pleasures of creation with musicians and audience alike.[24]

Attali, too, recognises the significance of jazz; indeed, he invokes the free jazz movement of the late 50s and 60s and highlights the efforts of several jazz organisations of the time (including Archie Schepp's Jazz Composers' Guild, the National Association for the Advancement of Colored Musicians, and the Jazz Composers' Orchestra Association) to develop further what he calls the *stage of composition*. But Attali then goes on to criticise and reject jazz, claiming that it was a failure because it did not succeed in actually bringing about the stage of composition. Despite a remarkably high degree of organisational activity above and beyond what was necessary for playing music itself, the free jazz movement proved incapable of fundamentally altering the ways jazz was recorded, distributed, and consumed by the music industry, much less altering the broader social relations surrounding the industry and the place of music within society at large. This criticism may appear unfair, given the immensity of the task and the paucity of means jazz musicians had at their disposal to address it; that it was even conceived of may be considered remarkable enough all by itself. But Attali can only offer this critique because he has suddenly stopped considering music to be *prophetic* of new social relations, as he started out proclaiming it to be. Instead, he now expects jazz to have actually changed social relations and the political economy of the music industry all by itself! If we remain faithful to Attali's original formulation, however, and consider improvisational jazz as nomad music to be a *herald* rather than the cause of new social relations, we may then want to ask what those new social relations entail; from where else, outside of music, they might arise; and, in a more speculative and utopian vein, under what conditions they might actually prevail.

The Nomad market and permanent revolution

Although Deleuze and Guattari themselves refer most often to nomadism in modernist and avant-garde art and literature,[25] they argue more broadly that contemporary capitalism promotes the emergence of no-madic social relations throughout society, while at the same time it severely counteracts and constrains them. Capitalism in their view is actively revolutionary, but only halfway; it is also extremely reaction-ary.[26] On one hand, capitalism constantly transforms and improves social production, and therefore also transforms consumption and social relations in general; but on the other hand, it maintains the subordination of labour, consumption, and society to the unremitting accumulation of private capital.

By comparing capitalism with two other social forms, Deleuze and Guattari distinguish an economic component of capitalism from a power component, and what is novel and perhaps surprising is that they consider economics to be the positive element of capitalism, and power (less surprisingly) to be the negative element. Economics, or more precisely the abstract calculus of the market, subverts the older power relations of explicit domination, and knits new social ties beneath the level of political authority, subjugation and representation. Yet capitalism at the same time installs a new form of power by yoking the dynamics of the market to private capital-accumulation. The power of private capital, in this view, acts as a brake and a limit to the dynamism of the market, which left unfettered would generate increasing freedom and material abundance.

In a more thoroughly historical set of studies of the emergence of capitalism in early modern Europe, Fernand Braudel has arrived at a similar conclusion, which he casts in terms of markets and anti-markets.[27] For Braudel, the free market exchange of commodities (excluding power-relations) continually enriches, diversifies, and enlarges human abilities and sensibilities.[28] Anti-market monopolies and oligopolies, however, because of their size, wealth, and/or political clout, can control the market to their own advantage, thereby limiting its dynamics according to the dictates of private accumulation – both qualitatively (what gets produced) as well as quantitatively (how much is available for public consumption). If we agree, in line with the conclusions of Braudel and Deleuze and Guattari, that a truly free market would sponsor new social relations of greater freedom, diversity, and material abundance once the power of the capitalist anti-market were eliminated, the question becomes: how do we drive a wedge between the power and economic components of capitalism? How do we eliminate the power of anti-markets and yet retain the free market and all its positive effects?

One answer – admittedly a speculative and utopian one, but fully within the logic of the foregoing analysis – is to eliminate the job-market but retain the commodities-market: in other words, eliminate wage-power. Capital depends on wage-power for its existence: eliminate the source of capital – wage-power – and capitalism is over.[29] One way to accomplish this – without reverting to craft or artisanal production and thereby sacrificing the richness and abundance of developed industrial and so-called 'post-industrial' production – would be to transform formerly capitalist enterprises, lock, stock, and barrel, into worker-owned cooperatives (on the model of the Mondragon cooperatives in Spain). Advanced processes of production, along with the technical division of power they entail, would continue as before, but without a hierarchical social division of power and without the anti-market limitations on public appropriation and enjoyment.

Under these – avowedly ideal – circumstances, both the producers' cooperatives and market society as a whole would operate on the nomadic model of improvisational jazz (or neo-Darwinian evolution): order would emerge 'from below', from the interaction of a multiplicity of social agents on the market, rather than being imposed or constrained from above by institutions of power and accumulated wealth. This 'nomad market' would respond to supply and demand, not to dictates of capital and the anti-market pressures of private accumulation; rather than to the restrictive valorisation of privately-owned capital, social production would be devoted to the continual improvement of production, consumption, and social relations themselves: this is the sense in which I take jazz improvisation to be a model for permanent revolution in society at large.

References

Attali, J. (1985), *Noise: The Political Economy of Music*, trans. B. Massumi, Minneapolis: University of Minnesota Press.

Bacon, F. (2000), *The Advancement of Learning*, Oxford: Clarendon Press.

Bailey, D. (1982), *Musical Improvisation: Its Nature and Practice in Music*, Englewood Cliffs, Prentice-Hall.

Braudel, F. (1973), *Capitalism and Material Life: 1400–1800*, New York: Harper and Row.

Canetti, E. (1962), *Crowds and Power*, New York: Viking.

DeLanda, M. (1996), 'Markets and Anti-Markets in the World Economy', in S. Aronowitz, B. Martinsons and M. Menser (eds), *Technoscience and Cyberculture*, New York; London: Routledge, pp. 181–94.

DeLanda, M. (1997), *A Thousand Years of Non-linear History*, New York: Zone Books.

Deleuze, G. (1994), *Difference and Repetition*, trans. Paul Patton, New York: Columbia University Press.

Deleuze, G. and Guattari, F. (1977), *Anti-Oedipus: Capitalism and Schizophrenia*, trans. R. Hurley, M. Seem and H. R. Lane, New York: Viking.

Deleuze, G. and Guattari, F. (1987), *A Thousand Plateaus: Capitalism and Schizophrenia*, trans. B. Massumi, Minneapolis: University of Minnesota Press.

Deleuze, G. and Guattari, F. (1994), *What is Philosophy?*, trans. G. Burchell and H. Tomlinson, New York: Columbia University Press.

Girard, R. (1977), *Violence and the Sacred*, Baltimore: Johns Hopkins University Press.

Girard, R. (1986), *The Scapegoat*, Baltimore: Johns Hopkins University Press.

Hjelmslev, L. (1961), *Prolegomena to a Theory of Language*, Madison: University of Wisconsin Press.

Holland, E. W. (1987), ' "Introduction to the Non-Fascist Life": Deleuze and Guattari's "Revolutionary" Semiotics', *Esprit Créateur* XXVII (2): 19–29.

Holland, E. W. (1999), *Deleuze and Guattari's Anti-Oedipus: Introduction to Schizoanalysis*, New York, London: Routledge.

Holland, E. W. (2003), 'Representation and Misrepresentation in Postcolonial Literature and Theory', *Research in African Literatures* 34 (1): 159–73.

Holt, J. (1976), *Instead of Education: Ways to Help People Do Things Better*, New York: Dutton.

Jarrett, M. (1999), *Drifting on a Read*, Albany: SUNY Press.

Kauffman, S. (1995), *At Home in the Universe: The Search for Laws of Self-organization and Complexity*, New York: Oxford University Press.

Lévi-Strauss, C. (1966), *The Savage Mind*, Chicago: University of Chicago Press.

Massumi, B. (1992), *A User's Guide to Capitalism and Schizophrenia: Deviations from Deleuze and Guattari*, Cambridge: MIT Press.

Serres, M. (1982), *Hermes: Literature, Science, Philosophy*, Baltimore: Johns Hopkins University Press.

Wittgenstein, L. (1953), *Philosophical Investigations*, New York: Macmillan.

Notes

1. On thought as experimentation and its relations with utopia, see Deleuze and Guattari 1994: 99–111.
2. Note that even when the figure of nomadic peoples is invoked, nomadism is for Deleuze and Guattari a matter not just of occupying space, but of algebra and affect as well; read in conjunction with *What is Philosophy?* (1994), it is clear that the nomad (like the schizophrenic) is for Deleuze and Guattari a conceptual persona, not a psychosocial type.
3. See *What is Philosophy?*, for Deleuze and Guattari's views on the distinction between philosophical and other kinds of concepts; on the controversy about what I here call selective external reference, see Holland (2003).
4. Deleuze's understanding of conceptual variation (difference in repetition) bears comparison with Wittgenstein's notion of 'family resemblances'; see Wittgenstein 1953.
5. We leave aside here Deleuze and Guattari's concept of the 'war-machine', despite its important relations with nomadism; examining the relations of the nomad to the war-machine and the state would be another way of differentiating the concept of nomadism in Deleuze and Guattari.
6. Deleuze and Guattari oppose *nomos* to both *polis* and *logos* in the nomadology plateau; see Deleuze and Guattari 1987, esp. 472.
7. To invoke another pair of terms from the meshwork or constellation of Deleuzo-Guattarian concepts engaging with nomadism, the state governs its space via 'striation', whereas nomadic space remains 'smooth'.
8. Illustrative of this mode of occupying space is the fact that grazing animals are distributed randomly (*disposés*) through the 'smooth' space of pasturage without the space itself being systematically divided up (*partagé*) or 'striated'; see the discussion of 'disposer' and 'partager' in Deleuze and Guattari 1987: 472.
9. From an informal talk; but see Holt 1976. This formula may be related to sociologists' distinctions between *gemeinschaft/gesellschaft* and primary/secondary social relations.
10. The *nomos/logos* distinction thus bears comparison in this context with Lévi-Strauss's distinction between engineering and *bricolage*; see Lévi-Strauss 1966.
11. In contradistinction to the Saussurian binary signifier/signified as well as the philosophical opposition between form and matter, Hjelmslev distinguishes between expression and content, each of which entails both form and substance (hence form of expression and substance of expression; form of content and substance of content); see Hjelmslev 1961.
12. In a similar vein, jazz guitarist Derek Bailey will argue that 'although some improvisers employ a high level of technical skill in their playing, to speak of 'mastering' the instrument in improvisation is misleading. The instrument is not just a tool but an ally. It is not only a means to an end, it is a source of material, and technique for the improviser is often an exploitation of the natural resources of the instrument . . . Almost any aspect of playing an instrument can reveal music . . . The instrument's responsiveness to its acoustic environment, how it reacts to other instruments and how it reacts to the physical aspects of performing, can vary enormously. The accidental can be exploited through the amount of control exercised over the instrument, from complete – producing exactly what the player dictates – to none at all – letting the instrument have its say' (Bailey 1982: 117–18).
13. See Serres 1982.
14. See DeLanda 1997, Massumi 1992, and Kauffman 1995.

15. Significantly, the notion of 'survival of the fittest' was not originally Darwin's (it was adapted from Herbert Spencer, and didn't appear until the fifth edition of *The Origin of Species*), even though it became one of the slogans most readily associated with his theory of evolution.
16. I am in what follows intentionally using a fairly loose definition of what counts as jazz, a topic that lends itself to controversy. I am not concerned, for example, with distinguishing European and African components or contributions to jazz; nor am I claiming that jazz is the only musical genre in which improvisation occurs, or that it always occurs there; nor I am taking into account either jazz composition or solo jazz performance, both of which certainly merit the name jazz. By jazz here I mean live group jazz improvisation, which involves musicians (1) working at most from a chord chart (not a score) if not from nothing at all, and (2) trading solos (usually of unpredictable length) between choruses or engaging in 'call-and-response' style conversations among individuals within the group. (Group jazz improvisation can of course be recorded, but the fleeting event of interactive creativity thereby gets frozen for eternity.)
17. See the beginning of the nomadology plateau (sect. 12) in Deleuze and Guattari 1987, and Notes 6 and 7 above.
18. Of course, there is always a – relatively – small margin of 'artistic interpretation' in classical music performance (compared, that is, to the large margin in improvisational jazz); and improvisation was an important genre especially in the early baroque period; but these important exceptions do not alter the basic distinction between the forms of social organisation and interaction of the jazz group and the modern symphony orchestra.
19. Compare what Derek Bailey has to say about the difference between improvising and performing from a pre-composed score: 'One reason why the standard Western instrumental training produces non-improvisers (and it doesn't just produce violinists, pianists, cellists, etcetera: it produces specifically non-improvisers, musicians rendered incapable of attempting improvisation) is that not only does it teach how to play an instrument, it teaches that the creation of music is a separate activity from playing that instrument. Learning how to create music is a separate study totally divorced from playing an instrument. Music for the instrumentalist is a set of written symbols which he interprets as best he can. They, the symbols, are the music, and the man who wrote them, the composer, is the music-maker. The instrument is the medium through which the composer finally transmits his ideas. The instrumentalist is not required to make music. He can assist with his 'interpretation' perhaps, but, judging from most reported remarks on the subject, composers prefer the instrumentalist to limit his contribution to providing the instrument, keeping it in tune and being able to use it to carry out, as accurately as possible, any instructions which might be given to him. The improviser's view of the instrument is totally different.' (Bailey 1982: 116)
20. Attali's four stages are not identical but bear comparison with those of Deleuze and Guattari in *Anti-Oedipus: Capitalism and Schizophrenia* (1977).
21. This view bears comparison with that of René Girard; see Girard 1977 and Girard 1986.
22. For a pertinent discussion of the invention of electronic instruments in the context of jazz improvisation, see Bailey's discussion of the Music Improvisation Company (Bailey 1982: 111–24).
23. Contrast the view of one Chinese professor hosting American jazz musicians, who was unable to understand what value could be attached to improvised jazz – precisely because so much of it went un-recorded; quoted in Jarrett 1999: 72.
24. Distinctive of jazz clubs are the high levels of interaction between musicians and audience through call-and-response patterns and of audience participation

through dancing. There are even clubs where audience members routinely step up and play or sing with the band. (Not everyone, of course, is inclined or welcome to do so, but the spirit of participatory enjoyment suggests that for those not able to play an instrument or scat-sing, dancing would be an alternative mode of participation.)

25. Artaud and Kleist are among the avant-garde figures they frequently mention.
26. Their view is like Marx's in this respect, though they would not call it 'dialectical' as he might; and unlike Marx, Deleuze and Guattari distinguish explicitly between the positive, economic component of capitalism and its retrograde, power component; see below, and Holland 1999, esp. pp. 58–60.
27. See Braudel 1973, esp. vol. 2. Drawing on Braudel, but exaggerating his differences with Marx, Manuel DeLanda also argues against the myth that capitalism started out competitive and became monopolistic; see DeLanda 1996. Whether the capitalist economy grows *increasingly* monopolistic over time (as Marx argued) is a different issue; but what is clear in Braudel is that monopolies were there from the beginning.
28. The political valence of Braudel's distinction between markets and anti-markets is similar to that between the technical and social division of labour (discussed above), though the scale is different: the social/technical division of labour is usually considered within an individual firm or specific industry, while the market/anti-market distinction applies to whole economies.
29. Having removed the *source* of capital in wage-labour, one would also want to reappropriate the accumulated *fruits* of the wage-labour heretofore exploited by capital, by simply cancelling all debt and transforming banks into cooperative credit unions. This would be no different in principle from, though it would represent a significant extension of, current proposals to cancel the debt of under-developed Third World countries.

Chapter 2

Is Pop Music?

Greg Hainge

> It is not really known when music begins.
> (Deleuze and Guattari 1987: 300)

In order to answer the question contained in this title, it will of course be necessary firstly to try and ascertain what music is. This, naturally, will be a very difficult task, for in its most absolute sense, music, as understood by Deleuze, in a move consonant with his entire philosophical project, *is*, strictly speaking, nothing, or, rather, the last thing it could be is nothing. Instead, music is a haecceity, which is to say that, like 'a season, a winter, a summer, an hour, a date', it is a becoming, a certain kind of affect at differing degrees of intensity, it is a 'this-ness', not a *thing* or *substance* or *subject* but a mode of individuation that has 'a perfect individuality lacking nothing' and that consists 'entirely of relations of movement and rest between molecules or particles, capacities to affect and be affected' (Deleuze and Guattari 1987: 261).[1] This description, which ostensibly traces the outline of a haecceity, exhibits a transparent relation to music in the most banal sense of this term, for music consists in this sense entirely of notes (the particles of music) and rests which draw relations of movement and rest between melody and rhythm, voice and instrument, instrument and instrument, harmony and dissonance, sound and silence, whilst music is commonly considered to be the art form most capable of *affect* at the same time as the apparent fixity of the musical composition – with its sacrosanct inscription as a *score* – has always and necessarily been more open to interpretation than other artistic expressions, never more so than in the era of the cover version and remix culture.

This pseudo-definition only tells us what music is as an *event*, but, it tells us little about the essential ontology of music, of how music comes into be(com)ing in the first place. And yet perhaps it tells us everything since for Deleuze becoming *is* everything, constituting an absolute outside which encompasses all that take places within it at the same time as it is inseparable from these events. Everything, then, is situated on and springs from a plane of consistency, otherwise known as a plane of desire (for it is necessarily productive) or a plane of immanence because becoming is nothing but immanence. Explaining how this reversal of Platonism does away with a stable foundation of being, Claire Colebrook writes, 'the supposed real world that would lie behind the flux of becoming is not, Deleuze insists, a stable world of being; there "is" nothing other than the flow of becoming. All "beings" are just relatively stable moments in a flow of becoming-life' (Colebrook 2001: 125).

The problem for most philosophical or artistic expressions, according to Deleuze, is that this plane of immanence can be conceptualised in two different ways. On the one hand, as he writes:

> The plane can be a hidden principle, which makes visible what is seen and audible what is heard, etc., which at every instant causes the given to be given, in this or that state, at this or that moment. But the plane itself is not given. It is by nature hidden. It can only be inferred, induced, concluded from that to which it gives rise. (Deleuze and Guattari 1987: 265)

Conceiving of the plane in this way, the relatively stable moments of the flow of becoming-life appear to be individuations, the enfolding of their aleatory outside being perceived as a finalised process resulting in an individuated entity and a perception of them as fixed forms separate from the (now transcendent) plane which exists, therefore, 'only in a supplementary dimension to that to which it gives rise'. As Deleuze suggests, 'the plan(e), conceived or made in this fashion, always concerns the development of forms and the formation of subjects' (Deleuze and Guattari 1987: 265).

'Then there is an altogether different conception of the plane', Deleuze continues, or an altogether different conception of the plane.

> Here, there are no longer any forms or developments of forms; nor are there subjects or the formation of subjects. There is no structure, any more than there is genesis. There are only relations of movement and rest, speed and slowness between unformed elements, or at least between elements that are relatively unformed, molecules and particles of all kinds. (Deleuze and Guattari 1987: 266)

To a certain extent, these two kinds of planes always exist together, for even though the latter is 'the plane of Nature' (Deleuze and Guattari 1987: 266), 'one continually passes from one to the other, by unnoticeable degrees and without being aware of it, or one becomes aware of it only afterward. Because one continually reconstitutes one plane atop another, or extricates one from the other' (Deleuze and Guattari 1987: 269). This is possible, for Deleuze, since if one does not allow the plane of immanence 'to play freely on the surface' but instead allows it to become deeply rooted in Nature, it suddenly appears to serve as a ground, a principle of organisation that stands in a transcendent relation to all that takes place upon it (Deleuze and Guattari 1987: 269). Whilst the plane of immanence is more 'natural', then, 'the plane of organisation is constantly working away at the plane of consistency, always trying to plug the lines of flight, stop or interrupt the movements of deterritorialisation, weigh them down, restratify them, reconstitute forms and subjects in a dimension of depth' at the same time as, conversely, 'the plane of consistency is constantly extricating itself from the plane of organisation, causing particles to spin off the strata, scrambling forms by dint of speed or slowness, breaking down functions by means of assemblages or micro-assemblages' (Deleuze and Guattari 1987: 270). These two planes thus serve as two abstract poles which draw differing degrees of intensity towards themselves. Judging by the above suggestion that music is a haecceity, it might be thought that music would be drawn, more often than not, towards the latter pole, that it would arise from the plane of immanence which is constituted by relations of movement and rest. Indeed, Deleuze calls this plane 'which knows only longitudes and latitudes, speeds and haecceities, the plane of consistency or *composition*' (Deleuze and Guattari 1987: 266; my emphasis), a name which, once again, would seem to imply a certain kinship to music. Such, however, is not the case, for in order for music to come into perception it would appear that a separation is effectuated between the plane and that to which it gives rise. Indeed, Deleuze explicitly states that 'the developmental or organisational principle [of music] does not appear in itself, in a direct relation with that which is developed or is organised: There is a transcendent compositional principle that is not of the nature of sound, that is not "audible" by itself or for itself' (Deleuze and Guattari 1987: 266).

This is not the case for all music, indeed, Deleuze suggests that 'to the transcendent, organisational plane of Western music based on sound forms and their development, we [should] oppose the immanent plane of consistency of Eastern music, composed of speeds and slownesses, movements and rest' (Deleuze and Guattari 1987: 270). Nor is this attraction of Western music towards the plane of organisation an absolute principle; as Deleuze writes, 'certain modern musicians oppose the transcendent plan(e) of organisation . . . to the immanent sound plane' (Deleuze and Guattari 1987: 267). Nonetheless, it is the transcendent plane of organisation which, according to Deleuze, 'is said to have dominated all of Western classical music' and that, it can be added, continues to dominate nearly all forms and genres of Western music (Deleuze and Guattari 1987: 267). This is to say that even when Western music is embarked upon a process of involution 'in which form is constantly being dissolved' (Deleuze and Guattari 1987: 267), there is nearly always a concomitant development of form that draws Western music towards a plane of organisation (Deleuze and Guattari 1987: 270). This may be due, in part, to Western music's reliance on a regular, pulsed metre that grounds it in '*Chronos*: the time of measure that situates things and persons, develops a form, and determines a subject' (Deleuze and Guattari 1987: 262); it may be linked to the dominance of 'pre-composed' forms as opposed to improvisational performance compositions (an opposition which finds an analogous series in the pre-recorded vs live binary of many contemporary popular musical forms); it may, as Deleuze suggests, have to do with music's relationship to the refrain (Deleuze and Guattari 1987: 300). What matters most in the final analysis, however, is that the *perceptible* (which is to say audible) forms of Western music, which as a virtual entity on an ideational level of intensity appears to be a haecceity, are consistently pulled towards a plane of transcendence and music is thereby imbued with a double and contradictory movement.

It is this movement that for Deleuze constitutes the very essence of music whose content, according to a passage in *A Thousand Plateaus*, is 'the refrain itself', yet which is described on this same page as 'a creative, active operation that consists in deterritorialising the refrain' (Deleuze and Guattari 1987: 300). As he elaborates, 'whereas the refrain is essentially territorial, territorialising, or reterritorialising, music makes it a deterritorialised content for a deterritorialising form of expression' (Deleuze and Guattari 1987: 300). In a nutshell, 'what musicians do should be musical' (Deleuze and Guattari 1987: 300), which is to say that whilst music makes use of the refrain, a type of sonic organisation which is often used by animals in order to provide an aural barrier that extends their physical presence, warning off competitors, it is not the objective of music to stake out a territory, to create an enclave shut off from the outside but, on the contrary, to *affect* as do the colours of a coral fish and birdsong, to deploy attributes intended to attract not repel (see Deleuze and Guattari 1987: 316–17). Whilst the coming into perception of Western music would appear in most cases to be dependent on a transcendent plane which can only produce fixed forms and not becomings, then, its power of affects, its musicality it might be said, comes from a properly musical process that consists in dismantling those very forms,

pushing them to their limit, submitting them to the diagonal or transversal as music reterritorialises upon itself *qua* music (Deleuze and
Guattari 1987: 303). Thus, 'the whole becoming of Western music, all
musical becoming, implies a minimum of sound forms and even of
melodic and harmonic functions', but given this, 'speeds and slownesses
are made to pass across them, and it is precisely these speeds and
slownesses that reduce the forms and functions to the minimum' (Deleuze
and Guattari 1987: 270). It is a question, then, of 'a material proliferation
that goes hand in hand with a dissolution of form (involution) but [which
is] at the same time accompanied by a continuous development of form',
as Deleuze writes (Deleuze and Guattari 1987: 270). Western music,
whilst dependent on the creation of forms, only becomes music through
the undoing of those forms and this double movement is music's very
ground of possibility and its salvation, it is what enables it to form a block
of expression and yet remain musical. This, then, is what music is, but is
this what pop is?

Here again a problem is encountered because the very definition of pop
music is a contentious issue on which, it would seem, there can be no
absolute consensus. For Ian Buchanan, pop is merely a codeword for the
populism inherent in the refrain, it is that which allows us a return 'home',
and as such a pre-requisite of pop is the inclusion of a refrain, 'a tune that
sticks in your head and can be easily whistled or hummed', as he says
(Buchanan 2000: 184). According to this definition, pop would indeed
appear to be music, in fact one might say that it is a kind of *ur-music* since
it is even more dependent on the territoriality of the refrain than other
musical forms. To believe this, however, would be to forget, as Buchanan
reminds us, that for Deleuze and Guattari 'the refrain is not music, it is
rather "the block of content proper to music"' (Buchanan 2000: 184,
quoting Deleuze and Guattari 1987: 299). Indeed, even though music
exists only 'because the refrain exists also, because music takes up the
refrain, lays hold of it as a content in a form of expression, because it
forms a block with it in order to take it somewhere else', the refrain is
ultimately 'a means of preventing music, warding it off, or forgoing it'
(Deleuze and Guattari 1987: 300). Whilst an analysis of pop's relationship to the refrain would appear to suggest that pop is not music, then,
this analysis does not in the end allow us to differentiate pop from other
musical forms and cannot then serve to define what pop *is*.

In their essay 'What I Hear is Thinking too: Deleuze and Guattari Go
Pop', Timothy Murphy and Daniel Smith take a different approach and
define pop as:

the regime of music production that is tied neither to the European composer/ concert tradition and its strict division of labor, nor to any of the various historical traditions of indigenous music making around the world, but rather to the *bricolage* of modern recording technology (electric/electronic instruments, studios, overdubbing, mixing, etc.) and its media of distribution. (Murphy and Smith 2001: para 2)

This definition of pop, whilst retaining the standard classical (read serious) vs. pop (read frivolous) division adds another dimension to the argument, for it suggests that pop is in fact opposed to both European classical *and* indigenous musical traditions, which is to say traditions that are constructed according to an entirely different set of principles, or even on a different plane – indeed, does Deleuze not oppose 'the transcendent, organisational plane of Western music based on sound forms and their development [to] the immanent plane of consistency of Eastern music, composed of speeds and slownesses, movements and rest' (Deleuze and Guattari 1987: 270)? What is more, in tying their definition of pop to its modes of production and distribution, Smith and Murphy might be said to overcome the very binary opposition that they establish, since many of the traditional modes they oppose to pop have altered their *modus operandi* to utilise the *bricolage* of modern recording technology and distribution so as to ensure their very survival. (We need only think of 'World Music' compact discs and the massive proliferation of live recordings of European classical works to see that this is the case.) Smith and Murphy's definition of pop then ends up turning this term into little more than a *porte-manteau* word which can contain any kind of music, a phenomenon that does not appear to worry John Corbett who suggests that 'all music is now popular' since the electronic colonisation of all music that equates to a kind of musical imperialism involves 'a complex treatment of the notion of "popularity" that cuts across three territories, blurring their boundaries [. . .] *Popular music as a statistical region* [. . .] *Popular music as a formal genre* [. . .] [and] *Popular music as anything recorded*' (Corbett 1994: 35; emphasis in original). Such a move, however, is very problematic, for it implies that the same criterion can be used to analyse the expressions of The Spice Girls, Kenny G, Scorn and the Dillinger Escape Plan, and this is patently not the case. Whilst all of these 'artists' could be classified as 'popular' because of the varying levels of commercial success that they enjoy, there is virtually no common ground between the The Spice Girls and Kenny G on the one hand (whom one would assume to be familiar to most readers) and Scorn and the Dillinger Escape Plan on the other.[2]

It would be unfair *completely* to dismiss Smith and Murphy's claims with regards to their definition of pop, however, for the answer to the question as to whether or not pop is music does indeed reside in the relationship of music to the market. Indeed, in order to arrive at an understanding of what pop in its truest sense *is*, it is necessary to intensify Ian Buchanan's statement that popular culture is 'more complexly bound to its milieu than other modes of art perhaps are' (Buchanan 2000: 176) and suggest that pop at its highest level of intensity is inextricably bound to its milieu, its plane and its territory. As a result, it no longer qualifies as music in a Deleuzian sense since the mode according to which it operates is not one in which it is desirable to perform the deterritorialisation of the refrain intrinsic to a properly musical expression.

What will here be called pop is pop at its most extreme level of intensity, pop as an idea and not a content of expression, much as Deleuze talks of music in its pre-expressive state. The reason why it is necessary to retain this abstraction in a definition of pop is precisely because it is a term that only seems to lead to polemic or a complete absence of meaning when it passes into actuality through embodiment in pop groups or musical genres. Any discussion around this theme that gives specific examples seems destined to be accused of resurrecting a high/low culture debate and, by inference, of making subjective value judgements. This is not to say that the comments regarding pop herein *cannot* be applied to specific instances of pop, merely that it is necessary for this secondary application to be carried out by each individual reader since subjective examples can only ever be just that and hence of little use in an attempt to answer an ontological question imbued with a high coefficient of objectivity.

In the Western tradition (which is, of course, that which gave rise to pop), the organisational principle of music does not, according to Deleuze and Guattari, appear in itself but, rather, remains inaudible. Music's audible forms relate to their plane, then, only as 'a transcendent unity or hidden principle' (Deleuze and Guattari 1987: 266). Such is not the case for pop in its highest form. For if pop can be said to be inextricably bound to its milieu, this is because, as its name suggests, it is born of a desire to become popular and populist and its forms of expression then take as their model the forms already existing within the milieu that constitute the popular. Whilst in Western music traditionally the plane cannot be given but only 'inferred from the forms it develops and the subject it forms, since it is *for* these forms and these subjects' (Deleuze and Guattari 1987: 266), then, it is rather the case with pop that the forms exist for the plane. This is the first sense in which pop does not conform to a Deleuzian conceptualisation of music, for even though Western music predominantly maintains a transcendent relation to the plane from which it springs, that plane is nonetheless a pure *musical* outside whereas the outside that constitutes the plane from which pop is created is *commercial*, which is to say that it is made up of the axiomatics necessary to appeal to a studied demographic and thus become popular. Even though pop comes into being through a manipulation and organisation of sonic content, then, those processes are only secondary effects of its primary organisational principle which is dictated by market forces. There is in pop's coming into expression, therefore, an excessive reliance on a transcendent plane or autonomous outside that has nothing to do with an artistic or musical becoming in which *'expressive qualities or matters of expression enter shifting relations with one another that "express" the relation of the territory they draw to the interior milieu of impulses and exterior milieu of circumstances'* (Deleuze and Guattari 1987: 317; emphasis in original).

Whilst pop, like Western music, entertains a transcendent relation to its plane, then, it is not able to resist the fixed forms created on this transcendent plane as does music because the plane of pop is precisely one that requires new expressions emanating from it *not* to resist its preexisting forms. The forms arising on the commercial plane of pop necessarily conform to an average ideal in order to be populist and hence part of the plane. Indeed, as Buchanan points out, there is a certain conformity inherent to pop that can then only be linked to the privileged status he accords pop's (non-complex) refrains which are a symptom of its very populism (Buchanan 2000: 180). This conformity extends even to the repeated instances of the refrain in a true pop song which are not, then, pushed to their limit, deterritorialised or reterritorialised *qua* music but merely banal Platonic copies of an original already devoid of music. On this count also, then, pop is not music, an assertion entirely in accord with Antoine Hennion's analysis of the formulaic nature of specific pop songs in his article 'The Production of Success: An Antimusicology of the Pop Song' (Hennion 1990).

This is not to say that there can be no such thing as popular music, that all popular music is necessarily populist, that no music that enjoys a healthy relationship to the market can qualify as music, that all popular music is content to produce only banal copies of the same and loath to deterritorialise the refrain. Such is obviously not the case and one need only examine some specific examples of popular music to understand that the popular *can* strive for a properly musical expression; that it *can* perform deterritorialisations of many of the punctual structures of pop and enter into a becoming-music in spite of its popularity; that it is not necessarily governed by populist tendencies.

On all of his albums (although to a lesser extent, perhaps, on some of the tracks featured on his 2001 offering, *Blowback* – which his official website describes as 'his most open, accessible and, yes, downright commercial album in six years', a fact which is explained by his return from the verge of insanity after the diagnosis and treatment of a disease that affected his immune system and psychological health),[3] Tricky performs rhythmic and linguistic deterritorialisations at odds with the ordered, predictable and punctual structures of pop – the former through the integration of what he has termed 'spastic jungle' rhythms into seemingly ordered and often sedate instrumentation, the latter through his minoritarian use of the English language. One of the most striking examples of these deterritorialisations can be found on his 1996 album, *Pre-Millennium Tension*, in the track 'Makes me wanna die'. This track starts off with the main vocalist, Tricky's former collaborator, Martina, singing the chorus, 'she makes me Wanna Die', half way through which the bass and high-hat breakbeat that remain constant throughout the song kick in, shortly followed by the sparse, electric guitar accompaniment that develops throughout the song, almost but never quite echoing the movements of the vocal melodies. The punctuality of the rhythm section, then, establishes a grid system on which the vocals and guitar slip and slide, each enunciating recurrent themes which never, however, recur at the same time as each other and thus deny the confluence of instrumental and vocal melodies common in pop on both a harmonic and rhythmic plane. In Deleuzian terms, it might be said that the forms of the song are submitted 'to temporal transformations, augmentations or diminutions, slowdowns or accelerations, which do not occur solely according to laws of organisation or even of development' (Deleuze and Guattari 1987: 270); indeed, the vocal and guitar lines, far from consolidating and concretising the organisation of the rhythm section (which is to say its structure, that upon which its form is premised) have a deterritorialising effect as they seem to warp and bend the regular, ordered metre of the pulsed beat.

It would appear that there is in the song 'Makes me Wanna Die', then, a properly musical block of expression that demonstrates the double movement of reterritorialisation and deterritorialisation immanent to Western music. What is more, consonant with the suggestion posited above that music, in Deleuze's formulation, is a haecceity, a system that is not fixed but, rather, a mode of individuation whose totality therefore cannot be given but rather remains open, constantly becoming, this song does not perform the expected, hermetic closure of a pop song that would fully individuate it, fix its form, separate it from its plane and render it transcendent. Rather, the ending of this track denies the listener a transcendent ending through resolution, the final vocal recurrence ('how could you dare? / who do you think you are? / you're insignificant / a small piece / an ism / no more no less / you try to learn the universe / can't even converse in universe / you know . . .') being brutally cut short as though the power cord had been severed, refusing both syntactic (previously, this lyric has continued: 'you know it's ironic / smokin' hydroponic') and melodic closure and leaving this final utterance to echo briefly in its own space, the apparent interiority of the vocal line returned to an absolute outside.

A similar phenomenon can be observed in David Sylvian's 'Brilliant Trees' from the 1984 album of the same name. This song does not (for its first section at least) follow a strict punctual rhythmic structure but rather the temporal contractions and expansions of Sylvian's voice in its interplay with the instrumentation – in which the absence of a rhythm section is conspicuous. In this song, melody as well as rhythm are deterritorialised. The last vocal line of the first instance of the chorus ('leading my life back to the soil') does not obey the melodic resolution it appears to lead to: Sylvian's voice, instead of repeating the final note with the last word of the phrase, raises up a minor third, thus creating an expectation of continuation, refusing the closure that the refrain (which draws fixed and closed territories) should provide. In the second coming of the chorus, although the rhythmic qualities remain consistent, the melody of the vocal line undergoes a change, providing the expected resolution, repeating the last note of the melody, the base note of the key in which the song is written. However, whereas this kind of resolution would, in pop, lead to the end of the song, in 'Brilliant Trees' it does not lead to a closed, hermetic end. It serves, rather, as a bridge into the second and final section of the song in which Sylvian's voice (which has acted as a complex attractor for the instrumentation up until this point, pulling the various instruments along in the wake of its own utterly contingent speeds and slownesses) is replaced by a very sparse and tribal sounding rhythm section which, whilst displaying a certain degree of punctuality, certainly does not obey the kind of regular pulsed metre that dominates the Western musical tradition. What is more, this rhythm section's punctuality seems constantly to be pulled away from its moorings by the other instrumental lines, Sakamoto's synthesiser and Hassell's trumpet following the logic of their own individual expression and that of the exchange in which they are engaged, their trajectories sliding over this rhythmic base yet utterly unaffected by it. This meandering instrumental section (which occupies the last four minutes of the track's eight and a half minutes) eventually peters out to nothingness, refusing neat closure not only to the song but also, since it is the last track, to the entire album.

Of particular interest in Sylvian's career for the present discussion, however, is the single he released following a hiatus in his solo work, for the era that produced *Brilliant Trees*, the double CD *Gone to Earth* (1985) and *Secrets of the Beehive* (1987) was followed by a period of ten years in which he released no solo albums. During this period he did, however, release a five-CD box set containing the majority of his solo work entitled *Weatherbox* (1989). To accompany this retrospective, Sylvian concurrently released a single ironically titled 'Pop Song' whose very cover art (a negativised image of a topless female) indicated that this single was not, in spite of its title, intended to signal a shift in Sylvian's career from artsy maverick to corporate whore eager to cash in. 'Pop Song' itself is, similarly, very unlike the kind of song that its title might evoke and is, perhaps, one of the most unmelodic of Sylvian's compositions, the music being based around microtones and the piano improvisations of John Taylor. The main instrumental line consists of a synthesiser bouncing back and forth, staccato, from an upper pedal note to (mostly) discordant relations: minor thirds, semitones, minor sixths and augmented fourths. Around this line, the other instruments follow the improvisational style of Taylor's piano playing, following no external pattern, logic or architectural structure, no simple attractor of the kind used by pop that would reproduce a fixed form known in advance. The only discernible logic in the instrumental lines comes not from conformity to a melodic convention known in advance (as is often the case in pop) but, rather, from the patterns of exchange established occasionally between them, which is to say their *relations*. Meanwhile, Sylvian's vocal line, based once more primarily around discordant intervals, follows its own logic and progression over all of this, singing of the everyday in Sylvian's inimical and distinctly non-everyday way ('Behind the iron gates / the shifts were worked in silence / Each weekend beckoned like Ulysses' sirens / And as the words were few / We'd listen to the radio / It was loud and irritated me so' (Sylvian 1999: 11). It proposes a different variation with every verse and returns to a semi-stable centre (for there is still variation) only in the recurrent refrain ('I'll tell you I love you, like my favourite pop song') whose polyvocal harmony is itself based around the kind of discordant interval entirely anathema to a pop song.

The *démarche* of Queens of the Stone Age on the track 'You Would Know' from their 1998 self-titled album is somewhat different. In this song – which starts out with the interplay of the sound of a ring-tone phone and a disjointed guitar line that remains constant throughout the song's verses – jumpy, stuttering instruments and vocals are gradually added to build a deranged verse structure which oozes a sense of menace from every orifice on its holey surface. Holey space, for Deleuze, is a space which communicates with both smooth and striated space, 'it is always *connected* to nomad [smooth] space, whereas it *conjugates* with seden-tary [striated] space' (Deleuze and Guattari 1987: 415). Holey space then is described by an abstract line which has two different modes of liaison: it can be 'a kind of rhizome, with its gaps, detours, subterranean passages, stems, openings, traits, holes, etc.' and on the other side its traits of expression can be put 'into a form or a code', its holes made to resonate together, its lines of flight plugged, its connections submitted to 'a whole regime of arborescent conjunctions' (Deleuze and Guattari 1987: 415). If holey space has a soundtrack, it could well sound like this song which seems as though its score were written by an itinerant hole-punch, its traits of expression (or instrumental lines) desperately trying to conform to a model which appears to be absent, constantly striving for a pattern to emerge from its wanderings. Indeed, this verse structure eventually builds into a beautiful, almost sublime melodic chorus that struggles into life, fighting the precarious Jenga-like foundations of the verse – which is to say that the verse is built from the progressive yet arbitrary accumulation of elements similar to each other but different enough to render each either entirely independent or else a cornerstone of the whole. The first unveiling of the chorus is a tease, allowing only a glimpse of what is to come, one enunciation of the refrain, 'You would know', a four-second soundbite that immediately falls away to two moans and a return to the holey verse structure. This then happens again, the first snatch of the chorus this time, however, giving way to eleven moans uttered over the instrumental backdrop of the verse structure, before there is a return to the chorus which is repeated again and again, expanded occasionally, as the instruments gradually organise themselves into a stable structure that locks itself ever tighter together as more layers are accumulated. This leads, in turn, to a solo instrumental section that develops the melodies and themes of the refrain, a passage that would normally act as a diversion before a return to the refrain proper. QOTSA do not allow us this closure, however, for at the very moment that the return of this refrain is sensed to be coming, a return which would signal the final and complete accomplishment of the chorus, the sublime moment of trans-cendent perfection, everything falls away to two single guitars playing the holey jumpy discordant style of the verse in a short final burst of slapstick that leaves the listener wanting more at the same time as thrusting him outside of himself rather than enclosing him in the warm homely blanket of the refrain.

Finally, since the number of possible enumerations of exceptions to the rule established (namely, that pop is not music) is potentially infinite, it will be useful to examine the case of Björk, an artist who has known an enormous critical and commercial success, who is truly popular, then. Björk deterritorialises the English language with her every utterance, ripping its signifiers from their syntactic chain with her Icelandic inflections whilst the idiosyncrasies and singularity of her musical vocalisations deterritorialise her songs' refrains by rendering them unrepeatable. The curious paths that her vocal lines follow are the product of her own interior music,[4] not of harmonic patterns that can be objectively grasped, and in those moments when a more predictable harmonic line threatens to come to the surface Björk invariably usurps it with a primal, seemingly impossible scream or guttural howl. Take, for instance, the hit single 'It's Oh So Quiet' off her 1995 album *Post*, a big band musical number whose perfectly orthodox choruses are consistently interrupted by a joyous piercing scream totally out of place in its context.

A more complete deterritorialisation of the refrain (which constitutes the content of music but which requires deterritorialising in order for that content to pass into expression as music) can be found on *Homogenic*'s (1997) 'Pluto'. On this track – the dirty beats, rhythms created from static and other digital dysfunctions and distorted vocals of which deterritorialise a transcendent idyll of high-fidelity reproduction – the simple melodic pattern of the refrain, rather than always returning to the same point, is intensified through pitch progression. The first time the refrain occurs, the melody line is repeated four times, ending in an non-final semitone drop which leads into a stuttering rhythm section that sounds like somebody trying to jump start technology on a cold morning. This eventually leads back into the verse structure which again guides us through to the refrain where the same melody line recurs four times, ending in the same semitone drop, but then continuing from the pitch where the first development of the refrain leaves off as the instrumental backdrop drops away to mirror the bridge passage of technology without a choke. This refrain, at a second level of intensity and pitch, is itself repeated four times. It then ends in a semitone drop, is picked up again at the point at which the second level refrain leaves off and is repeated nine times at this third level of intensity. During this third level of intensity, the refrain is repeated so many times on the backdrop of looped stuttering rhythms that the music is forced into a locked groove that is only broken when Björk's voice breaks the punctual pattern of the refrain at the end of the ninth enunciation with a new melodic variation which ends in a throwaway scream that allows the song, for a brief moment, fully to develop its rhythmic pulse before it slowly shudders to a halt. Even at the very point of death of this album's penultimate track, however, Björk does not allow us (and especially those who would skip this track, one of the album's most 'difficult') entirely to shut this intensity and dysfunction off for good, for the index cut that divides the compact disc into tracks has been made in such a way that the final track of the album – 'All Is Full of Love', a track in which can be found a haven of calm, a certain degree of resolution and sublime hermetic closure – begins with a fraction of a second of the final technological death spasm of its neighbour.

It would no doubt be possible to enumerate many more examples of popular music which instigate a properly musical expression, but it is not necessary, for these examples have shown some of the ways in which popular music can enter into a becoming-music. What these examples have also shown, however, is that the term 'pop' is even more problematic than originally thought. For these songs, being properly musical, cannot of course be true pop in spite of the fact that they are recorded by people commonly referred to as pop artists (with the possible exception of David Sylvian who – disingenuously, fully aware of the term's problematic nature – applies the term 'pop' to one of his own songs). Herein lies the rub, for whilst these artists are included within the category of what is generally termed pop because of their popularity, it does not follow from this that they entertain the same relationship to the commercial and popular plane as does 'real' pop. This is to say that the amusicality of pop has nothing to do with the level of commercial success that a particular expression enjoys but, rather, with the nature of the relationship between that expression and the commercial and popular plane which, in the case of pop, is genetic and causal. If a popular musician is content to produce an expression which is formulated according to the commercial plane of pop and which therefore cannot diverge from the forms pre-existing on that plane – for such would be to risk exclusion from that plane – then that expression will not be music (within a Deleuzian paradigm and perhaps others also) but, rather, pop. If, however, a popular artist chooses to create an expression which does not conform faithfully to pre-existing forms, which does not adhere to a model known in advance but, rather, transforms existing models and forms so as to produce an expression both singular and new, then that expression will indeed be musical.

Many may sense an apparent hostility towards pop in this discussion, yet any such hostility is not intended; whilst it has indeed been argued that pop is not music within a Deleuzian paradigm, this is done not so as to dismiss any further consideration of pop as a subject worthy of critical attention, but merely to suggest that from within this paradigm an attempt to analyse pop as a musical expression is bound to fail since pop operates according to an entirely different mode from music – a distinction which requires us to differentiate, therefore, between popular music and pop (or perhaps this should be written Pop). Pop cannot be analysed as a musical expression because it does not spring from a plane of desire that would necessarily be productive, always generative of the new – as are all art and philosophy for Deleuze by necessity – but, rather, from a plane which does not appear to desire difference, which tends only to produce conformity of varying degrees of divergence. Pop, then, operates in a fashion very similar to Muzak, which, similarly, is not music.

Muzak is (not-)music as pure function, (not-)music which exists only as a means to convert the individual into consumer. Muzak is sometimes termed 'business music' since it is designed to programme on a subliminal level behavioural patterns within a commercial environment, be it by increasing workers' output or increasing shoppers' spending (see Gifford 1995). As Muscio, a Muzak arranger, has commented, 'our [Muzak's] service actually lies in its sequential arrangement to gain certain effects and to serve a functional purpose' (quoted in Lanza 1995: 155). It is not only in this commercial imperative that Muzak resembles the form of Pop music analysed above, however, for Muzak, like Pop with its homely refrains, is also programmed to appeal to (or, rather, not offend) the largest number of people possible. As Gifford writes:

> Arranging a song for Muzak is like cooking for 50 people. Suzuki [a Muzak arranger] has to please everyone to some degree, but it's more important that he offend nobody. His job is to take the edges off of songs. Vocals are removed and replaced by a suitably anonymous instrument, usually piano, guitar, woodwinds or vibes. Punchy rhythm parts are deflated a bit; distorted guitars and overly brassy horns are filed down. High, squeaky passages are lowered an octave, and dissonant chords are sweetened. (Gifford 1995)

Whilst the suggestion that pop is nothing more than Muzak again may seem a somewhat contentious and aggressive gesture, and particularly in light of this quotation which appears to describe the very epitome of blandness, it does find credence in the fact that Muzak, although its infamy is still widespread and in spite of the cheesy symbolic capital that its name still evokes, is, in fact, heard less and less in those commercial spaces where one would previously have heard (subconsciously, of course, for one is not supposed to *hear* Muzak) its piped-in anaesthetic tones. Indeed, in the shopping malls, supermarkets and hotel lobbies of the new millennium, one is far more likely to hear Pop. Rather than there being a direct functional equivalence between Muzak and Pop, then, it is perhaps rather the case that the latter has superseded the former and become even less musical in the process.

Many readers will no doubt still sense in this line of argument a latent hostility towards Pop. If such exists, it is perhaps only because there sometimes resides a similar hostility in Deleuze's thought where the popular, as Buchanan writes, is 'the undesirable other, or, worse, an enormous homogenising machine depriving art of its place and value in contemporary society' (Buchanan 2000: 175). To dismiss the popular in this manner, however, is to allow philosophy to be governed (and hence destroyed) by its enemy: opinion. If popular art forms appear to constitute somewhat of a stumbling block for Deleuze and for philosophy more generally, then, this is perhaps because philosophy has repeated the common mistake of conflating Pop and the popular. For as long as Pop (and this term can be extended, of course, to encompass other popular forms apart from pseudo-musical ones) is analysed according to the same set of principles articulated to artistic forms that can only produce the new, a sense of frustration will necessarily be felt, for they simply do not operate in the same manner, even when they share certain characteristics such as the refrain. For Deleuze, the refrain in music expresses the internal music of the individual which subsequently finds an auto-objectivity in its expression and reception when, as Deleuze writes, *'expressive qualities or matters of expression enter shifting relations with one another that "express" the relation of the territory they draw to the interior milieu of impulses and exterior milieu of circumstances'* (Deleuze and Guattari 1987: 317). When functioning in this manner, the expressive qualities of the territorialising refrain 'find an objectivity in the territory they draw' (Deleuze and Guattari 1987: 317). This can only happen, however, when the expression that draws the territory is an inherent enunciation of the individual whence issues that expression, when the territorialising expression is the becoming-expressive of qualities proper to the individual (see Deleuze and Guattari 1987: 316), when, it might be said, the music has soul. If the motivation behind the territorial expression of Pop issues not from an internal imperative but from an external imperative, an axiomatic of the strata of Capital, it cannot become auto-objective and will instead merely become an auxiliary of the apparatuses of capture of the Capitalist machine.[5] This does not inherently make Pop 'better' or 'worse' than a truly musical expression, but it does mean that it needs to be analysed according to its own immanent terms, for such is the guiding or founding principle of all Deleuzian analysis.

References

Buchanan, I. (2000), *Deleuzism: A Metacommentary*, Edinburgh: Edinburgh University Press.
Colebrook, C. (2001), *Gilles Deleuze*, London: Routledge.
Corbett, J. (1994), 'Free, Single, and Disengaged: Listening Pleasure and the Popular Music Object', in J. Corbett, *Extended Play: Sounding off from John Cage to Dr. Funkenstein*, Durham and London: Duke University Press.
Deleuze, G. and Guattari, F. (1987), *A Thousand Plateaus: Capitalism and Schizophrenia*, trans. B. Massumi, Minneapolis: University of Minnesota Press.
Gifford, B. (1995), 'They're Playing our Songs', *Feedmag*, October 1995, available online at http://www.feedmag.com/feature.html, 8 August 2001.
Hennion, A. (1990), 'The Production of Success: An Antimusicology of the Pop Song', in S. Frith and A. Goodwin (eds), *On Record: Rock, Pop, and the Written Word*, New York: Pantheon Books: 185–206, reprinted from *Critical Studies in Mass Communication*, 3 (1) (1986).
Lanza, J. (1995), *Elevator Music: A Surreal History of Muzak, Easy-Listening and Other Moodsong*, London: Quartet Books.
Murphy, T. S. and Smith, D. W. (2001), 'What I Hear is Thinking too: Deleuze and Guattari Go Pop', *Echo: A Music-Centered Journal*, 3 (1): para. 2, available online at http://www.humnet.ucla.edu/echo, 16 January 2002.
Sylvian, D. (1999), *Trophies II: The Lyrics of David Sylvian*, London: Opium (Arts).

Discography

Björk (1995), *Post*, One Little Indian.
Björk (1997), *Homogenic*, One Little Indian.
Queens of the Stone Age (1998), *Queens of the Stone Age*, Loosegroove Records.
Sylvian, D. (1984), *Brilliant Trees*, Virgin Records.
Sylvian, D. (1985), *Gone to Earth*, Virgin Records.
Sylvian, D. (1987), *Secrets of the Beehive*, Virgin Records.
Sylvian, D. (1989), *Weatherbox*, Virgin Records.
Sylvian, D. (2001), 'Pop Song', Virgin Records, 1989. Also included on *Everything and Nothing*, Virgin Records.
Tricky (1996), *Pre-Millennium Tension*, Polygram.
Tricky (2001), *Blowback*, Hollywood Records.

Notes

1. For the sake of readability, I shall refer to Deleuze even when the ideas discussed can be found in a work co-authored with Félix Guattari.
2. Scorn is the result of the illogical career progression of Mick Harris from drummer in überthrash metal outfit Napalm Death to post-industrial grindcore merchant in the band Scorn to king of dark ambient dub in Scorn the one-man outfit. The Dillinger Escape Plan meanwhile is an extreme hardcore unit from

New York heavily influenced by free jazz structures and rhythms and whose sound can only be described in highly metaphorical ways, perhaps as being like the noise of a high-speed train carrying Charlie Parker and Jaco Pastorias from New Orleans to New York at the very moment when, passing over a bridge, it jumps its rails and ploughs head-on into the lines of gridlocked commuter traffic below.

3. http://hollywoodrecords.go.com/tricky/index.html, 3 April 2003.

4. This becomes especially apparent when one is able to observe her compositional method. Various documentaries and clips on the internet, for instance, have shown her walking along a beach or sitting at her laptop screaming and singing according to a properly improvisational compositional ideal that springs not from a pre-formed notion of what a song is to be but what it could become at any instant.

5. It is important to stress that the individual and the strata of Capital cannot be unproblematically opposed to each other in a simple dualism as, respectively, internal and external, even if this terminology seems merely to echo Deleuze's own vocabulary when he talks of the relationship between expressive qualities and their territory. The individual always retains a transversal relation to the social, political and economic field within which it is produced. It is always merely a folding of subjectification and hence only a partial object. Nonetheless, to think through this opposition in terms of internality and externality is useful inasmuch as it shows the extent to which the strata of Capital, positing itself as an outside to all production, can reproduce only stunted forms of subjectivity, reflections of the personological, familial, structural and institutional models that it favours, subjectivities whose internality is defined precisely by their externality.

Chapter 3

Deleuze, Adorno, and the Composition of Musical Multiplicity

Nick Nesbitt

To approach the relation of Deleuze and music in the short space of this chapter, I want to focus on the musical implications of what I understand to be the primary enabling concept of Deleuze's work, that of 'internal difference': the *internal, non-relational* non-identity of an object. To do so, I wish to compare it to the dialectical thought of Theodor Adorno, whose work is both contemporary to Deleuze's elaboration of an explicitly *non-dialectical* concept of difference and the most highly developed *philosophy* of music of the twentieth century. Unlike Adorno's voluminous writings on music, Deleuze's rejection of dialectical thought as false abstraction and his investigation of internal difference, the '*différence de soi avec soi*' ('the difference of a self with itself') (2002: 35; 2004: 27), is an abstractly philosophical investigation carried out in many guises throughout his work. Neither a musician nor a philosopher of music, Deleuze understood his work to be the production of *concepts*, as he reminds us from his earliest articles (Deleuze 2002: 28; 2004: 33) to *What is Philosophy?* (Deleuze and Guattari 1994: 5). Instead of describing the various moments at which Deleuze talks about music, moments that (with the possible exception of the 'refrain') I see as still somewhat metaphorical illustrations of the concepts he is elaborating, I wish to look at a range of musical phenomena from the perspective of Deleuzian *internal difference* to explore whether it might hold new ways of conceptualising musical activity. If we can understand musical composition as the attempt to work through in each instance the specificity and autonomy (identity) of a set of musical events, then the concept of internal difference may offer the most productive point at which to approach Deleuze's relation to music. Deleuze himself never *compares* the figures he describes (philosophers, writers, musicians, painters, and so on), but rather addresses each on its plane of consistency, in the singularity of its internal difference, as it were. If, in placing Deleuze in descriptive relation to Adorno's negative (musical) dialectics, my procedure is thus wilfully unDeleuzian (comparative, dialectical), it nonetheless could be said to follow Deleuze's own prescription: to take concepts as various tools, and see what they might bring to our understanding of various (musical) events.

Deleuze and Adorno appear to stand in irreconcilable opposition. The former the philosopher of immanence and the univocity of being, the latter the foremost thinker of irresolvable contradictions and negative dialectics, they look to very different precursors and speak entirely different philosophical languages that allow for precious little communication to occur. Yet to abandon each to his proper plane of immanence – in which the truth of each may be expressed without dissent – would be to abandon a critical standpoint in deference to the history of philosophy. Instead, I think it is possible to compose a (dissonant) relationship between these two seemingly antagonistic thinkers. To do so, I think it is only possible to avoid purely metaphorical, impressionistic comments on Deleuze and Adorno's relation to music if we approach these thinkers on their own terrain, that of conceptual reflection.

Deleuze begins his philosophical project not simply with the affirmative thrust of his later works, but as an explicit critique of Hegelian dialectical difference. Deleuze judges the dialectic 'abstract' and 'empty' insofar as 'the Being of Hegelian logic remains merely *thought* being' (1983: 157, 183, my emphasis). Hegelian difference remains an *external* conceptualisation of difference 'with another thing' (a spatial difference), 'its difference with everything that it is not' (a difference of contradiction) (2004: 42). In contrast to a Hegelian dialectical notion of difference, Deleuze follows Henri Bergson and, ultimately, Spinoza, in articulating an internally identical notion of difference in his two 1956 articles 'Bergson 1859–1941' and 'La conception de la différence chez Bergson', both recently republished in the collection *L'Ile Déserte et autres Textes* (2002). There we find Deleuze's presentation of internal difference that all Deleuze's later, better-known works will take as a given as they go on to explore its vast implications. In 'Bergson 1859–1941', Deleuze offers his most succinct formulation of internal difference: 'La durée est ce qui diffère ou ce qui change de nature, la qualité, l'hétérogénéité, ce qui diffère avec soi.' At its most succinct: 'Duration is . . . what differs from itself' (Deleuze 2002: 34; 2004: 26).

How can we understand such an apparently impossible, self-contradictory statement? If duration is what *persists* in time in some sort of identity, then it is just the opposite of difference; to endure is to remain the same. In consonance with the project he will articulate in *Logique du sens*, the logical contradictions of a Deleuzian internal difference form an attempt to force human apprehension to overcome the subject–object logic of a classical dialectical logic.[1] The internal difference of Deleuze's early writings is already one of those *objets impossibles* (the round square, unextended matter), the *événement pur* that precedes and makes possible logical cognition (*le bon sens*) itself (Deleuze 1969: 49; 1990: 35). To think internal difference is to subject oneself to the destructive force of the contradiction, to run up against a logically impossible *problème-épreuve*, a zen *koan*, the point of which is to attempt to break through the sedentary fixations of subjectivity, to perceive the plane of the pure event, the transcendental plane of the univocity of being that itself founds the fixed, self-same subject: 'la personne . . . forme produite à partir de ce champ transcendental impersonnel' (Deleuze 1969: 161, 141; 1990: 136, 116).

Deleuze himself spends little time attempting to define the concept of internal difference, either in these early articles or the later *Différence et répétition* (1968), quickly passing on in each case to take his original question ('Comment la durée a-t-elle ce pouvoir?' as an *a priori* given) ('The question can be put another way: if Being is the difference of a thing, [si l'être est la différence de la chose], what results from this for the thing itself?') (Deleuze 2002: 34; 2004: 38). The examples of internal difference Deleuze offers are generally either mathematical or biological. All depend on a logic of abstraction and purification in which Hegelian negativity and contradiction are displaced outside of any singular entity, leaving that entity free to operate as a singular productive machine. *Bergsonism* informs us that 'The number, and first of all the mathematical unit [*l'unité mathématique*] itself, are the model of that which divides without changing its nature' (Deleuze 1966: 34; 1991: 14, translation modified). Deleuze's biological illustrations of internal difference share a similar degree of abstraction. While internal difference is implicit in Bergson's concept of an internal *élan vital* that Deleuze sees as the 'cause profonde des variations' (Deleuze 1966: 55), Deleuze further develops this biological model in his article 'Gibert Simondon, L'individu et sa genèse physico-biologique' and his talk 'La méthode de dramatisation', recently translated as 'The Method of Dramatization' and published in *Desert Islands and Other Texts* (Deleuze 2004: 94–116). This force of internal differentiation, which takes on the various guises of *élan vital*, Will to Power, or Spinozian *potentia*, occurs when a cell, for example, divides itself to become a different individual while retaining its generic (in the sense of *genus*) identity.

Rather than mounting a sustained critique of the Deleuzian notion of internal difference, an undertaking that would take us far from the field of music, here let us simply accept as Deleuze does *internal difference* as an operative concept, and attempt to unfold its implications for a Deleuzian understanding of musical difference.[2] Deleuze proceeds analogously to Spinoza's sudden beginning of the *Ethics* via a definition rather than a search for an unmediated foundation: 'Par cause de soi', Spinoza writes in the first line of the *Ethics*, 'j'entends ce don't . . . la nature ne peut être conçue qu'existante' (Spinoza 1954: 1; 1919: 45). Whether such entities as Spinoza's *potential* – what Negri calls 'productive being' (Negri 1999: 46) or Deleuze's account of internally differentiated singularities – *actually* exist remains unquestioned. Deleuze, like Spinoza, simply begins *in media res,* as Negri so aptly puts the matter in his study of Spinoza (Negri 1998: 47). If we presume such singularities to exist, Deleuze asks, what implications then unfold from this presupposition? There is no reason to think that if internal difference is a problematic, under-theorised, and somewhat mystified ground to Deleuzian thought, and I think that it is, that this need invalidate a thought that so depends upon it in its functioning. Perhaps, as Adorno argued, every philosophy must proceed to do its work starting from any number of necessary givens or grounds, and that it would be 'infantile' to hold this against a philosophy instead of viewing these quite simply as enabling concepts whose *function* we must investigate (Adorno 2001: 15–16). In this view, Deleuzian internal difference is no different from the Kantian categories or Hegel's assumption that as we progressively come to understand the world, we will in fact find it to reveal its rationality. Internal difference is quite simply the *a priori* that allows the many productive Deleuzian machines to function. Let us follow some of them at work in the field of music.

Musical Difference – Dialectical, Internal, and Ethical

In a general sense, the problem of internal difference can be said to be *the* problem Western concert music addresses from Wagner's *Tristan* (1857) through to the period in which Deleuze constructs his properly philosophical notion. The concept of internal difference transforms our understanding of music in opposition to a classical model of harmonic analysis. First conceived by Rameau (*Traité de l'Harmonie Réduite à ses Principes Naturels,* 1722) and codified by Hugo Riemann (*Katechismus der Harmonielehre,* 1891), in this classical model, every chord is defined only in its subordinate relation to a tonic (I) chord. Quite schematically, in a composition in C major, every chord is defined and differentiated only in its subordinate relation to the C major chord. A given chordal or harmonic moment bears no autonomous, self-sufficient identity; it merely *represents* its function in that key. D minor 7 (II–7) or B half-diminished (VII⁰) are only functions of what they are not: C major (I). All harmonic movement proceeds teleologically, to that final tonic chord that will close any rigorously classical composition. This structural logic of functional harmony constitutes a pre-constructed language that, like Saussurean linguistics, interpellates the individual composer who constructs his or her musical object in dialogue with those structural norms. The various analytical degrees that Rameau and Riemann identified (I–VII, tonics, subdominants, dominants, and so on) function in a hierarchal, differential, and structural relationship, each taking on its meaning via its place in a given harmonic form. In this classical model, a C major chord is the tonic chord (I) in a composition in C, but that same C major chord functions as the subdominant (IV) in a composition in G major.

In response to this heteronomous relation, the dehierarchisation of harmony – the elimination of functional referents such as the tonic and dominant that teleologically reduce all musical harmony to *relationships* – received its first shocking sounding in Western concert music in the 'Tristan chord', whose extreme ambiguity broke any clear, classical logic of harmonic relation. While sounding utterly 'right' in Wagner's composition, it could be analysed as simultaneously belonging to five extremely distant tonalities all at once (Abromont 2001: 311).[3] Here was a chord that, like Deleuze's concept of internal, non-relational difference itself, was quite literally undecidable in terms of classical analysis; its function continues to this day to generate extensive, contradictory, and often puzzled commentary in musicological circles. In and of itself, it constitutes a plane of internal difference that suddenly, since 1857, has simply stopped (trained) listeners from thinking in terms of musical function and relation. Like Deleuze's concept of internal difference itself, the Tristan chord forces us to abandon relational thinking. How can one single harmonic event be so many contradictory things at once; in other words, how can it be internally, and not relationally differentiated? Like the entities Alice finds on the other side of the looking glass, we may not understand how the Tristan chord functions logically and relationally in Rameau and Riemann's world, where any chord can (ideally) only be one thing at a time, in its self-same identity,[4] but function it does indeed, as a polyvalent entity unto itself.

This tendency culminated in 1920 in Schoenberg's absolute dehierarchising codification of twelve-tone harmony. There, none of the twelve notes of the chromatic scale bears any relation of dominance or superiority over any other; each is an internally differentiated entity unto itself, each of which must simply follow another in a predetermined order. Wagner, however, was not the demiurgic initiator of this dehierarchisation of harmony. The move from mediaeval modal harmony (as in Gregorian chant) – in which each degree of a given modal arrangement of a scale (Ionian, Dorian, and so on) bore a specific role or *gestus* in relation to the other modes – to equal temperament itself gradually brought about the attainment of strict functional equivalency of all twelve keys by the 1850s. Though many musicians claim certain keys are more suited to expressing one or another musical emotion, this is presumably because a given key is habitually linked with certain compositions (say, Chopin's Op. 53 in A flat: 'Heroic'). Wagner extended this equivalency of all twelve chromatic keys (a composition in A flat major is objectively no more suited to expressing 'heroicism' than one in D sharp major) into a progressively freer scheme of unlimited chromatic modulation (the movement from one tonality to another) *within* a composition. In true equal temperament, no key retains an individual colour or identity, and this implies in turn that all twelve possible modulations can occur in a given compositional structure. The increasing chromaticism of Chopin and Wagner merely extended the structural equivalency of equal temperament first into overarching key relationships and then into the smallest elements of musical composition, including vertical harmonic structures (incorporation of progressively more distant – or 'dissonant' – harmonic extensions in chords), and horizontal intervallic structures, each eventually coming, by the time of Schoenberg, to incorporate freely the twelve notes of the chromatic scale.

Conversely, long before Wagner's Tristan chord, the mediaeval modes could be said to constitute an early model of internal musical difference, since each mode (that is, the various possible dispositions of whole and half step intervals in the diatonic scale) takes on its own distinctive 'mood' or character. Each becomes what Deleuze and Guattari, speaking of art and music in particular, call 'autonomous and sufficient [musical] beings' insofar as 'the composition of created sensations preserves itself in itself [*se conserve en lui-même*] (1994: 168, 164, translation modified). Whether such an anthropomorphism of musical 'affect' is more than the authors' rhetorical flourish, whether a musical 'subject' might actually stand autonomously in relation to human subjectivity seems doubtful, though great music can convince us it is possible. In any case, Deleuze and Guattari's conception of musical subjectivity follows quite exactly Locke's description from 1694 of the self: the subject is 'that which can consider itself the same thinking thing in different times and places' (Locke 1998: 148). Only, and this of course makes all the difference, the determining element in Locke's concept of the subject, self-consciousness, has been subtracted by Deleuze and Guattari from their concept of self-same, immediate musical expression. The mediaeval expression of Deleuze and Guattari's 'autonomous musical beings' attained its most advanced state in the Cistercian Chant, codified and theorised in Guy d'Eu's *Regule de Arte Musica* (c. 1132). Each Cistercian melody forms an independent, self-same 'modal unity,' each of which possesses its own particular personality or '*dispositio*' (Abromont 2001: 387). For the first time in the West, the second Cistercian Reform generated a music autonomously from Gui d'Eu's productive machine, a theoretical deduction that created the musical monad that is Cistercian Chant through an objective '*prise de conscience* of the individual in his autonomy' (Maître 1995: 409). This reform undertook a purification of musical practice that banished from a given melody all 'contradictory elements', overthrowing the uncertainty of historical (Gregorian) tradition in deference to the pure perfection of reason (Maître 1995: 60). Gui d'Eu diagrams this purified auto-differentiation as a modal circle, internally rationalized and free of contradiction, in a process of eternal self-differentiation: The '*dispositio* [of the seven modes] is ordered within a circle [*in circulo ordinatur*], which, in the image of eternity, has neither beginning nor end ... Wherever you begin [within the circle], you find one type generated by one of its neighbours and generating another [in turn]' (d'Eu 1995: 140–1).

From another perspective, the move away from the church modes and the adoption of the mean-tone scale amounted in effect to the constitution of Deleuzian planes of internal difference. Instead of evenly spreading the inaccuracies of the upper notes of the harmonic series throughout the chromatic scale,[5] the mean-tone system of the sixteenth century made all the lower intervals perfectly consonant, while displacing the cumulative inaccuracies of the Pythagorean scale upon a single note (B sharp) which itself then became unusable, the howling 'wolf fifth' (Abromont 2001: 335). In a very schematic sense, then, one could say that the mean-tone system constituted a pure plane of immanent non-contradiction following the same exclusionary procedure at work in Deleuze's Nietzschean 'expulsion of the negative' from a conception of singularity (Deleuze 1962: 199).

A musical version of Deleuze's univocal Spinozianism occurs in the Impressionist turn to the musical mode as the vector of musical construction. The terminological overlap between the Spinozian 'modes' of being and the more specifically musical usage is penetrating. The modal musical constructions of Debussy (as in the C whole-tone harmony of 'Voiles') turn from a relational method of structuration – in which themes progress into variations in a teleological process of development with harmony built around cadential moments of tension and release – to one in which a single set of scalar material determines a (relatively) static field of harmony and melody (cf. Ulehla, ch. 8). In this sense, all conceivable modes are precisely *virtual* in Deleuze's structuralist sense,[6] since there exists a concrete and limited number of mathematically possible combinations of a given set of notes (most commonly the twelve notes of the chromatic scale). This abstract material constitutes the univocal being of a musical universe, while each musical mode constitutes a single plane of consistency in that musical universe. Still, even the most rigorously 'modal' composition of this period is not absolutely internal in its difference; Debussy's experiments, for example, are only comprehensible in both their internal logic and as moments in the history of music in relation to the most progressive developments in functional harmony at the turn of the twentieth century.

The innovations of Schoenberg and his students Berg and Webern constitute an alternative attempt to compose internally differentiated, monad-like musical objects. Already in Brahms, the externally imposed single metre that determines the rhythmic totality of a composition begins to be replaced by constantly shifting metrical patterns, while Brahms's construction of musical development itself increasingly arises out of the interval structures internal to musical motifs in a way that directly begins the move to serialism, abandoning all development driven by a composition's mere rhythmic momentum (Ulehla 1994: 12, 21–4). At every level – rhythmic, harmonic, and timbral – Schoenberg and his students pursue Brahms' innovations, working to throw off externally imposed forms and replace them with internally generated distinctions. The period of 'free-atonal' composition – more accurately composition freely using the twelve-tone scale previous to Schoenberg's development of the twelve-tone serial row – refers to a method of composition in which all twelve chromatic tones are employed without reference to a transcendent diatonic scale or need for specific resolutions. In this sense, this is a music of sheer immanence in which each musical moment arises out of another without reference to an external source of formal or stylistic authority, an ideal first approached in Schoenberg's *Erwartung* (1909). 'In the new music that counts,' wrote Adorno in his article 'The Function of Counterpoint in New Music':

> it is as untrue that the subject has merely emancipated itself as it is that music has simply invoked objectivity. Its ideal is autonomy. It adheres to nothing that is alien to its own impulse, its own coherence, and that has

been merely imposed upon it. It desires to become objective out of its own subjectivity, through the unreserved immersion in its unique self, without external supports and borrowings. (Adorno 1999: 134)

Adorno here identifies in free atonality a model of internal musical difference founded upon the autonomous musical event. And yet – most obviously in their close relation to Brahms, Wagner, and Mahler – these composers' relation to their inherited material (sonata form, functional harmony, orchestration, theme and variation technique) is dialectical. Each, and above all the Berg whose *Wozzeck* and *Lulu* Deleuze invokes on numerous occasions, worked *through* such musical inheritances in their pursuit of musical autonomy. The sheer immanence of twelve-tone composition is itself mediated, reducible to neither a Deleuzian absolute purging of representation and reflection, nor to a simple development and outgrowth of Viennese Classicism. Viennese Modernism is at once relational and what Alain Badiou has called a 'purely singular event' (Badiou 2001: 41).

The relation between a Deleuzian music of internal difference and Adorno's musical dialectics is complex, at once one of identity and difference. This becomes clear in Adorno's late study *Alban Berg: Master of the Smallest Link* (1991). In a sense, one might call this Adorno's most Deleuzian musical study, closest that is to a work in which one 'think[s] of [an author] so hard that he can no longer be an object' (Deleuze and Parnet 1987: 119). In contrast to the polemical partisan politics (Schoenberg vs. Stravinsky) of Adorno's earlier *Philosophy of Modern Music,* the Berg study combines a total immersion in the smallest details of Berg's music with a notable modesty as Adorno lovingly recalls his former teacher. Like Deleuze's monographs, *Alban Berg* reincarnates as an aesthetic semblance Berg, the biographical and musical 'character'.

Adorno understands Berg to have proceeded in a musical dissolution of dialectics analogous to his own negative dialectics. If the latter undermines the machine-like functioning of official dialectics (thesis/antithesis/synthesis) in a self-critique of antinomical thought, Adorno's Berg subjects the classic sonata form to immanent critique. Berg's first orchestral piece (Op. 6) approaches 'liquidation of the sonata' (Adorno 1991: 82) by itself composing an aesthetic semblance of the natural through expressionist means. The piece's 'unceasing variation' arises from the void of silence in its opening measure, through pianissimo unpitched percussion (tam-tam, cymbals), then pitched percussion (tympani), then brass, strings and bassoon in a composition in which 'the development technique has become total; there is not a single note that is not the result of strict motivic development' (Adorno 1991: 106). The imitation of nature that Adorno calls 'Berg's commitment to the organic' (Adorno 1991: 20) – in which (sonic) life appears to arise out of nothingness, expands and then contracts back into nothingness – occurs at both the micrological and formal levels in this composition; Berg's aesthetic semblance of nature is achieved with the most complex and highly developed technical means.[7] From them, Berg creates a composition in which, 'with vegetative force, almost rank, [the music] expands in all directions' (Adorno 1991: 72).

To understand why Adorno's claim that 'the first movement [of Op. 6] is liquefied sonata in the extreme' (Adorno 1991: 107) constitutes as well a critique of the dialectic, one need only consider the explanation of sonata form given in the first edition of the *New Grove Dictionary of Music* (Webster 1980: 497–508). James Webster's article describes 'a two-part tonal structure, articulated in three main sections . . . Sonata form is a synthesis of binary and ternary principles: it integrates three sections into a two-part structure' (Webster 1980: 497). These sections – the exposition, development and recapitulation – correspond directly to the abstract form of dialectical syllogism (thesis/antithesis/synthesis). The binary nature of the musical material corresponds in turn to the movement of affirmation and negation, the 'tremendous power of the negative' that marks the movement of the Hegelian dialectic (Hegel 1977: 19). In this sense, the sonata form reproduces on the musical plane the movement of spirit in which 'Spirit becomes object because it is just this movement of becoming an *other to itself* . . . in which the immediate, the unexperienced, i.e. the abstract . . . becomes alien from itself and then returns to itself from this alienation, and is only then revealed for the first time in its actuality and truth' (Hegel 1977: 21). Furthermore, Webster describes in astonishingly Deleuzian terms the single Deleuzian plane of '*Affekt*' (psychological state, rhythmic profile, texture, etc.) that developed 'in uniform texture' in earlier Baroque music, where 'contrast appears only in opposing planes (solo and *tutti*, loud and soft and so on)'. In its place, sonata form introduced dialectical negation into Classical music – with Beethoven as its pinnacle of expression – at the same moment Hegel's notion of determinate negation enters philosophy (Webster 1980: 498).[8]

In contrast, in Berg's Op. 6, the dialectical driving force of the sonata form is absent. Instead, the achievement of totality in Berg's musical object is 'compelled by the events themselves – that is, by the musical design . . . Individual events have their individual sound without concern for a preconceived totality' (Adorno 1991: 52). The parallel Adorno's description offers with Deleuze and Guattari's notion of a musical subject that 'stands on its own' (Deleuze and Guattari 1991: 155) is striking. Moreover, in the motivic economy of *Wozzeck,* specific musical figures (the captain's English horn phrase first heard in bar 4, Wozzeck's 'Wir arme Leute' phrase) constitute themselves as subjectified musical sound-concepts, or what Deleuze and Guattari call 'conceptual personae [*personnages*]' (Deleuze and Guattari 1994: 24).

The music of Alban Berg, and *Wozzeck* in particular – which both Deleuze and Adorno take as one of the signal interventions of the twentieth century – leads, however, to a distinctly antagonistic relation between Deleuzian and Adornian thought. There is no way, I think, to understand *Wozzeck* within the scheme of a Deleuzian 'ethics' of the Will to Power and *potentia* as the latter is laid out in Deleuze's Nietzsche and Spinoza studies. Adorno opposes Berg quite explicitly to any Nietzschean 'affirmation' or 'health':

> Berg assumes a position in extreme antithesis to that which musical tradition calls healthy, to the will to live, to the affirmative, to the repeated glorification of that which *is.* The concept of health, inherently as ineradicable a part of prevailing musical criteria as it is of Philistinism, is in league with conformism; health is allied with what in life is stronger, with the victors. (Adorno 1991: 5)

In this passage dense with implied references, Adorno gestures on the one hand to a dimension of Nietzsche Deleuze suppresses and banishes from the anti-Hegelian, purified, positive plane of consistency that is his *Nietzsche*: the Nietzsche who, in undertaking his symptomatology of nihilism, identifies himself not with the healthy, but with the *sick*:

> In the midst of torments that go with an uninterrupted three-day migraine, accompanied by laborious vomiting of phlegm, I possessed a dialectician's clarity *par excellence* . . . Need I say after all this that in questions of decadence I am *experienced*? . . . Who knows how much I am ultimately indebted . . . to my protracted sickness! (Adorno 1991: 222–3 and 229, emphasis in original)

Simultaneously, Adorno's evocation of 'the victors' points as well to Walter Benjamin's 'Theses on the Philosophy of History' (*Illuminations*). Benjamin's seventh thesis looks back sadly over the carnage of history to conclude that:

> the nature of this sadness stands out more clearly if one asks with whom the adherents of historicism actually empathise. The answer is inevitable: with the victor . . . Whoever has emerged victorious participates to this

day in the triumphal procession in which the present rulers step over those who are lying prostrate. (Benjamin 1968: 256)

From its basic orientation to its smallest compositional details, Berg's music expresses this empathy and suffering; it is music 'radical and shocking in its partiality for the weaker, the defeated: the figure of Berg's humanity. No music of our time was as humane as his; that distances it from [the actual cruelty of] humankind' (Adorno 1991: 5). While moments such as Marie's D minor viola motif that begins Act Three of *Wozzeck* stand out for me in their expression of an overwhelming suffering and empathy, Berg lovingly held onto the (musical) past in every dimension of his work. He reworked and reanimated the deadened, reified material he saw as he glanced behind him at the wreckage of (musical) history. Berg refused to throw away the sonatas, rondos, marches, lullabies, suites, passacaglias, fugues, and fantasias (to name only a few of the forms reworked in *Wozzeck*) that he had inherited simply because history marches on (cf. Jarman 1989: 42). Every measure of his music incarnates this 'tolerance for what has been, which he allows to shine through, not literally, but recurrently in dream and involuntary memory' (Adorno 1991: 8).

The contrast between Berg and one of Deleuze's primary musical references, Pierre Boulez, is striking. While Deleuze and Guattari make many decisive conceptual applications of Boulez's writings and music in *A Thousand Plateaus* (cf. Bogue 1991), I wish to focus here instead on the inherent Deleuzism of Boulez's 1963 book *Penser la Musique Aujourd'hui*. Not only does Boulez offer Deleuze a sonic model for an immediate, non-representational plane of consistency, the 'sound block that no longer has a point of origin . . . the immanent sound plane, which is always given along with that to which it gives rise' (Deleuze and Guattari 1987: 296, 267), but Boulez forms the ideal musical interlocutor for the Deleuze of *Nietzsche et la Philosophie* (1962) precisely because the musico-theoretical concepts the composer elaborates function following the same logic of isolation and abstraction that underlies Deleuze's early thought. Whether Boulez actually creates non-referential sound-events in compositions such as *Pli selon Pli*, as Deleuze and Guattari claim, is a question that, while beyond the scope of this article to address in detail, seems highly tendentious given the nature of that composition's explicit, if complex, relation to Mallarmé's poem. Still, it is striking how closely Boulez's argument in *Penser la Musique Aujourd'hui* follows on a musical plane Deleuze's Nietzschean 'ethics' of prophylactic purification of relational difference and negativity.

Penser la Musique Aujourd'hui was adapted from a series of lectures Boulez first gave at the summer courses in modern music at Darmstadt, Germany. The Darmstadt courses brought together the now-famous founders of postwar Serial Music, including Boulez, Messiaen, Karlheinz Stockhausen, and Luigi Nono, while Adorno himself played an important role in the development of theoretical reflection on serialism with Darmstadt lectures such as 'Vers une musique informelle'. Boulez's text makes plain his goal of an absolute musical interiority, purified of all relations to extra-musical criteria. Boulez's fundamental normative goal is to 'found musical systems on exclusively musical criteria' (Boulez 1963: 29). In his musical Cartesianism, he affirms the 'absolute necessity of a logically organised consciousness' (Boulez 1963: 33). Boulez poses as a musical puritan, scandalised by worldly temptation, as he encourages his interlocutors to:

> discipline our mental universe in such a way *that we may have before us no denials to confront us* [*que nous n'ayons pas devant nous de reniements à affronter*] . . . Let us strictly organise our musical thought: this will deliver us from contingency and the transitory. Isn't this the principal refusal that we must oppose to the oh so seductive, yet thoroughly vain, temptations? (Boulez 1963: 33, my emphasis)

Like the Deleuze of *Nietzsche et la Philosophie,* in which the will to power acts to 'expulse the negative' (Deleuze 1962: 199), Boulez strives to purify his musical plane of all negativity ('no denials to confront us') so that he may proceed univocally. The serial musical world Boulez constructs is quite literally univocal, an apartheid-like space (Darmstadt as much as the serial composition itself) in which no dissenting voices can deny the validity of the Serial musical procedure.

Boulez's essay appeared precisely in the period following the breakup of the Darmstadt group triggered by the dissident, resolutely humanist voice of Luigi Nono. Without ever mentioning them by name, Nono's 1959 Darmstadt talk *Presenza Storica nella Musica d'Oggi* was a direct attack on the rationalist interiority of his fellow Darmstadt serialists, Boulez and Nono's close friend Stockhausen in particular.[9] Nono – whose 1955 composition *Il Canto Sospeso* combines Serialist techniques with text from the letters of those condemned to die for their resistance to European fascism – castigates in his talk:

> the tendency . . . to refuse to integrate an artistico-cultural phenomenon in its historical context, that is to say to refuse to consider it in *relation* to its origins and to the elements that formed it, neither in *relation* to its participation in present reality and its efficacy over it, nor in *relation*

to its capacity to project into the future, but exclusively *in itself* and *for itself*, as its own end, and only in relation to the precise instant in which it manifests itself. (Nono 1987: 239, my emphasis)

In contrast to Nono's attempt to link a radical ethical project to the most advanced musical procedures, Boulez's strict structuralism (he approvingly quotes Louis Rougier's statement that 'what we can know of the world is its structure, not its essence' (Boulez 1963: 31)) absolutises the banishment of transcendental knowledge from artistic practice, and thus any relation of music to ethics. Boulez's structuralism describes a musical 'universe' that is strictly 'relative', in which 'structural relations are not defined once and for all according to absolute criteria; they organise themselves, according to varying schemas' (Boulez 1963: 35). If this is a 'logic of relations' (Boulez 1963: 113), it is not the exterior, dialectical relations of form and meaning, art and society, truth and expression, that interest both Adorno and Nono, but a relation of strict interiority. Boulez's notion of the series – the combinatory sequence (of pitches, but also in postwar serialism of rhythmic and timbral material) that determines a composition – posits a self-sufficient entity: the series 'possesses intrinsic characteristics – they depend . . . on its structure, on the isomorphic figures it contains, on the symmetries it harbors, and, consequently, on the selective powers it holds' (Boulez 1963: 113). The only exteriority Boulez admits is that of an infinite regress of further structural relations that organise the 'disposition of structures in relation to one another'. From these structural dispositions, seemingly with no dialectical interaction with inherited material – musical, social, philosophical or otherwise – 'one arrives directly at [compositional] form' (Boulez 1963: 150).

Boulez presents a musical system in total abstraction from extramusical meaning, and indeed from musical subjectivity (as hearing, imagining, sounding) in any form: 'In the serial system . . . no function [in a series] reveals itself as identical from one series to another, but each function depends solely upon the particular characteristics [of that series] and the fashion in which they are exploited' (Boulez 1963: 48). Boulez gives no explanation of how the internal differentiation of a series's identity might (or might not) depend on immanent universals that transcend a particular series, whether of human auditory physiology, a historical, comparative musical memory and practice (as in his own music's critical relation to Schoenberg and Webern), or the immanent universality of musical materials (notes, timbres, rhythms, and so on) that transcend any given composition. Boulez can only maintain his incredible contention that 'the series . . . is not arbitrary' (Boulez 1963: 92) because its notion has been purged of any relation to exterior facticity. This exclusionary logic – 'the ensemble delimited by the original series excludes . . . the arbitrary, because it implies consequences necessarily tied to a selection based upon sonorous realities' (Boulez 1963: 93) – functions only because all 'realities' save the 'sonorous' have been excised from consideration. Through this purging, Boulez's sound-world strives to constitute a plane of immanence shorn of any historical content that would introduce contradiction to its univocity. 'A responsible universe is able – without exterior action, with no other agency than the intrinsic – to assure the coherency of the text' (Boulez 1963: 149).

In conclusion, let me turn to another field of advanced musical production in effect in this same period (early 1960s) as all the texts we have considered up to now. This is a field that demonstrates, I think, both the continued explanatory force of both Deleuzian and Adornian conceptions of musical difference, and yet, through its instantiation of a concrete, intersubjective musical ethics, transcends certain limitations of both Deleuze and Adorno. For if the insufficiency of a Deleuzian 'ethics' of interiority is its patent refusal to construct an ethical *relation* to others, Adorno's negative dialectics runs up against its limit in its inability to consider from within (that is to say, in sympathy with) the most advanced products of vernacular Modernism, and, more specifically, jazz.

In comparison with the structural complexities of Boulez's *Pli selon Pli* (1962), the strictly contemporary musical production of John Coltrane may seem crude and underdeveloped. Coltrane's music, however, stands out in twentieth-century Western music – with Berg's *Wozzeck* perhaps its only equal – in its production of a substantive ethical voice from the most highly developed interaction with musical materials. In contrast to both Boulez's mathematical musical abstraction from social content and Adorno's unwillingness to posit any substantial, non-aesthetic relation between the isolated artist (Schoenberg) and an absolutely untrue society, Coltrane constructed an uncompromisingly radical development of the African diasporic vernacular that still functioned as a fundamental ethical intervention in the American Civil Rights movement. Coltrane's music was no Brechtian agitprop, and his work proceeded along strictly musical lines that would seem to allow for no unambiguous 'social' reading. And yet, though many traditionalists reacted violently to his innovations, a vast community of listeners from white jazz critics and club-goers to a large section of the African American vernacular community conversant in the language of jazz and the blues understood Coltrane's music quite unambiguously to create the aesthetic semblance (a Deleuzian 'personnage musical') of the freedom and autonomy of an unfree subject (cf. Early 1999; Lock 1988).

Like Deleuze in his chosen field, Coltrane produced an endless stream of musical concepts, completely refashioning the aesthetic norms of jazz at least three times in the years between the time he joined Miles Davis in 1955 and his death in 1967. A composition such as 'Impressions' reveals a many-layered reflection on musical difference that addressed within the sphere of musical reflection the problem of difference as it existed in the African American community in the mid-twentieth century. 'Impressions' was perhaps the signature composition of Coltrane's live performances with his classic quartet (McCoy Tyner, Jimmy Garrison, Elvin Jones) in the period 1960–4. The piece serves as a vehicle for reflection upon difference in more than the vague sense that Coltrane's playing gave articulate voice to the existential concerns of minorities involved in the fight for social justice in the 1960s. As an aesthetic object, 'Impressions' constructs a modal plane of immanence for Coltrane's improvisations in a manner similar to the modalism of early twentieth-century composers such as Debussy.[10] Constructed in AABA form, the harmonic scheme of 'Impressions' is extremely simple: eight bars of D minor Dorian repeated once, eight bars of D sharp minor (commonly notated as its enharmonic equivalent E flat Dorian), then a return of eight bars of D minor.

While other modal jazz compositions of the period frequently specify solos over a single tonality (as in the C minor modality of Coltrane's beautiful ballad 'Lonnie's Lament'), 'Impressions' is ingeniously structured to engender maximum differentiation of musical material with the simplest of means. By modulating a half-tone up from D to D sharp in its bridge, the A and B sections maintain a non-identity of harmonic material.[11] On the one hand, each section thus constitutes a (sonic) univocal plane of consistency, one located a half-tone above the other. There is no harmonic preparation for the modulation from one plane to the other, a preparation that in traditional harmony gradually relates and initiates this passage. Moreover, the non-identity of the two modes makes their shift extreme, with no common tones to relate one tonality to the other. The harmony simply shifts immediately from one absolutely internally consistent mode to the other and back. Each *mode* forms its own *monad*.

And yet these planes are nonetheless in complex relation. Deleuze himself fudges the notion of internal difference with his concept of 'resonance' (Deleuze and Guattari 1991: 28). Clearly, to say that planes of consistency 'resonate' between one another is to undercut any strict notion of their *absolutely* internal difference, musical, conceptual or otherwise. A body can only resonate with another if they have certain characteristics in common. A composition such as 'Impressions' demonstrates this resonance concretely. Each of its two modalities takes on meaning only in relation to its non-identical other. In a strictly modal composition with unchanging tonality, the absolute non-identity of the notes of the composition's mode turn into an absolute identity and non-differentiation in a static harmonic field. In 'Impressions', in contrast, the movement between two tonalities constantly reinforces the absolute difference of one field from the other. In this sense, if one took the entire thirty-two-bar form as a totality, rather than each single modal plane, the composition could be said to differentiate itself internally; the Dorian mode differentiates itself (D, then D sharp, then D again) while maintaining its identity as, precisely, the Dorian mode (an identical distribution of intervals). This absolute interiority, however, is a pure abstraction. 'Impressions' might be said to demonstrate conversely the functioning of relational difference itself. As soon as we begin to consider 'Impressions' as an actually existing, performed, improvised entity, it is no longer possible to maintain a Deleuzian quarantine on relational musical difference. What both Deleuze and Boulez excise from the concept of music is precisely human experience, the instantiation of music as a complexly rendered social totality. This is precisely where Coltrane can offer a penetrating interjection for our understanding of musical difference.

As its thirty-two bar form becomes internalised by the performer, 'Impressions' begins to be heard in a movement of relational tension and release. In fact, its harmonic form is understandable as a single extended cadence rather than as two absolutely distinct sonic planes: with D minor functioning as tonic, the extreme tension of the E flat-7 serves as an implied tritone dominant (flat II alt.). Furthermore, in performance, McCoy Tyner and Coltrane constantly introduce harmonic movement in relation to the piece's two abstract, static tonal planes. Coltrane rarely restricts himself to the six notes of the Dorian scale for more than the first chorus of his solos on 'Impressions', as he superimposes alternate chord changes and patterns to lead out of the tonality toward increasingly extreme chromaticism (Porter 1998: 218–30; Liebman 1991: 25–8).[12] McCoy Tyner's comping behind Coltrane builds a modal plane of consistency using the smooth (Deleuze and Boulez would say *lisse*), equidistant fourth-based chords that arrest a sense of harmonic motion with a static Dorian plane, but here as well, Tyner constantly introduces chromatic alterations, parallel chord constructions that depart from the Dorian mode, and altered and tritone dominant transitions that smooth the work's single modulation.[13]

If Coltrane stands out as one of the greatest artists of the twentieth century, it is surely for his capacity to combine aesthetic innovation of the highest level with an unparalleled force of expression. Coltrane developed to the most extraordinary degree, to a degree previously undreamt of, Deleuze's Spinozian encomium to the possibilities of 'what a [sounding] body can do'. Coltrane at once instantiates Spinoza's ethical maxim and drives it beyond the interiority of a monad-like single saxophone/body via the communicative, intersubjective social force of musical sound. Coltrane's music is uncompromising in its breakthrough beyond the virtual to explore the possible, yet it remains more than pure expression; it communicates, wordlessly. This music instantiates productive, radically constituent musical subjectivity as a critique of the alienation and violence of what Toni Negri, following Spinoza, calls *potestas* or 'constituted Power'. For Coltrane, this transcendantal Power lay not only in the reigning violence of Jim Crow America, but in the sedimented forms of musical expression itself. In Coltrane's practice, musical expression is not to alienate its power of construction to transcendent, received norms (including any pre-existing stylistic genre such as bebop or tonality itself) but instead to reinvent in each moment of expression the dimensions of emancipated subjectivity (as in 'Brasilia' from 1965 or the free exploration of thematic cells in Coltrane's last recording, *Interstellar Space*).[14] Though many jazz musicians shared this radical programme in the 1960s, arguably only Coltrane was able fully to engage the constructive possibilities of this emancipation through his unparalleled technique and grasp of musical material, historical, theoretical, and expressive. He combined the most advanced systematic research into vernacular musical Modernism with the deepest expressive potential of what Houston Baker has called 'blues voice': not a stylistic norm (of which Coltrane was of course an unparalleled master) but a mode or 'matrix' of (social) expression (Baker 1984: 3).

The musical *character* of John Coltrane thus offers a semblance of an emancipated subject constructed in sound. 'Impressions' is not autonomy itself, but its representation in sound, the impression music can convey that that autonomy is more than merely possible, or rather that it is rather virtual and immanent, awakened in the struggle to sound a transcendental possible ('A Love Supreme'). These unimaginable sounds are to a degree actually and truly free, even if those who hear them are not, and the tale of autonomy Coltrane tells is therefore not merely utopian, but can take on at least the immanent, empirical form of aesthetic expression. This music thus stands as a truth Adorno could never allow himself to hear, that an advanced musical construction could retain intersubjective, moral purchase in an American vernacular community. It is equally the truth of a Deleuzian notion of internal (musical) difference, as it constructs for us selfsame musical entities that (consciously) refer only to themselves, to the working through of their (musical, existential) problems, and in this utter, windowless interiority, resonate outward across, time and space, culture and race to express fully 'what a [living] body can do' – whether that body is black, social, human, or simply a vector of organic organisation – and to demonstrate that what we took to be utterly impossible and utopian is in fact virtually at hand.

References

Abromont, C. (2001), *La Théorie de la Musique*, Paris: Fayard Henry Lemoine.
Adorno, T. W. (1973), *Negative Dialectics*, trans. E. B. Ashton, New York: Continuum.
Adorno, T. W. (1991), *Alban Berg: Master of the Smallest Link*, trans. J. Brand and C. Hailey, Cambridge: Cambridge University Press.
Adorno, T. W. (1999), *Sound Figures*, trans. R. Livingstone, Stanford: Stanford University Press.
Adorno, T. W. (2000), *Problems of Moral Philosophy*, trans. R. Livingstone, Stanford: Stanford University Press.
Adorno, T. W. (2001), *Kant's Critique of Pure Reason*, Stanford: Stanford University Press.
Badiou, A. (2001), *Ethics: An Essay on the Understanding of Evil*, trans. P. Hallward, New York: Verso.
Baker, H. A. Jr (1984), *Blues, Ideology, and Afro-American Literature: A Vernacular Theory*, Chicago: University of Chicago Press.
Benjamin, W. (1968), *Illuminations*, trans. H. Zohn, New York: Schocken Books.
Berg, A. *Wozzeck* (score), Vienna: Universal Edition No. 12100.
Berg, A. *Drei Orchesterstucke, Op. 6* (score), Vienna: Philharmonia No. 432.
Berliner, P. (1994), *Thinking in Jazz: The Infinite Art of Improvisation*, Chicago: University of Chicago Press.
Bernstein, J. M. (2001), *Adorno: Disenchantment and Ethics*, Cambridge: Cambridge University Press.
Bogue, R. (1991), 'Rhizomusicosmology', *Substance* 20 (3): 85–101.
Boulez, P. (1963), *Penser la musique aujourd'hui*, Paris: Ed. Gonthier (Gallimard).
Buchanan, I. (2000), *Deleuzism: A Metacommentary*, Durham: Duke University Press.
Deleuze, G. (1962), *Nietzsche et la philosophie*, Paris: Presses Universitaires de France.
Deleuze, G. (1966), *Le Bergsonisme*, Paris: Presses Universitaires de France.
Deleuze, G. (1968), *Différence et Répétition*, Paris: Presses Universitaires de France.
Deleuze, G. (1969), *Logique du sens*, Paris: Les éditions du minuit.
Deleuze, G. (1981), *Spinoza: Philosophie Pratique*, Paris: Les éditions de minuit.
Deleuze, G. (1983), *Nietzsche and Philosophy*, trans. Hugh Tomlinson, New York: Columbia University Press.
Deleuze, G. (1990), *The Logic of Sense*, trans. Mark Lester and Charles Stivale, New York: Columbia University Press.

Deleuze, G. (1990), *Pourparlers*, Paris: *Les éditions de minuit*.
Deleuze, G. (1991), *Bergsonism*, trans. Hugh Tomlinson and Barbara Habberjam, New York: Zone Books.
Deleuze, G. (1993), *The Fold: Leibniz and the Baroque*, trans T. Conley, Minneapolis: University of Minnesota Press.
Deleuze, G. (1994), *Difference and Repetition*, trans. Paul Patton, London: Athlone Press.
Deleuze, G. (2002), *L'Ile déserte et autres texts*, Paris: *Les éditions de minuit*.
Deleuze, G. (2004), *Desert Islands and Other Texts* (1953–1974), Cambridge, MA: Semiotext(e).
Deleuze, G. and Guattari, F. (1987), *A Thousand Plateaus*, trans. B. Massumi, Minneapolis: University of Minnesota Press.
Deleuze, G. and Guattari, F. (1991), *Qu'est-ce que la philosophie?* Paris: Les éditions de minuit.
Deleuze, G. and Guattari, F. (1994) *What is Philosophy?*, trans. Hugh Tomlinson and Graham Burchell, New York: Columbia University Press
Deleuze, G. and Parnet, C. (1987), *Dialogues*, trans. H. Tomlinson and B. Habberjam, New York: Columbia University Press.
Deliège, I. and Paddison, M. (eds) (2001), *Musique Contemporaine: Perspectives Théoriques et Philosophiques*, Paris: Mardaga.
D'Eu, G. 'Regule de arte musica', in Claire Maître (1995), *La réforme cistercienne du plain-chant: Etude d'un traité théorique*, Brecht: Cîteaux, pp. 108–233.
Early, G. (1999), 'Ode to John Coltrane: A Jazz Musician's Influence on African American Culture', *Antioch Review*, 57 (3): 370–85.
Hardt, M. (1993), *Gilles Deleuze: An Apprenticeship in Philosophy*, Minneapolis: University of Minnesota Press.
Headlam, D. (1996), *The Music of Alban Berg*, New Haven: Yale University Press.
Hegel, G. W. F. (1969), *Hegel's Science of Logic*, trans. A. V. Miller, Atlantic Highlands: Humanities Press International.
Hegel, G. W. F. (1977), *Hegel's Phenomenology of Spirit*, trans. A. V. Miller, Oxford: Oxford University Press.
Jarman, D. (1989), *Alban Berg: Wozzeck*, Cambridge: Cambridge University Press.
Liebman, D. (1991), *A Chromatic Approach to Jazz Harmony and Melody*, Rottenburg: Advance Music.
Lock, G. (1988), *Forces in Motion: The Music and Thoughts of Anthony Braxton*, New York: Da Capo Press.
Locke, J. (1998), *Identité et Différence: L'Invention de la Conscience*, Bilingual edition presented, trans. E. Balibar, Paris: Seuil.
Maître, Claire (1995), *La réforme cistercienne du plain-chant: Etude d'un traité théorique*, Brecht: Cîteaux.
Negri, A. (1998), *Spinoza: L'Anomalia Salvaggia, Spinoza Sovversivo, Democrazia ed Eternità in Spinoza*, Rome: Derive Approdi.
Negri, A. (1999), *Insurgencies: Constituent Power and the Modern State*, trans. Maurizia Boscagli, Minneapolis: University of Minnesota Press.
Nietzsche, F. (1969), *Ecce Homo*, trans. W. Kaufmann, New York: Vintage Books.
Nono, L. (1987), 'Prezenza storica nella musica d'oggi', in *Nono*, trans. E. Restagno, Torino: Edizioni di Torino, pp. 239–45.
Paddison, M. (1993), *Adorno's Aesthetic of Music*, Cambridge: Cambridge University Press.
Porter, L. (1998), *John Coltrane: His Life and Music*, Ann Arbor: University of Michigan Press.
Spinoza, B. (1919), *The Chief Works of Benedict de Spinoza*, trans. R. H. M. Elwes, London: G. Bell and Sons.

Spinoza, B. (1954), *Oeuvres complètes*, Paris: Gallimard.

Ulehla, L. (1994), *Contemporary Harmony: Romanticism through the Twelve-tone Row*, Rottenburg: Advance Music.

Webster, J. (1980), 'Sonata Form', in the *New Grove Dictionary of Music and Musicians*, Washington: Macmillan, pp. 497–508.

Notes

1. Whether this stigmatised dualism corresponds to Adorno's reworking of dialectical logic into a 'negative dialectics', and whether it even corresponds to Hegel's own dialectical thought is a question beyond the scope of this article, that I address elsewhere.
2. I undertake such an interrogation of internal difference in my article 'Deleuze and Adorno, Alone Together'.
3. The more 'distant' one key is from another, the fewer notes they share in common.
4. This is a grossly simplified vision of an ideally pure 'classical harmony'; to take the most obvious counter-example, 'pivot chords' that prepare a smooth modulation from one key to another depend upon their inherent ambiguity (the same chord holds different functional places in both the original and target keys) to lead the listener's ear from one tonality into another. That said, such a chord does not truly hold simultaneous, contradictory identities like the 'Tristan chord', rather it shifts smoothly from its first identity to a second as the listener identifies the passage to a new key.
5. As one proceeds through the various intervals of the Pythagorean scale, these progressively grow more and more out of tune, and intervals must be 'tempered' to allow the use of harmonic modulation in a composition. This was obviously unimportant for mediaeval church music, which generally remained in a single key or 'mode', but became an increasingly pressing concern as composers came to include more and more distant modulations (that is, moving to keys with fewer common notes) in their compositions.
6. 'Structure is the reality of the virtual' (1968: 270).
7. Dave Headlam (1996: 187–93) charts in particular the extremely close network of voice-leading connections Berg develops in the harmonic material of Op. 6 No. 1, connections that, I would add, link the sonic material like the dense vines of the 'primeval world' Headlam evokes (187).
8. As Webster's formulation suggests, the links between Deleuze's Leibniz and Baroque music are penetrating, and remain to be developed beyond the cursory points Deleuze brings out in the final chapter of *Le Pli*.
9. Nono would confirm this in his 1987 autobiographical interview with Enzo Restagno: '[The talk] was wrongly understood as my attack on [John] Cage, when in reality it was an attack on the academicism that was developing in Europe, in Darmstadt in particular ... When I finished reading my talk, Stockhausen reacted with extreme violence against me, because he felt himself personally attacked, and he was right' (15).
10. The song's melody actually draws upon melodies by Morton Gould and Maurice Ravel (Porter 218).
11. D Dorian: D, E, F, G, A, B, C; D sharp Dorian: D sharp, F sharp, G sharp, A sharp, B sharp, C sharp (this difference is not absolute: the B sharp is of course the enharmonic equivalent to C).
12. This is particularly clear on the newly released recording of 'Impressions' from 19 November 1962 in the collection *Live Trane: The European Tours*.

13. For an example of this process, see Paul Berliner's 1994 transcription and analysis of Tyner's comping on an earlier modal improvisation, 'Softly, as in a Morning Sunrise' (689–708).
14. See Porter (1998: 276–88) for an analysis of Coltrane's solo constructions from this later period.

Chapter 4

Affect and Individuation in Popular Electronic Music

Drew Hemment

Popular electronic music and the sonic machinic

> It may be that the sound molecules of pop music are at this very moment implanting here and there a people of a new type, singularly indifferent to the orders of the radio, to computer safeguards, to the threat of the atomic bomb. (Deleuze and Guattari 1987: 346)

The sound molecules of popular music have implanted very little in Deleuze's writing, only encountered obliquely if at all.[1] Where Deleuze does approach music directly he rarely strays beyond the orbit of Boulez and the Vienna School, and even then it is often encountered only as a theoretical motif. The section of *A Thousand Plateaus* from which this quote is drawn intimates that popular music might hold out an answer for a problem grappled with by the likes of Kafka, Klee and Mallarmé, namely a people's and the artist's alienation from their world and from each other. I have elsewhere (Hemment 1997) sought to explore the kind of people popular music might implant 'here and there', borrowing on the understanding of a minor literature Deleuze excavates from Kafka to propose a thinking of a *minor music*. But here I am interested more in a consideration of popular music, and of popular electronic music in particular, *as music*, in the relations of movement and rest between these particles, their capacities to affect and be affected.

In so doing, I shall mention the oblique references to music contained in Deleuze's collaborative work with Guattari in *Capitalism and Schizophrenia*, but rather than attempting to unify these as some kind of comprehensive musical theory, I shall filter them through a way of engaging in the technological apparatus and aesthetic forms of popular electronic music suggested by Deleuze's work on cinema.[2] The development of electronic music during the twentieth century in many ways echoes that of cinema, and yet unlike cinema it has remained largely untheorised. Extensive discourses surround disciplines such as electro-acoustic and computer music, scientific fields such as acoustics and psycho-acoustics, and some of the canonical figures of art music, such as Cage, Stockhausen, Schaeffer, or, for Deleuze's part, Boulez and the Vienna School. But a corresponding attention to popular electronic music has emerged only recently and in an incipient form. In Deleuze's two volumes on cinema he develops a relational conception of movement and time whose material basis is the cinematic apparatus and whose *modus operandi* alternate between a 'movement-image' for which time is con-strained by physical movement and a 'time-image' where time is freed from such constraints to become a temporality of multiplicity. In a similar way I shall look at the relations between movement and rest, speed and slowness within popular electronic music. As to be expected, a different set of terms emerge from this analysis, commensurate with the distinct material conditions of electronic music. As a starting point, I shall look not at the synthesiser, which Deleuze suggests (in reference to the procedure of Varèse) to be an idiomatic musical assemblage (Deleuze and Guattari 1987: 343), but rather the phonograph and recording technology. My approach, then, is to examine how this assemblage created the material conditions for electronic music, working this per-spective through to an understanding of the sonic affects it engenders in the same way that Deleuze examines the formation of the cinematic image by scrutinising the technical apparatus of camera and film. I will then look at how in electronic music there is a fundamental interrelation between materiality and time, texture and rhythm, and seek to explicate these through the terms *texture-affect* and *time-affect*. The first relates to music as the perception of surface events, of materiality or texture as nuance, unfolding in the time of an eternal present, whereas in the second materiality is perceived as a temporal event, and music occurs as a materialisation of time or the temporalising of matter, an incorporeal transformation.

I am interested here in looking beyond a naturalist understanding of music or recorded sound to consider the kind of individuation at stake in popular electronic music; that is to say, in exploring the relations of movement and rest between the molecules of electronic music, by way of approaching music as *affect*, as an intensity that carries an ability to affect and be affected. My thinking is informed here by Deleuze's and Guattari's understanding of 'haecceity' as the kind of individuality we find in seasons or dates, as opposed to subjects or things, and that 'consist[s] entirely of relations of movement and rest between molecules or particles, capacities to affect and be affected' (Deleuze and Guattari 1987: 261). Here haecceity is understood not as an abstract mode of individuation, as if autumn could exist without the falling of leaves, but rather as something that acts upon or through material bodies and substances. And I shall argue that the kind of individuation at stake in music can, accordingly, be treated neither abstractly nor naturalistically, but must allow for the multiplicity of indeterminate circuits through which electronic music passes, and that are composed by its passing. Deleuze continues that such individualities, or haecceities, 'are not simply emplacements, but concrete individuations that have a status of their own and direct the metamorphosis of things and subjects' (Deleuze and Guattari 1987: 261). And he notes, within his specific example of demonology, 'the importance of rain, hail, wind, pestilential air, or air polluted by noxious particles, favourable conditions for these transports' (Deleuze and Guattari 1987: 261). In investigating the mode of individuation of electronic music, therefore, we need also to ask, what is the pestilential air of electronic music?

We need some kind of mass spectrometer to glimpse the range of particles that inhabit this pestilent air. Deleuze's understanding of the 'machinic assemblage' as a set of dispersed, mutually implicating networks which include bodily, technological and cultural components is particularly suited to a study of the assemblages of technologies, sounds and bodies found in electronic dance music, and can be invoked to expand, or rather explode, the *frame* within which music is conventionally viewed. In considering music the tendency is to focus on completed works, whether they be notated compositions or recorded songs or tracks. With recorded music in particular the way in which the medium, packaging and sleeve notes enclose it – just as a painting is contained by its frame – emphasises a particular understanding of music as a finished piece. However, this elides the way that in playback the final statement is deterritorialised and set adrift in multiple, uncertain circumstances that can never be fully prescribed in advance, and also the way that the recording presents only a snap shot of musical materials and codes circulating in technological networks. In contrast, a focus on assemblage suggests a thinking of music in terms of *event*, where event is not understood as the single instance in which it is played or heard, but rather a dispersed terrain that includes multiple, mobile nodes. I shall henceforth refer to this expanded field, this mass spectrometer, as the *sonic machinic*.[3]

The very *impurity* of popular music leads us towards a thinking of the many forces that compose the musical field. But this also helps us approach other forms of music from outside the framework of conventional musicology, the sonic machinic offering a perspective from which to consider the *conflictual* field of musical forces that conventional musical discourse elides or represses. Western 'classical' music can also be said to be composed within an expanded field, insofar as it presupposes technologies of instrument construction and auditorium design, and a whole micropolitics of playing and listening, but this wider field is obscured by the Modernist conception of the individual genius. The same may be said of other forms of contemporary music, such as electroacoustic, which, in remaining bound to the striated space and rarefied air of academic institutions and their laboratories, presents a sonic radicalism that is like an internal combustion engine with no connecting rod, its parts whirring spasmodically, disconnected from any gears or bearings, not even disturbing the air around it. If music is a transcoding machine, and rhythm the in-between of communicating milieus, then musical affect occurs in the transmission of torque, in the change of speed or direction through the engagement with other parts or machines. Electro-acoustic does of course make connections between different sound engines, from microphones that capture found sound, to tape and its splicings, and the algorithms and speaker arrays of ambisonics, but the perspective of the sonic machinic helps us highlight the way that it operates between a highly circumscribed set of technical milieus. If this disconnection can be read as standing for the experimental, *qua* a freeing from the tyranny of 'emplacement', then it is not the kind of experimentation that I find at work in Deleuze, for this is a freeing that is necessary but not sufficient. It is a very easy form of experimentation that is often celebrated in writing *about* Deleuze, which indeed is reinforced in this context by the limited points of reference of his own musical theory. Lines of flight can descend into black holes, but they can also effect connections and transformations.

1877: The Edison defect and the rupture of recording

Until the rise of recording, sound was essentially fleeting and intangible, floating above the site of its making, before fading inevitably away.[4] Every performance of a song or scored composition would be different, varying according to circumstance, musicians, instruments and acoustics, just as the sound heard depended upon the size, shape and even atmospherics of the space, as well as relative position of the listener with respect to the source. In contrast, recording changed this by capturing a singular snapshot, replacing the aura of the artwork with the permanence of the 'audio document' (Chanan 1995). This is viewed as an objectification that has stripped music of its spontaneity and nuance, and left it poorer as a result, a misgiving Paul DeMarinis (1993) gives voice to under the motif of the 'Edison effect'. But what the perspective of documentary realism and the Edison effect obscures is the way in which any finality is undone by a play of deterritorialisation and reterritorialisation that opens up a new realm of indeterminacy on another level. This play of slippage and momentary rest can be seen as a latency in the very imperfections of the medium – the Edison *defect* – that are productive of a new kind of music and another sonic realm, in what we might call the *rupture of recording*.

Listen to one of Edison's early recordings and what strikes you is not so much the words transported from another age, as the surface of noise that obscures them, a surface of static over which recognisable shapes – a human voice, the words to a poem – flicker like shadows. Edison intended his phonograph to offer a transparent window onto past events, to record for posterity business transactions or the last words of a dying relative. But within the inconvenient cloud of interference can be heard the first hints of the subsequent century of sound waiting to unfold, for this inherent imperfection contained within itself a *musical potential* that would come to be explored during the course of the twentieth century within electronic music, in a counter-history marked by accident, manipulation and reuse that detached itself from the *telos* of representational technologies.

Moreover, in preserving sound as a material trace, recording created an artefact that is available to be reworked, and so a second order domain of sonic transformations. Envisaged as a means of storing and documenting audible events, the tradition of recording inaugurated by the phonograph ruptured the metaphysics of sonic presence and opened up the interstitial spaces of copies and recordings. This opened the door to a new kind of music making, one based in a foregrounding of interference, citation and secondary processes, a *plastic art* working within and through the grain of the machine. This has persisted through a path of increasing abstraction, from grooves cut in cylinder or disc, through magnetic imprint on tape, to strings of 0s and 1s, and can be discerned in everything from Cage's rudimentary experiments with turntables, through *musique concrète*, the street phonography of hip hop, 'versioning' and the remix, to the real-time digital shaping of sound.

Just as the closure of the artwork has been interrupted, so the self-identity of live performance has been displaced by the event understood as a kind of *connectivity* between flows and intensities that pulse across a virtual plane of inscription. As recording technologies are also *distribu-*

tive technologies, the potential for manipulation has been doubled by an increasing scope for participatory involvement and intervention. With the supplanting of the phonograph by the gramophone, the music industry emerged based upon a logic of mass production and an individualised listening experience. But from its earliest moments this has been undercut by cultures of participatory use, from the rise of the jukebox in the penny arcades, through to the immersive, collective spaces opened by the sound system, the street poetics of break dancing made possible by the ghetto-blaster, and even the surreal 'walkman party' noted by Hosokawa (1984). These potentials for manipulation and distribution have coincided at various points, from the DJ transforming a playback device into an instrument, to the distributed events made possible by file sharing and streaming – radicalising the document and making manifest an understanding of event as something virtual and yet concrete.

The rupture of recording has made possible a new kind of music and also has induced a wider dislocation in perception and culture. In a sense then a parallel might be drawn with McLuhan's *The Gutenberg Galaxy* (1962), where he outlines the wholesale reconfiguration of culture around the linearity of the literary text following the rise of the printing press in the fifteenth century. Whilst technology is not seen here as an autonomous agent of change, still the rise of recording technologies initiated by Edison's phonograph in 1877 is seen to have wholly shifted the coordinates through which music, culture and the body are played and replayed.

Simulacra and surface-affect

In preserving a material trace that could be endlessly reworked, the rupture of recording made possible a practice of music as the production of surface-affects, where distortion comes to supplant fidelity as the guiding aim. We have seen that this surface of noise was already present in the earliest instances of recording. But I shall here seek to show how this imperfection gradually came to be approached not as static obscuring a prior event, but as event and as music itself, at the precise point at which the recorded sound became neither original nor copy yet both. Here the lack of transparency in recording, the surface of noise or imperfections of the medium, is not so much an error to be corrected by technological progress but a point for departure. This recalls Deleuze's understanding of simulation, in which the simulacrum – literally, the 'bad copy' – breaks from the binary of original and copy in the production of difference.[5] It is within the simulacra that indeterminacy and nuance once again flicker within the sonic machinic, as a practice of music as the manipulation and production of texture emerges, understood as real movement or concrete duration. The concept of the simulacrum therefore at once helps us elucidate an ontology of recorded sound, and gestures towards a kind of music making through which we can begin to discern the outlines of the surface-affect.

The move away from documentary realism's pursuit of the ideal copy and towards the production of simulacra first emerged as a question of music with issues surrounding microphone placement. Prior to the introduction of electrical techniques, acoustic recording had been dominated by debates about whether resonance (indirect, 'impure' sounds) should be included to increase richness and 'authenticity'. Two strategies developed, one aiming to reproduce concert hall (auditorium) acoustics through careful use of space and microphone placement, the other situating musicians very close to the mikes in an acoustically dead studio to create a flat sound 'true' to the virtual environment of the studio – something exploited in particular by the impossible proximity of the crooner. It was here that the realism of recording reached a paradoxical point at which its logic began to unravel. With the first of these two strategies it was claimed that the placement of mikes and musicians could create 'realistic' acoustic images, that it could *reproduce the orchestra in your own home*. But this was just the beginning of the move towards the 'calculated effects' (Chanan 1995) of simulation, for the attempt to reproduce the authentic sound of a live auditorium performance – the 'unobtainable ideal of realism' (Chanan 1995: 58) – required complex strategies and an increasing use of artificial tricks and techniques. On the other hand with the latter strategy of dead miking, the 'true' studio environment became dislocated from any naturalistic structuring of space or time and progressively became the site of ever-greater deterritorialisations of the artists', engineers' and public's audio sense.

What we might term a 'studio art' came of age when producers surrendered the transparent reproduction of live performance and instead explored the potential of the recording medium in its own right. The key shift away from documentary realism and towards the productivity of the simulacra came with developments in electrical recording. Once sound was converted to a set of electrical signals, studio technicians were able endlessly to manipulate variable parameters. Within the commercial field of studio production this was originally used to clean up and 'enhance' recordings in attempts to emulate the 'real' live sound. However, the techniques developed soon came to be used to produce original effects that never would have been attempted in a live performance. The incidental noises and imperfections later came to be exploited in the production of chimeras and previously unimagined sounds, as electronic music bifurcated from the tradition of studio production that sought a transparent reproduction of performance. Perhaps the earliest example within mainstream pop music is the Elvis Presley recordings at Sun Studios (rock here viewed as *proto-electronica*) which utilised various tricks and techniques to add effects to the original recording, such that the effects rather than song structure came to define the resultant sound. But the sense of music being transformed from the transport of song and voice into the production of a surface affect is most clearly captured in the 'wall of sound' developed by the Los Angeles based producer Phil Spector in the early 1960s, which was based in setting each sonic element at an equivalent level on the mixing desk without the individuation of each being lost. There has subsequently been a general displacement of the site of creativity from the moment of 'live' performance to the no-place of the studio, and a corresponding drift from the creation of original audio statements towards the production of simulacra through the processing of previously recorded sounds, analogue signals and abstracted codes. Rather than developing narrative or exposing the logical structure of a sound world, the surface of a sonic terrain is explored.

Within mainstream pop, however, textural affect still remained a support for the voice and the song, subordinated to the linear, narrative regime of Western music. A decisive break came with the echo chambers of 1970s Jamaican dub. Here the surface engenders *depth*, the punctual system of counterpoint and harmony overwhelmed by molecular flows sounding a smooth plane that is anything but flat, the molar system of the song sucked into the vortex of echo and delay. Here the simulacrum breaks from the logic of original and copy, in the production of a plurality of uncertain nuance and oblique reference. Dub was parasitical upon the musical output of North America, but in putting it through the remix machine of studio and mixing desk the designation of copy was lost in the profusion of many 'versions'. And just as recording precipitated a mutation in sound type, the increase in decibel level made possible by the wiring of speakers and amps dislocated musical participation and generated a mode of music dominated by rhythmic surface and textural spaces. Arising a world apart from the European avant-garde, in the laboratories of dub the transmission connects and the wheels turn, effecting deterritorialisations that leak beyond the narrow definition of the musical. Consisting at its most basic of turntables, mixer, amps, speakers, DJs, MCs and crew, the sound system was at once a highly efficient machine and a kind of connectivity, an assemblage of bodies, technologies and sounds, a molecular system that connected at many points, mapping the sonic machinic and displacing the hierarchical studio and economic system with the sonorific pack.

Another well documented case, one which highlights how the sonic machinic broke from the telos of representational technologies, is the assemblage of acid house and the Roland TB-303. Indeterminacy in music had been extensively explored by Cage and Fluxus, but with the Roland TB-303 it arose in an implicit way within a culture of misuse. This piece of studio equipment was designed to produce an accurate reproduction of bass-guitar lines to be used in studio sessions, but notoriously bad at what it was intended for, it was very good at making mistakes. Its programming procedures were so complex that the operator's intentions would become lost and unexpected results appear out of the confusion – 'bad copies' that proved more interesting than what was intended. Soon the misuse became the norm, as the unique squelching sounds produced by its filters came to define a whole genre of music – acid house – mapping out a template first sketched in 1985 by DJ Pierre, Spanky and Herbert J with Phuture's 'Acid Trax'.[6] In the place of the despotic studios of dub there emerged the 'bedroom producer', deterritorialising yet further studio production. The 303 – like the drum machine which generated the rhythmic codes of house in the 1980s, the Roland TR-808 – was bought cheap on the second-hand market following its premature discontinuation because of its failure to emulate real instruments. Here we see machines which failed in their representational function of simulating real instruments being used to construct a new musical regime characterised by intensive, insistent rhythms, and dominated by the multiplying and layering of textures and surface.

The misuse of these machines created the *sound* of the different musical forms, the sonic character by which a track would stand out from the flows of corporate sense data, but it also informed the time-structure of the music. With sequencers and drum machines in particular, a very specific constructionist approach was engendered, in which percussive and sonic codes were layered upon one another, each based in the repetition or 'looping' of discrete segments. And driving this aesthetic was the regular pulse of the beat, which in its purest form took the shape of the constant 'four-to-the-floor' rhythm, incorporating four regular beats to the bar, or a main beat in 4/4 time. The 4/4 beat is a punctual system, understood as 'the musical codes at a given moment' (Deleuze and Guattari 1987: 299), that falls on the wrong side of the distinction, drawn from Boulez, between tempo and non-tempo, pulsed and non-pulsed time, metre and rhythm (see Deleuze and Guattari 1987: 262). The dominance of the drum machine made readily accessible a material expression of raw repetition, but only by displacing an indeterminate temporality with the insistent regularity of the mechanistic and metronomic beat. A similar case may be made for digital systems which reproduce the time independent variables inherited from traditional models of music, as with compositional software such as Cubase which only allow sounds to be recorded within separate tracks and replayed in linear time. In each case, in being tied to a rigid temporal grid music is impoverished, obeying the infinite precision of the electronic or digital clock and often rigidly quantised into standard units.[7]

To stop analysis at the point of this impoverishment is premature, however. Firstly, because a focus on time code neglects the expanded field within which the musical event takes place, the expansion of the musical. While art music enshrines a finalised expression (often by shifting the site of music to the score itself), and headphone music aims for an ideal of audibility, in electronic dance music the art-work is diffracted by a network that involves multiple levels of synthesis and complexity, the many spaces between the beats tripping you up and undermining the regularity of the pulse. But secondly, and more interestingly, the molecularity of surface texture itself can effect deterritorialisations that problematise the neat distinction between pulsed and non-pulsed time and the dualisms of the avant-garde. The first electronic studio tracks of disco (such as Peech Boys, 'Don't Make Me Wait') used the early sequencing technologies to produce the constant 'four-to-the-floor' rhythm as a material force, whilst house DJs such as Frankie Knuckles increased the percussive power of the tracks by layering a regular beat straight from a Roland 808 drum machine over the mix, forging a sensibility that would be widely emulated even when more sophisticated studio technologies became available that were capable of lending far greater nuance and sophistication to the regular electronic pulse.[8] Here something interesting occurs: the metronomic pulse is transformed into a force of rupture when it is pushed to a limit of sheer, intensive repetition, the mechanistic grid of digital clock time is punctured by an intensity, the succession of abstract instants postponed by the arrival of the present as a non-identical moment that is productive of difference. The impure pleasures of beats based music offer a euphoria of measurement, but in a way that subverts the punctual system and its own precision. Any sense of linear succession or sequence is undone by the insistence of a now that we might compare to the Bergsonian *eternal present*. Whilst this does not undo Deleuze's and Guattari's distinction between *Aeon* and *Chronos* (1987: 262), it does complicate it, forcing us to look beyond the simple dualism to which they themselves often succumb. For in these instances the complication is manifested in a kind of temporal minimalism that is productive of a surface-affect, where nuance and inflection are heard *because of* a reduction of indeterminacy on another level. 'Sobriety. Sobriety.' I have focused here on the emergence through the history of twentieth-century popular music of a nuance within the simulacrum that occurs here as an intensive textural or rhythmic surface, and that can be obscured by a too-neat distinction between pulsed and non-pulsed time, metre and rhythm. This is not something that is unique to popular electronic music, however, as within Reichian minimalism as much as Detroit techno or contemporary electronica we could point to a sophisticated exploration of sonic texture pursued through subtle rhythmic or melodic variation. What we find here is that the expression of surface is heard not despite a rhythmic simplicity, but because of it. The subordination of time becomes a condition of the textural affect. And that affect – the bad copy or simulacrum – is experienced not as outside of time, but as a movement or duration, where movement occurs not in the jumps between one location (frame) to another as in Deleuze's analysis of cinema, but as material flow. Recalling Bergson's understanding of *durée* as concrete movement, music returns as a pulsing line of flight, a surface affect.

De-composition and time-affect

The rhythmic template of the 'four-to-the-floor' was an elegant piece of code, beautiful in its simplicity.[9] In the expanded field rhythm is less like a computer algorithm than biological code such as DNA, as biological code is context dependent and gives rise to organic forms infinitely more complex than the information it contains.[10] In this sense its beauty stems not from the abstract time code of the rhythm, but from its material insistence and its interaction with its environment. This highlights the fact that the temporality of rhythm is indissoluble from its material support, and also that the piece of music is composed in the spaces between intersecting planes, planes of 'composition' in a narrow sense but also of amplification, corporeality, sexuality, and so on. In the course of the 1980s house music and techno migrated out of the black and gay clubs of Chicago, New York and Detroit, and spread like a meme to Europe and in particular the UK. Musical culture in Europe was transformed, but as the music migrated out of the Balearic bolt holes and illegal warehouse parties of Ibiza, London and Manchester into the legal sector, and was reterritorialised by entrepreneurs who introduced sophisticated marketing and macro-economics, this context irrevocably changed. As a narrowly defined version of 'dance music' entered a reciprocal colonising relationship with the commercial music sphere, to the extent that they became almost synonymous, the axis shifted and the assemblage came apart. Its connecting rod shattered, the four-to-the-floor shed its pestilence and all that was left was the bland quantised grid: the *difference engine* of the four-to-the-floor came to sound different, no longer productive of difference but of the same. In the early 1990s, this corporatisation of the music was met by an infusion of a different set of rhythmic sensibilities (most notably when hardcore fused with ragga to produce jungle), as the conditions were created for the emergence of musics that explored different quotients of deterritorialisation. Many artists developed extremes of rhythmic complexity in a conscious distancing from the tyranny of the four-to-the-floor, one example from this period being Bedouin Ascent's Dysfunktional Beats label, the *modus operandi* of which is rhythmic indeterminacy.[11] While of course this was not the first time greater rhythmic complexity had been explored in popular music, there was a certain opening here that led to a multiplication of distinct regimes of making music and of corporeal engagements in sound and rhythm, characterised by a shift to more dense and complex rhythmic patterns, and a wider use of percussive samples that encode multiple temporalities.

To appreciate this shift, and begin to consider how it might be indicative of what I am calling the time-affect, we need to give further consideration to rhythm, not just in the sense of different 'beats' but also in the wider sense of the repetition of the recording and of molecules of sound. In the Western tradition the influence of repetition has been occluded as non-serious and not worthy of attention, and within music it has either been effaced or disguised.[12] Raw repetition poses a double threat insofar as it cuts into and disrupts narrative development and rational thought, and presents a surface of open play. The carnality of rhythm creates a pulsing surface of intensity, a flow of desire not directed towards a climax or resolution. Repetition is, of course, not unique to beats based music. In *Studying Popular Music*, Richard Middleton contrasts the kind of repetition found within Western art music with that of Afro-American music and rock. The latter is based on the repetition of small discrete units or riffs, which he terms 'musemes', whereas the former privileges the continuous, narrative development of themes. While Western art music is also based in a repetition of a kind, the units involved – figures and motifs – tend to be longer, harmonically more elaborate, and in their composition they are functionally subordinate to a coherent whole. The musematic repetition of Afro-American music is opposed to the *discursive* repetition of art music and other bourgeois forms, its determination of time cyclical rather than linear. In the context of recorded music we might point to the rise of the DJ and the isolation of the *break*. Put most simply, the break is a dynamic, driving section within a song, a rhythmic segment – such as a drumming solo – that captures the particular motion of the music. Here the museme may be seen as a directional vector, a block of space-time that contains its own coordinates within itself whilst simultaneously opening a window onto the whole. It is a key segment of the genetic code which contains within itself a diagram of the motility of the track and from which the rest of the audio motion may be deduced. As such it could be composed of any number of instruments or sounds. Though fundamentally rhythmic, it does not have to be strictly percussive, but could be any sound or combination of sounds which contains a particularly powerful or vivid motion. In its very construction and form the break is marked by its iterability. It is a 'heterogeneous block of space-time' (Deleuze and Guattari: 1987), a window onto another world and another temporality that does not lose its difference in being repeated, but rather amplifies it within a rhythmic assemblage. In the form of the break, the museme occurs not as an abstract unit of division but as an iterative fragment torn out of its context and outside the closure of any whole, that is less atomistic than combinatory, and which maps out a rhythmic surface through its repetition.

But where Middleton's concept of the museme is of less use is in thinking beyond the unity of the musical fragment. It is helpful here to compare the understanding of the 'sound object' developed by Pierre Schaeffer, who with Pierre Henry was one of the founders of *musique concrète*. In his formulation, in capturing or preserving a material trace recording created the sound object as something that is available to be reworked and recombined rather than a final statement. Already apparent within John Cage is an understanding of *bricolage* as the clash of elements that resist fusion into a unitary entity (Nyman 1974: 36). Experimenting firstly with disc recorders, and then later with tape, Schaeffer and Henry et al. took this further by combining sounds taken from different spatio-temporal locations, with distinct acoustic properties and different temporalities. Pre-composed, non-musical or environmental sound-objects were recombined solely on the basis of their phenomenological qualities, disregarding the natural source. However, *concrète* is distinct in that it works on composite sonic objects which it encounters pre-formed and ready-made: the general iterability which emerges within the remix or the tendency within electronic music to render samples almost unrecognisable is here limited by a specific ideological determination of what counts as a 'concrete' sound: 'For *concrète*, sounds are conceived as indivisible, non-assembled entities, which are made or found, fixed in a medium, then shaped and combined in a concrete process. This axiomatic unity of the individual sound is fundamental to the process of *concrete*' (Hodgkinson 1998: 4). Electro-acoustic music would subsequently depart from this axiomatic unity, and similarly within popular electronic music another stance to the sound object emerged, one that is not unlike simulation in the way that it is productive of non-identical surface affects, but which operates more directly upon time and that generates its affects by virtue of an iterative process.

To think beyond a reductionist concept of rhythm, we need therefore to look more closely at this iterative process, and at a practice of what I shall here term *de-composition*, in which the museme or sound object becomes deterritorialised or de-composed within a mimetic art of sound. Here it is not just a question of looping or repeating indivisible units, but of reworking them in a nomadism where the nature of the musical fragment changes along with the territory that it traverses.[13] In de-composition, difference-in-repetition displaces an economy of imitation and re-pre-sentation, and the practice of music comes to be seen in terms of turning a prism to reveal different facets or aspects of a field of possibilities.[14] Such a mimetic form of music explores the inherent potentialities of a sonic phylum in the same way that a sculptor works upon the grain of wood or the contours of stone. Here the focus on recording technologies highlights a very specific modality of sonic transformation, and a way in which the inaudible can be made audible. We might compare here what Deleuze and Guattari say in relation to the sequencer (which they suggest might be considered as the assemblage of the 'musical machine of consistency' of Varèse's 'exemplary' procedure): 'By assembling modules, source ele-ments, and elements for treating sound (oscillators, generators, and transformers), by arranging microintervals, the synthesizer makes audible the sound process itself, the production of that process, and puts us in contact with still other elements beyond sound matter' (Deleuze and Guattari 1987: 343). What I have termed de-composition, the repetition-in-difference of the sound object, similarly does not so much reproduce the sonorous, as render sonorous (cf. Deleuze and Guattari 1987: 346), and what it makes audible is the deterritorialisation of the material trace.[15] This might be related to Deleuze's and Guattari's comments on metallurgy, which they note bears a distinct resemblance to music: 'What metal and metallurgy bring to light is a life proper to matter, a vital state of matter as such, a material vitalism that doubtless exists every-where but is ordinarily hidden or covered, rendered unrecognizable'

(Deleuze and Guattari 1987: 411). My interest is less in the exposition of a latent interiority or a hidden material vitalism, as in how the practice of music might be compared to the smelting and moulding of musical substances such that what is heard is the very smelting process itself. Music becomes a process of working upon material bodies in various metastable states, of de-composing and re-composing composite objects, and crafting them into forms with differing relations of speed and rest. From the perspective of the Edison defect, which highlights the openness and iterability of the recording, its secondary and impure nature, we can see a range of different quotients of deterritorialisation and reterritorialisation, passing through a spectrum running from the naturalism of field recordings through the referencing of plunderphonics to the music of kid606 where sounds are swept up into a euphoric cascade of references half glimpsed, misquoted and misread.

We have seen before how the layers of static first heard in Edison's early recordings prefigured a form of music as the manipulation of surfaces of noise or the productivity of simulacra. But here we see how the Edison defect also opens onto a form of music based in the difference-in-repetition of the sound object, and it is this radicalised understanding of rhythm that came to the fore with the demise of the difference engine of the four-to-the-floor. And where this is different from the perceptual regime of the surface-affect is in the way in which it radicalises time. The distinction is not simply that between flow and discontinuity, surface and rupture, for it is rather that the time warp of the Edison defect – the untimely return of the sound object – opens up an indeterminate space in which many temporalities can emerge. The rupture of recording is already plural. Firstly, it detaches a block of space-time from the unfolding of the world, the sound from the time and place of its first having sounded.[16] Different points in musical history or non-musical events can therefore be referenced and juxtaposed, breaking or mutating the unity of past–present–future, making time an object of perception by confounding the anticipation of succession. Secondly, the editing techniques that developed through the twentieth century opened new departures from the constraints of sequential time. Sound cut up, looped, reversed. But also, and most interestingly, in wresting the audio image out of time, the recording process freezes and isolates a fragment of time, making possible the capture – and reworking – of a plurality of temporalities encoded in individual sounds or passages of music. In morphing a movement in sound the perception of the very passing of time can be toyed with or subverted; time brought into view by being taken out of focus in a twist of the lens. This may be seen in the way that the scratch of the turntablist extracts from the encrypted vinyl groove an extended palette of noise, morphing a concrete duration into a movement elsewhere. And also in the way in which timestretching – made possible by the sampler and exploited extensively within electronic music, most notably in drum'n'bass – smears the sound object by extending or contracting its enveloping frame, mutating its temporal structure and exposing the sonic potentialities that lay dormant in its virtual space. Much in the way that Deleuze found the time-image to provide a direct perception of time within cinema, timestretching and the scratch might be said to present a direct perception of time. We see the emergence of a temporality of multiplicity, time-affect.

Postscript: music within the expanded field

To conclude, we may say that Deleuze's stance towards cinema suggests a way of discerning distinct modes of individuation or regimes in electronic music, albeit regimes that are often intertwined. On the one hand we have forms of music in which a surface of sound is fashioned out of an unfolding present, or a rhythmic surface is constructed out of the repetition of percussive code. Conversely, we have forms of music where the iteration of sonic fragments betray a perception of time, either through a referencing of other times, or through a distortion of time that makes that time manifest, such as in timestretching. The difference is that between time subordinated to surface, and surface subordinated to time. Ultimately, the two regimes converge, just as at a quantum level rupture and flow become indistinguishable. They offer but two understandings of the multifarious ways in which time and materiality coexist in the production of musical intensity or affect.

While there are clear resonances with Deleuze's understanding of the movement-image and time-image, my interest has not been to look at the extent to which the different terms correspond, but rather to see how Deleuze's method offers an approach that can be usefully applied to popular electronic music. Within the scope of this essay I have given only a somewhat superficial analysis, and it would be interesting to take this further and look more closely at the differences and similarities between movement-image and time-image on the one hand, and surface-affect and time-affect on the other, by way of exploring convergences and parallelisms between the technical and cultural apparatuses of cinema and electronic music. This could be expected to be a productive area of inquiry given the multiple connections that already exist, and it would be interesting to look at how these modes of individuation migrate in film sound tracks or music videos, or at how modes of individuation might emerge in audiovisual arts, or for that matter in dance or performance, that are distinct from those of cinema and electronic music.[17]

For Deleuze the shift from the movement-image to the time-image is not a matter of progress but a question of historical circumstance, and of the corresponding ways in which time is experienced or encountered in different historical moments. Similarly in music, surface-affect and time-affect are a function of wider cultural shifts and the dislocations in perception they engender. What I hope to have shown is that this is not a crude matter of technological determination, any more than in returning to the phonograph the aim is to create a hierarchy of technological artefacts. Nor is this the concern only of an isolated sphere of art or music practice, but rather of an expanded field where aesthetics, corporeality and resistance coincide, the smooth plane of the sonic machinic. In more than one way, the surface of static encountered in Edison's early recordings presented art music with its other, while the subsequent development of popular electronic music, its pestilence and impurity, has highlighted the constricted and striated space that art music, including that of Boulez and the Vienna School, occupies.

References

Benjamin, W. (1968), *Illuminations*, trans. H. Zohn, New York: Schocken Books.

Canning, P., 'The Crack of Time and the Ideal Game', in C. Boundas and D. Olkowski (eds), *Gilles Deleuze and the Theatre of Philosophy*, London: Routledge, pp. 73–98.

Chanan, M. (1995), *Repeated Takes: A Short History of Recording and its Effect on Music*, London: Verso.

Deleuze, G. (1986), *Cinema 1: The Movement Image*, trans. H. Tomlinson and B. Habberjam, New York and London: Continuum Publishing.

Deleuze, G. (1989), *Cinema 2: The Time-Image*, trans. H. Tomlinson and R. Galeta, London: The Athlone Press.

Deleuze, G. (1993), *The Fold: Leibniz and the Baroque*, trans. T. Conley, London: The Athlone Press.

Deleuze, G. (1994), *Difference and Repetition*, trans. P. Patton, London: The Athlone Press.

Deleuze, G. and Guattari, F. (1983), *Anti-Oedipus*, trans. R. Hurley, M. Seem and H. R. Lane, Minneapolis: University of Minnesota Press.

Deleuze, G. and Guattari, F. (1987), *A Thousand Plateaus*, trans. B. Massumi, Minneapolis: University of Minnesota Press.

Deleuze, G. and Guattari, F. (1990), 'What is a Minor Literature?' in R. Ferguson, M. Gever, T. T. Minh-ha and C. West (eds), *Out There: Marginalisation and Contemporary Cultures*, New York: The Museum of Contemporary Art and MIT Press.

DeMarinis, P. (1993), *The Edison Effect*, San Francisco: Art Institute.

Goodwin, A. (1990), 'Sample and Hold: Pop Music in the Digital Age of Reproduction', in S. Frith and A. Goodwin (eds), *On Record: Rock, Pop and the Written Word*, London: Routledge, pp. 258–73.

Hemment, D. (1997), 'E is for Ekstasis', *New Formations: Uncivil Societies* 31 (Spring/Summer): 23–38.

Hemment, D. (1998a), 'Audiovisual Theory', *On Magazine* 5 (3): 30–1.

Hemment, D. (1998b), 'Corpus of Sound: Bodycoder and the Music of Movement', *Mute*, 10: 34–9.

Hemment, D. (1998c), 'Dangerous Dancing and Disco Riots: The Northern Warehouse Parties', in G. McKay (ed.), *DiY Culture*, New York and London: Verso, pp. 208–27.

Hodgkinson, T. (1998), 'Migraines of a Caustic Ear: Problems in *Musique Concrète*', *Resonance* 6 (2).

Hosokawa, S. (1984), 'The Walkman Effect', in R. Middleton and D. Horn (eds), *Popular Music Vol. 4: Performers & Audiences*, Cambridge: Cambridge University Press, pp. 165–80.

McLuhan, M. (1962), *The Gutenberg Galaxy: The Making of Typographic Man*, London: Routledge.

Middleton, R. (1990), *Studying Popular Music*, Milton Keynes: Open University Press.

Nyman, M. (1974), *Experimental Music: Cage and Beyond*, London: Macmillan, Studio Vista.

Patton, P., (1994), 'Anti-Platonism and Art', in C. Boundas and D. Olkowski (eds), *Gilles Deleuze and the Theater of Philosophy*, New York: Routledge, pp. 141–56.

Notes

1. For the purposes of this paper I shall use the terms popular electronic music and electronic dance music interchangeably.
2. See Deleuze 1986, 1989.
3. As with the 'sound machine' of Varèse's procedure, the sonic machinic 'molecularizes and atomizes, ionises sound matter, and harnesses a cosmic energy' (Deleuze and Guattari 1987: 343). But unlike the assemblage Deleuze cites as an example, the synthesiser, it is not reducible to particular technologies or techniques, but is rather a kind of connectivity or circuitry linking nodes of many different natures.
4. Notation might be claimed to be an exception, which preserves music but only by representing it in a visual form on the written page.
5. This understanding of simulation is distinct from the popular understanding of the artificial recreation of the real, as embodied in a 'flight simulator', and also from the 'simulation theory' associated with Baudrillard and Virilio, which tends to become fixated on the collapse of representation and define itself against an epistemology it claims to have been lost.
6. Written in 1985, released 1986.
7. This remains the case in drum 'n' bass, which has been the object of much discussion centring around the vectorial attributes of the break, for the breakbeats are also programmed, their molecular incisions subordinated to meter. In this sense their deterritorialisations are reterritorialised within a striated space, where, as Deleuze notes, 'the measure can be regular or irregular, but it is always assignable' (Deleuze and Guattari 1987: 553).
8. Ultimately a machine-like precision came to be equated with funkiness when the rigid and stiff rhythms of European electronic groups such as Kraftwerk were

imported into black music through the electro of Africa Bambaata and Detroit techno, and we could also point to the energetic milieu of pounding, distorted kick drums on tracks such as Cristian Vogel's 'Defunkt' (Solid Records).

9. A code is understood here not as a set of symbols (the beats in 4/4 time), but as a rule set or function for translating one symbolic notation into another. Thus the four-to-the-floor code describes the function (something like, 'apply regularly alternating sequence in 4/4 time to generate surface affects between sound molecules or between bodies'), and we see it operating when Frankie Knuckles transforms a flat metronomic pulse by increasing the density of the beats or in the way in which bodies translate the beat into movement.

10. In biological code, 'meaning is entirely dependent upon environment' (Peter J. Bentley (University College, London), conference presentation at *Code: The Language of our Time*, Ars Electronic 2003, Linz).

11. It is not helpful here to reduce the discussion to an opposition between drum machine and sampler; artists have always sought to stretch the limits of the technically possible, and the limited horizons of sequencers and drum machines have been tested for as long as they have been used in music.

12. We might cite here Plato's exclusion of music from the *Polis*, the idealised acoustic spaces of the modern concert hall, or even the prohibition within recent British law of repetitive beats, or, to be more precise, amplified music played in social contexts which 'includes sounds wholly or predominantly characterised by the emission of a succession of repetitive beats'. (Criminal Justice and Public Order Act 1994, Part V: Powers in relation to raves, 63 (1) (b).)

13. We might compare Deleuze's and Guattari's comment that 'Music is a creative, active operation that consists in deterritorialising the refrain' (Deleuze and Guattari: 1987, 300), and point to the diversity of forms in which this occurs: combined into the heterogeneous plateaus of West African polyrhythmic drumming, repeated in the subtly evolving syncopated patterns of Reichian minimalism, or, even, hugely extended and magnified in the drones of La Monte Young or the eternal now-time created by Merzbow by sculpting layers of static.

14. This is also an opening to an outside; for the recording is an opening onto the world, as is evident in the way that the inclusion of *found sound* has come to be a staple of electronic music, but also in the way in which, during the course of the twentieth century, and through the field recordings of Bartók in particular, recording led to an opening of the Western ear to non-Western musics, sounds and sonic sensibilities.

15. Insofar as recording technology made possible a *materialisation of musical memory*, we might say that the flickering figures of de-composition give material expression to an audio unconscious latent within mnemonics of the material trace as a field of virtual potentialities, much in the same way that Benjamin spoke of photography opening the optical unconscious (Benjamin 1968).

16. In a relative not absolute way: the cylinder decomposes in time, the disc and data degrade.

17. See for example my discussion of *kinesonics*, or the relationality of music and movement (Hemment 1998b), or of audiovision (Hemment 1998a).

Chapter 5

Violence in Three Shades of Metal: Death, Doom and Black

Ronald Bogue

The role of violence in contemporary culture has often been raised in discussions of popular music, and this question is particularly germane to three closely related forms of heavy metal music known as death metal, doom metal and black metal. The music of all three forms is extremely loud, sombre and modal, highly percussive, and often fast, with vocals generally delivered in guttural shouts, grunts, moans, screams or whispers. The lyrics frequently offer images of mayhem, dismemberment, bodily decay, and disease. And in the case of black metal, a few of its better-known artists have been convicted of arson and murder. Deleuze says little directly about popular music, and his analyses of music as an art are less copious than those of other arts, especially literature and cinema. Nonetheless, his thought, especially as developed with Guattari, provides an incisive means of articulating the issues surrounding the social dimension of music in general and those related to violence in these three forms of heavy metal music in particular.

Deleuze and Music

Deleuze's most extended treatment of music is to be found in Plateaus 10 and 11 of *A Thousand Plateaus*, where he and Guattari develop the concept of music as the 'creative, active operation that consists in deterritorializing the refrain' (Deleuze and Guattari 1987: 300).[1] Deleuze and Guattari's fundamental goal is to situate music within the processes of the natural world and conceive of it as a specific mode of engaging patterns of action, relation and development. The refrain may be defined loosely as any rhythmic pattern that forms part of a network of relations among creatures and their environment within a milieu, territory or social domain. Each organism traces a 'developmental melody' as it grows, matures and eventually dies, and the regular rhythms of its activities function as so many motifs in counterpoint with the motifs produced by surrounding organisms and inorganic forces. Organisms possess varying degrees of autonomy in relation to their environment, milieu creatures being closely tied to their surrounding world, territorial animals less so, and certain species (such as humans) even less so again (in that humans, though showing territorial tendencies, finally are capable of inhabiting spaces in much more unfixed and shifting patterns than such territorial species as the stickleback fish or the Australian grass finch). Relative degrees of autonomy among organisms are made possible by the 'deterritorialisation' of refrains, by the uncoding or unfixing of rhythmic patterns within one context, and by their 'reterritorialisation' within another. The song of the Stagemaker bird, for example, is a sonic pattern that has been 'deterritorialised' from any single function – say, that of signalling danger – and has been 'reterritorialised' as a multi-functional refrain integrated within diverse refrains traced in the activities of nest-building, mating, food-gathering, predator-signalling, territorial defence, and so on. The Stagemaker's song emerges within its territory as part of its lifeworld, and the bird's overall degree of autonomy, its relative flexibility in the organisation of a given block of space-time, is a function of the deterritorialisation and reterritorialisation of its multiple refrains.

Human music is significantly less fixed in its function than is birdsong, and music's greater degree of deterritorialisation is inseparable from the general degree of flexibility of the human species in its relation to its lifeworld. Human music may be involved in any number of activities – courtship, war, ritual, worship, lament, labour, celebration, dance, intoxication, amusement – but music possesses no necessary relationship to any of these, and it tends toward an autonomy that is beyond any function other than its own process. Indeed, music's reterritorialisation of sound is largely a recoding of sound in terms of itself, that is, in terms of formal systems such as those of traditional harmony and counterpoint in Western tonal music. Yet human music is not simply a collection of deterritorialised refrains, for it is also a deterritorialising force that interacts with non-musical rhythmic patterns and provides them with sonic analogues within musical works. For Deleuze and Guattari, all deterritorialisation proceeds via a process of becoming-other, a passage between entities or categories that sets them in metamorphic disequilibrium. In Olivier Messiaen's use of birdsong in his musical compositions, Deleuze and Guattari find an apt example of music's function as a deterritorialising force interacting with refrains in a process of becoming-other.[2] In many of his compositions, especially those of the 1950s and 1960s, Messiaen constructs motifs from various birdsongs, rendering them with what he regards as great accuracy. Yet he observes that the high pitches, rapid tempos, and peculiar timbres of birdsongs require that he enlarge the intervals between tones, slow the tempos, and find substitute timbres among human instruments in order to provide musical counterparts to the original birdsongs. The result, Messiaen concedes, is a music filled with birdsongs that the most practised of ornithologists can seldom recognise. For Deleuze and Guattari, Messiaen's interaction with birdsong is a paradigmatic instance of the musical process of becoming-other, a becoming-bird in which something passes between the fixed coordinates of human music and birdsong to produce new sounds. Messiaen's musical rendering of the bird's refrain deterritorialises that refrain, extracts it from its territorial function, and then incorporates it within a musical composition that unfolds along its own lines of development. Messiaen does not imitate the birdsong but provides a sonic analogue of the song, thereby giving musical embodiment to the extra-musical force of the bird's territorial refrain.

A musical becoming-other is not simply a matter of undoing fixed refrains, however, for in becoming-other one engages a dimension of reality that is qualitatively distinct from ordinary experience. Deleuze and Guattari differentiate between two domains in the real world, an actual domain of commonsense spatio-temporal entities and processes and a virtual domain of pure becoming and self-differentiating difference. The virtual may be conceived of loosely as a field of vectors of potential development and metamorphosis, each vector a line of continuous variation along which an actual process of development and metamorphosis might unfold. The virtual is immanent within the real, and every concrete, commonsense process is an actualisation of an immanent virtual line of force. Consider, for example, the genesis and growth of a biological entity. The initial single-cell ovum is crisscrossed by multiple lines of potential cleavage, only one of which is actualised upon fertilisation. As the single cell divides into two, potential lines of further division emerge within each of the new cells, again only one of which is actualised as each new cell in turn splits in two. Rather than seeing this process of division as the mechanical implementation of a preprogrammed blueprint, Deleuze and Guattari treat it as the unfolding of an immanent vector of differentiation, whereby a virtual, self-differentiating force is continuously actualised within concrete developmental processes.

'The world is an egg,' Deleuze says in *Difference and Repetition* (1994: 251), in that this process of actualisation of virtual lines of force is manifest throughout the real. Usually, the virtual domain of becoming and self-differentiating difference escapes us, but in moments of disequilibrium and disorientation we gain access to that realm. Then we encounter a world not of discrete objects, fixed coordinates and chronometric time, but of flows and fluxes, topological spaces and floating durations. Entities within this virtual domain may be characterised solely by 'pure relations of speed and slowness between particles' and by 'pure affects' (Deleuze and Guttari 1987: 270), or powers of affecting and being affected by other elements. The time of the virtual is not that of *Chronos*, or regularly measured clock time, but that of *Aeon*, a time like that of an infinitive, 'to swim', 'to sleep', a becoming that is unfixed and non-pulsed, unfolding in no specifiable direction and in relation to no clear coordinates. In *A Thousand Plateaus*, Deleuze and Guattari designate the domain of the virtual by various names, including the 'body without organs', the 'plane of consistency', and the 'smooth space of the nomadic war machine'. By calling it a body without organs, Deleuze and Guattari stress the affective nature of the virtual and its connection to the human body, but they caution that the body without organs is not strictly speaking an individual or human body, for the body without organs is immediately social (capital, for example, is the body without organs of the capitalist social formation) and it is always made up of flows and fluxes that include human and non-human elements alike. By labelling the virtual a plane of consistency, Deleuze and Guattari avoid associations with the human body entirely and highlight abstract continuities between elements, while insisting that the elements are irreducibly multiple and held together only through a loose cohesion, or glue-like consistency, emerging from relations of speed and affective intensity. And by speaking of the virtual as a smooth space (as opposed to one that is 'striated', or graphed and gridded), which is generated by the nomadic war machine, they emphasise the fluid, ever-changing quality of the virtual, as well as its connection to forces of transformation and potential destruction.

Thus, when Messiaen enters into a process of becoming-other and deterritorialises a birdsong refrain, he engages a virtual line of continuous variation that is immanent within the real, and that specific line of variation, or vector of potential development and differentiation, is interconnected with other such lines across a plane of consistency, or field of virtual vectorial forces. Messiaen's goal (and that of all composers generally, and of modern composers especially) is to capture these virtual forces, 'the forces of an immaterial, nonformal, and energetic Cosmos' (Deleuze and Guttari 1987: 342–3), and give them sonic embodiment. He seeks to render sonorous that which is non-sonorous, to address 'a problem of consistency or consolidation: How to consolidate the material, make it consistent, so that it can harness unthinkable, invisible, nonsonorous forces', such as those of 'Duration and Intensity' (Deleuze and Guattari 1987: 343). In one sense, then, Messiaen's compositions are directly connected to the actual material world, in that he generates thematic material through a deterritorialisation of actual birdsong refrains. But in another sense, his compositions partake of a different realm – the virtual – rendering sonorous the non-sonorous forces immanent within the real. In this regard, his compositions may be seen as sonic bodies without organs, palpable planes of consistency that render perceptible what usually escapes perception – the speeds, affects, and floating time of the virtual. I believe that the music of death, doom and black metal groups likewise aims at the creation of sonic bodies without organs, or palpable planes of consistency, though of a decidedly different quality from those of Messiaen.

The Music of Death, Doom and Black Metal

Death, doom and black metal are sub-genres of heavy metal music, a form of popular music whose origin most commentators trace to the 1969–70 release of Led Zeppelin's *Led Zeppelin II*, Deep Purple's *Deep Purple in Rock*, and Black Sabbath's *Paranoid*.[3] Of these three, Black Sabbath's was the album that fostered the development of death, doom and black metal. England's Venom produced what some regard as the first death metal album, *Welcome to Hell*, in 1981, with other early efforts in a death vein including those of Los Angeles' Slayer (*Show No Mercy* (1983), *Hell Awaits* (1985), and *Reign in Blood* (1986)), Switzerland's Hellhammer (*Apocalyptic Raids* (1985)), and Florida's Death (*Scream Bloody Gore* (1987) and *Leprosy* (1988)). By the early 1990s, death had become established as a prominent form of heavy metal music, leading performers during the 1990s including Morbid Angel, Deicide, Cannibal Corpse, Obituary, Monstrosity, Cryptopsy, Suffocation, Dying Fetus and Vader. At present, several hundred death bands are performing and recording worldwide.

Devotees of doom metal often cite as early instances of the sub-genre mid-1980s albums by Saint Vitus and Candlemass, the title of Candlemass's 1986 *Epicus Doomicus Metallicus* perhaps inspiring the sub-genre's eventual designation. But only in the early 1990s did doom become firmly established as an important form of heavy metal music, as groups such as Paradise Lost (*Lost Paradise* (1990)), My Dying Bride (*As the Flower Withers* (1992) and *Turn Loose the Swans* (1993)), and Anathema (*Serenade* (1993) and *Enigma* (1995)) fused elements of death metal with the sombre, slow-paced strains of groups such as Saint Vitus and Candlemass. Though perhaps less popular than death metal, doom continues to thrive, with at least 200 groups active in the Americas and Europe.

Black metal is often said to have arisen alongside death metal, Sweden's Bathory showing characteristics of the sub-genre in such releases as *The Return . . .* (1985), *Under the Sign of the Black Mark* (1987), *Blood Fire Death* (1988), but the groups most closely associated with the establishment of black metal as a distinct category, Norway's Mayhem, Burzum, Darkthrone, and Emperor, developed their music in direct response to death metal. These groups' releases from the early 1990s inspired the formation of hundreds of black metal bands in the next decade, black metal now perhaps rivalling death in popularity among metal audiences. In addition to Darkthrone, Emperor Burzum and Mayhem, important black metal groups active in the last decade include Dark Funeral, Enslaved, Gorgoroth, Immortal, Impaled Nazarene, Marduk, Rotting Christ, and Satyricon.[4]

Fundamental to death, doom and black metal, as to all heavy metal music, is the highly amplified sound of electric guitars, electric basses and drums. The basic sound is aptly named 'heavy metal', for both words convey something essential about the music. It is heavy in that it is emphatically percussive, 'thick' in texture, and highly amplified in the lower registers. It is metal in that its sound is dominated by a particular gamut of high distortion, low frequency 'grinding', and 'crunching' timbres produced by amplified solid-body electric guitars. The language of timbres, of course, like the language of tastes or smells, is crude at best, but whether one can precisely name the sound or not, one can easily discriminate a basic 'feel' to the sound of all death, doom and black metal. What is crucial is that the core sound of the sub-genres bears little relation to any sounds produced by conventional acoustic instruments, including the guitar. It is decidedly 'unnatural', non-organic, metallic. If rock 'n' roll generally depends for its existence on electric industrial technology, death, doom and black metal take as their fundamental sound that of the electric guitar treated as an electric industrial machine.

Death, doom and black metal do not imitate the sounds of industrial machines, but they produce sonic analogues of the sounds, rhythms and patterns of the modern technological lifeworld. In this sense, death, doom and black metal may be seen as music that attempts a deterritorialisation of the diverse refrains of contemporary industrial machine culture. But such an observation, besides being rather clichéd (though nonetheless true, I believe), says little about the music beyond its basic timbral qualities. If music deterritorialises non-musical refrains, it also reterritorialises sounds within conventional systems of relations: 'it is through a system of melodic and harmonic coordinates by means of which music reterritorialises upon itself, *qua* music' (Deleuze and Guattari 1987: 303). Deleuze and Guattari argue that genuine creativity in music requires not simply a deterritorialisation of refrains in the outside world, but also a deterritorialisation of the conventions of standard musical practice, which in the case of metal music, are those of traditional seventeenth- to nineteenth-century Western tonal harmony and counterpoint. Deleuze and Guattari advocate what they call a 'generalised chromaticism', a deterritorialisation 'affecting not only pitches but all sound components – durations, intensities, timbre, attacks . . . By placing all its components in continuous variation, music itself becomes a superlinear system, a rhizome instead of a tree, and enters the service of a virtual cosmic continuum of which even holes, silences, ruptures, and breaks are a part' (Deleuze and Guattari 1987: 95). Yet they recognise as well that a deterritorialisation of all musical components at the same time leads only to a muddled chaos of white noise:

> Sometimes one overdoes it, puts too much in, works with a jumble of lines and sounds; then instead of producing a cosmic machine capable of 'rendering sonorous', one lapses back to a machine of reproduction that ends up reproducing nothing but a scribble effacing all lines, a scramble effacing all sounds. (Deleuze and Guattari 1987: 343–4)

All elements of music must be open to experimentation, but only a selected few may be worked with at a time. What is needed is 'a maximum of calculated sobriety in relation to the disparate elements and the parameters', a 'sober gesture, an act of consistency, capture, or extraction that works in a material that is not meagre but prodigiously simplified, creatively limited, selected' (Deleuze and Guattari 1987: 344–5). And as Deleuze and Guattari observe of literary experimentation in *Kafka: Toward a Minor Literature*, innovation may proceed through proliferation (as in Joyce) but also through ascetic impoverishment (as in Beckett). Hence, in musical as in literary experimentation, not only does innovation require a limitation of the elements to be subjected to deterritorialisation, but it also may operate through a deliberately ascetic impoverishment of elements, an intensification of musical components through their simplification.

Death, doom and black metal explore a deliberately restricted range of possibilities within heavy metal music, each in its own way. Although the relationship between the three sub-genres is complex and shifting, perhaps the easiest means of characterising them is first to delineate death metal practices and then to approach doom and black metal as responses to death.[5] One finds in death metal a concerted effort to eliminate all sweetness, tenderness, and niceness from popular music – witness the repeated description of the sub-genre by its performers and listeners as 'extreme' and 'brutal' – and to fashion a music of frenetic speed and constant intensity. The intensity of the music is conveyed through the sheer volume of the sound, variations in volume level arising almost exclusively through brief antiphonal exchanges of solo power chords between guitarists or shifts from chord sections to monophonic sections played in unison by bass and guitars. The bass generally doubles the guitar motifs, providing a full low- frequency reinforcement of the guitars' deep sounds, while the 'bite' of the guitar attack ensures a relatively clear articulation of the rapid figures executed by the guitarists. The drums emphasise virtually every subdivision within each high-speed rhythmic motif, the highly amplified double kick-drums frequently delivering a near sub-sonic punch to each note of the prestissimo bass-guitar figures. The sound is not simply processed by the ears but also felt in the body (especially the chest), and though the ears might subordinate elements of a rhythmic motif into accented and unaccented components, the body feels each element as a distinct percussive event. The result is a music that is experienced as an unrelenting, high-speed assault of low-frequency and mid-range pulses grouped in massive blocks or slabs of sound.

Death's harmonic palette is quite limited. Major triads are avoided, and even minor triads tend to be replaced by the open fourths and fifths of power chords. Motifs generally are based on the intervals of the blues pentatonic scale (E–G–A–B–D in the key of E), with frequent emphasis given as well to the intervals of the minor second (E–F) and augmented fourth (E–A#) characteristic of the 'exotic' Phrygian and Locrian modes. There is little genuine harmonic movement in death compositions; standard blues progressions and even common metal progressions (e.g., C–D–Em in E) give way to tonic-centered sections of monophony or polyphonic sections based on a single chord or on a repeated alternation of two or three open fifths that reinforce the tonic within each phrase unit. Death compositions are usually organised in discrete sections, each section based on a complex rhythmic motif. And if a shift in tonality occurs, it coincides with a sectional break, such that the shift provides little sense of a movement linking one tonal area to another, instead merely signalling an abrupt break between tonal blocks. The sectional organisation seldom conforms to the standard verse–chorus–bridge structure of popular songs; rather, section follows section in a paratactic sequence of multiple, loosely related units, one unit simply being added on to the next. The result of these harmonic and structural practices is that in death songs a curious stasis pervades the ubiquitous high-speed motifs. Each section is like a plateau of intense constant energy, with its own mood (generally minor-modal, sometimes vaguely non-Western), full of motion but going nowhere in particular, section following section in a series of discontinuous shifts from one plateau to another, those shifts themselves possessing no identifiable developmental drive or direction.

Ultimately, this interplay of speed and stasis points toward the presence of two different kinds of time in death metal, the time of Chronos and that of Aeon, as well as two different ways of understanding the concept of speed. In *A Thousand Plateaus*, Deleuze and Guattari cite Pierre Boulez's distinction between pulsed and non-pulsed time in music (Deleuze and Guattari 1987: 262), pulsed time being the time of conventional metres and regular beats, non-pulsed time being the floating, unmarked time exhibited in certain modern compositions (Boulez's among them) in which, for example, performers freely execute motifs within a given duration (say, fifteen seconds) at their own pace, with no pulse provided by the conductor. Deleuze and Guattari link this distinction to one drawn often by Messiaen between metre and rhythm.[6] Metre, for Messiaen, denotes a regular, measured repetition of equal pulses, whereas rhythm is a matter of incommensurable durations, irregular sequences of unequally spaced pulses. In Messiaen's judgement, a march is the least rhythmic form of music, and it is rhythm, not metre, that he regards as the vital force of musical time. What Deleuze and Guattari call Chronos, the time of the commonsense, actual world, is a pulsed, metrical time of regular repeated intervals, whereas Aeon, the time of the virtual, is a non-pulsed rhythmic time of irregular, incommensurable intervals.

It is on the basis of this distinction between pulsed, metrical Chronos and non-pulsed, rhythmic Aeon that Deleuze and Guattari make what might at first seem a paradoxical opposition of movement and speed. Speed, they argue, is not necessarily a matter of a quantitative measure of movement. Indeed, 'a movement may be very fast, but that does not give it speed; a speed may be very slow, or even immobile, yet it is still speed. Movement is extensive; speed is intensive' (Deleuze and Guattari 1987: 381). To phrase the distinction somewhat differently, we might say that there is a quantitative speed of measurable velocities germane to the actual (an 'extensive' speed, in that it belongs to the realm of Cartesian spatio-temporal extension), but that there is also a qualitative speed that defies measure and opens us to the intensive dimension of the virtual.

Qualitative speed is movement out of control, and it may be encountered in extremes of mobility and immobility. Deleuze and Guattari suggest the nature of those extremes in their remarks on Kleist, who gives 'time a new rhythm' in literature. His fiction and drama present 'an endless succession of catatonic episodes or fainting spells, and flashes or rushes. Catatonia is: "This affect is too strong for me", and a flash is: "The power of this affect sweeps me away", so that the Self (*Moi*) is now nothing more than a character whose actions and emotions are desubjectified, perhaps even to the point of death' (Deleuze and Guattari 1987: 356). A rush is an acceleration that runs out of control, catatonia a vertiginous suspension of time, and the two extremes ultimately shade into one another. Just as the spokes of a wheel, moving faster and faster as the velocity of the wheel's rotation increases, at a certain point begin to blur and form a single, still shape, so acceleration beyond commonsense perception at a certain point is transformed into a constant, vibrating hum that para-doxically seems to freeze duration while still participating in a dimension of becoming. In this sense, every intensive moment of temporal disequili-brium, even a frozen, catatonic stupor, is a moment of qualitative speed.

Nearly all music involves both metre and rhythm, both pulsed and non-pulsed time; few compositions dispense entirely with evenly repeated beats and regular measures. In Deleuze and Guattari's analysis, this is not surprising, for Chronos and Aeon, though qualitatively distinct from one another, are only experienced as tendencies within an inextricable mix-ture of the two. There is no experience of chronometric time that does not have at least a tincture of vertiginous becoming within it, and no experience of a floating, suspended time that does not retain at least a hint of some regular measure. What varies in music is the handling of metre and rhythm, pulsed and non-pulsed time, and the relative emphasis placed on each factor. All rock 'n' roll has its roots in the regular metres of dance music, and death metal is no exception. The 'givens' of rock 'n' roll are the standard metres (2/4, 3/4, 4/4, 6/8, 9/8, 12/8) and four-, eight-, twelve-, and sixteen-bar rhythmic groupings of Western dance forms, and death musicians accept these conventions, attempting in individual sec-tions of their compositions to exploit a specific rhythmic motif within a standard metre, imbue it with an emphatic 'heaviness', and render it at a high rate of quantitative speed. But they also manage to create effects of qualitative speed, and through several techniques and practices.

As we have already seen, one method is to avoid virtually all harmonic movement and any developmental organisation of sectional units, there-by imparting to each high-speed unit a concomitant aura of atemporal stasis. A second, less common, technique is to repeat a hyper-regular figure until it becomes a hypnotic, trance-like drone (a strategy one meets in minimalists like Philip Glass, as in any number of jam bands). More important is a third technique of structuring songs in discrete rhythmic blocks that are connected by no common measure but simply placed in abrupt juxtaposition to one another. Rather than gradually accelerating or decelerating between sections, or doubling (or tripling, or halving) the pulse from one section to another, or using a common pulse to move, say, from a duple to a triple metre – all standard techniques for relating one metrical unit to another – death musicians frequently change tempo or metre from brief section to brief section (each section generally lasting between fifteen and thirty seconds) in such a way that there is no logical relation between sections, each coexisting with the others as an autonomous temporal unit. What one encounters in compositions of this sort is a series of self-contained, intensely pulsed rhythmic units punctuated by a sequence of erratic, spasmodic jolts, fits and starts. If in each discrete section a hyper-Chronos of quantitative speed is manifest, the time *between* each section is that of an Aeon of qualitative speed and incommensurable rhythm. And yet a fourth device, used sparingly but to telling effect, is to accelerate a rapid duple figure until the individually distinct rhythmic elements of the bass, guitar and drum parts merge in a non-pulsed tremolo of whirring chaos. In these moments, quantitative turns into qualitative speed, the previously pulsed units blurring in a tremolo rush that is at the same time a catatonic skid.

The music of doom metal might be characterised as death metal on Qualudes, death slowed to a funereal pace and stretched out in songs lasting sometimes as long as twenty-five or thirty minutes. The same minor-modal harmonies prevail in both, as do static chord relations within sections and loose paratactic structures linking sections to one another. The basic timbres of doom resemble those of death, and most doom metal, despite its slow pace, is insistently 'heavy'.[7] But doom has a melodic component that is largely absent in death. Even monophonic motifs in death, despite their linearity, tend to function less as melodies than as percussive bass lines, whereas in doom the guitars and bass frequently articulate extended legato lines that conform to standard notions of 'tunefulness'. Often the legato lines are doubled by a violin, flute or female vocalist, instruments and sounds almost never used in death. The melodies of doom, however, exploit a narrow range of expressivity, their function being primarily to establish a sombre, modal exotic mood and provide continuity within sections. Doom seeks above all to create atmospheric auras, to imbue each section with its own 'feel' while at the same time maintaining the heaviness of an emphatically pulsed sound.[8] Doom melodies serve to meld components within a section and give them a floating, hazy continuity, thereby creating what Deleuze and Guattari call a 'haecceity', a 'thisness', an atmosphere like a 'season, a winter, a summer, an hour, a date', with an identity that partakes of the time of Aeon, 'the indefinite time of the event, the floating line that knows only speeds' (Deleuze and Guattari 1987: 261–2). The atmospheric speed sought by doom, ultimately, is the qualitative speed of catatonia, the immobile speed of a paradoxically intense suspended animation.

Black metal comes in two varieties, one fairly close to death, the other with some similarities to doom. Like doom, black metal shares the timbres, harmonies, sectional construction and overall organisational structure of death. Much of black metal, like death, is fast paced, although the range of tempos in black tends to be broader than that in death. What many black metal bands reject is death's emphasis on virtuosity and musicianship. They strive for a messier, grungier sound, something more chaotic and raw than the precise and intricate percussive complexities of death. Such groups tend to emphasise a rhythmic figure at greater length and change tempo less frequently than do death bands, and they often replace death's quick monophonic lines with rapid flat-pick reiterations of massive, muddy triads. One extreme of black metal, then, might be very loosely designated grunge death (Burzum and Mayhem being examples of this strain). The other extreme might be thought of as fast doom. In this form of black metal, legato melodies executed by a violin, flute or organ often lend continuity to a high tempo section, and at times synthesisers are used to provide a vaguely choral, sustained harmonic 'wash' to a section (early Emperor provides numerous examples of this latter practice). But what is common to all black metal is a concentration on mood and atmosphere. Many black metal musicians dress in black robes and wear exaggerated white-and-black 'corpsepaint' on their faces, and though such practices are strictly extra-musical, they point to the basically ritual and theatrical conception of black metal music, which is meant to evoke vague auras, climates and affective settings. Like doom, black metal seeks to elicit the floating time of a catatonic Aeon, and at the same time, like death, it pursues both quantitative speed and the qualitative speed of a hyper-accelerated rush.

Voice, Words and Action

In a special issue of *Guitar Presents*, Marc Shapiro characterises death metal with what he calls a fairly simple equation: 'It's guitar tuned down so low that only dogs can hear it. It's songs about the Devil, revenge from the grave, death by garden tools and other tales from the dark side delivered, for the most part, in a Linda Blair/ *Exorcist*-like satanic growl.' (Shapiro 1993: 8) The satanic growl is indeed a distinctive feature of much death metal, and many doom and black vocalists adopt the same low-pitched, guttural, raspy, bark of death. Some black metal vocalists opt for incessant full-voiced or high-pitched screams over the death growl, and doom performers often combine growls, screams and grunts with deep murmurs and slow whispers. But what is common to most death, doom and black metal is the anti-melodic, non-natural treatment of the voice (though so-called 'clean' vocals have been gradually showing up in a few groups over the last decade). If, as Deleuze and Guattari assert, 'the first musical operation' is 'to machine the voice' (Deleuze and Guattari 1987: 303, translation modified), that is, to deterritorialise the voice from its ordinary, 'natural' speaking function, then death, doom and black vocalists are fundamentally – indeed, primally – musical in their anti-lyrical non-singing, in that their growls, screams and grunts simply push music's denaturalisation of the speaking voice to extremes (which most listeners hostile to the sub-genres would deem beyond the limits of the musical).

Though death, doom and black vocalists articulate words, seldom are the words readily understandable, especially in live performance, and even in the slowest tempos of doom. The most important function of the vocals is to provide a broadly affective, percussive reinforcement of accents and phrases, to fuse vocal noises with the instrumental sounds and create semi-human, semi-machine, blocks of sound. Nonetheless, lyrics do exist (most groups provide lyrics sheets with their CDs), and they have an important musical purpose. As Shapiro suggests, death lyrics tend to focus on the dark side, the grave, corporeal decay and physical violence. These staples of horror films are common in black metal as well, with satanic themes being somewhat more prevalent in black than in death. Doom lyrics often offer sepulchral expressions of Poe-esque *Liebestod* (My Dying Bride's lyrics read largely as an extended explication of the group's name), though frequently doom bands simply voice melancholy sentiments of vague despair and hopelessness (November's Doom is one such group). Although the lyrics of the three sub-genres often summon up dramatic *tableaus*, they seldom offer plots or stories, for their main purpose is to evoke emotions, moods and attitudes through highly charged images, raw, profane diction, and diverse first-person expressions of anti-social desire. In section four of *A Thousand Plateaus*, 'Postulates of Linguistics', Deleuze and Guattari argue that words do not represent things so much as *intervene* in things, performing 'incorporeal transformations' of bodies through speech-actions (Deleuze and Guattari 1987: 86). Similarly, death, doom and black lyrics intervene in the music, providing an affective specificity to what is only vaguely generated by the music. There is no inherently evil, violent, or even aggressive music (loud, yes, assertive, perhaps, but not inherently aggressive), and what the lyrics attempt is to narrow the sound's range of affective associations, imbue the music with more precisely delineated moods grounded in concrete situations – situations, as it happens, that frequently involve evil, violence and aggression.

Not all songs, however dwell on violence and mayhem. Doom lyrics as a whole tend to involve violence less than do those of death and black, and even within death and black there are wide variations in the frequency and intensity of violence in the lyrics. Satanic motifs are not uncommon in death and black lyrics, but they are far from ubiquitous, and often such motifs evidence less an obsession with evil than a fascination with non-Christian, broadly pagan sensibilities, a fascination shared with bands that draw themes and imagery for their songs from Norse mythology (Emperor, among many Scandinavian groups), Babylonian mythology (Morbid Angel) or Egyptian mythology (Nile). It is clear, then, that there is no inherent relation between the music and the lyrics, that the manifest continuities in musical practices across the subgenres do not have equally consistent continuities in the handling of lyrics. Yet when lyricists do choose to focus on violence and mayhem, one may well ask why, in such cases, if the music is not inherently violent or evil, has it been co-opted for violent or evil purposes? The difficulties of relating representations of violence (especially in film, fiction or art) to actual violence are well-known, and they are no less problematic in the case of death, doom and black metal music. Clearly, much of the impetus behind these lyrics is to shock and offend – to offend fundamentalist Christians with satanic hymns, to offend liberals with sexist profanities, to offend just about everyone with descriptions of putrefying flesh, evisceration, blood and gore. Often, the lyrics seem to function merely as the expression of a defiant anarchistic hedonism or the cathartic release of strong emotion. Occasionally, the performers adopt a mimetic stance and argue that they are not advocating violence but simply reflecting the violence around them in their songs. And frequently one detects an ironic, and at times parodic, sense of humour in the excesses of the imagery and the exaggerated postures of the songs' personas (not unlike the humour one finds in many horror films).

All of which suggests, not that art is separate from life, but that the connection between the two is complex and determinable only in specific circumstances. Representations of violence need have no relation to violent actions, but they may, though specifying causal relations must be approached with great caution and may well prove impossible. Consider the notorious case of the Norwegian black metal scene in the late 1980s and early 1990s, documented at length in Moynihan and Søderlind's sometimes lurid *Lords of Chaos: The Bloody Rise of the Satanic Metal Underground.*[9] Here are the facts. On April 8 1991, the lead singer of Mayhem, 'Dead' (Per Ohlin), committed suicide with a shotgun blast to the head. Before the police arrived, 'Euronymous' (Øystein Aarseth), Mayhem's founder and lead guitarist, photographed Dead's corpse, later bragging that he also ate pieces of Dead's brain and gathered scraps of Dead's skull to use as necklace decorations. In May 1992, the first of some forty-five to sixty church burnings took place, most of the subsequent incidents occurring over a three-year period, at least one-third with documented connections to the black metal scene. On 21 August 1992, 'Faust' (Bård Eithun), then drummer of Emperor, murdered Magne Andreassen, a gay man who, according to Faust, approached him for sex. On 10 August 1993, 'Count Grishnackh' (Varg Vikernes), guitarist of Burzum, murdered Euronymous. Later that month, Grishnackh and Faust were arrested for their respective murders. In September 1994, both were found guilty; Grishnackh was sentenced to twenty-one years in prison, Faust to a fourteen-year term. In subsequent trials, other black metal scene members were convicted of arson, including Samoth, Emperor's lead guitarist, who received a two-year sentence.

What is evident from Moynihan and Søderlind's account is that during this period in Oslo black metal music was an important part of a genuine 'scene', a multidimensional social milieu in which musicians lived with one another, performers and fans socialised with one another at concerts and especially at Euronymous's record store, Helvet, and participants embraced modes of dress, discourse and interaction commonly associated with evil, death, the demonic, and other dark forces. Euronymous was a charismatic promoter, recording and distributing CDs of various black metal bands, cleverly boosting Norwegian black metal in fanzine interviews that stressed the evil, dangerous nature of the music and of the performers (especially himself). Grishnackh, Euronymous's junior by six years, was an equally charismatic, forceful individual, and the two of them became friends for a while, eventually assembling around themselves a conspiratorial group of arsonists intent on demonstrating to each other how evil they could be. Grishnackh clearly resented Euronymous's popularity and eventually came to regard Euronymous as a poseur (as well as a dishonest business associate). When Grishnackh learned that Faust had killed someone, he seemed to envy Faust's status as a murderer, and some of Grishnackh's associates attribute his slaying of Euronymous as much to a desire for renown among his peers as to personal and professional animosities.

To deny that black metal music had any connection with the Norwegian black metal scene and its incidents of arson and murder would be foolish. But to claim that the music or the lyrics somehow caused the crimes would be equally absurd. A unique culture involving a shifting network of individuals with a host of interests, motives and desires took shape in a particular place and time, and music was an inextricable component of that culture. In Deleuze and Guattari's ethological terms, black metal functioned as a complex of refrains in counterpoint with numerous extra-musical refrains in a specific social and natural lifeworld. Just as a bird's song may combine with postures, actions, and surrounding materials (trees, twigs, worms, and so on) in patterns involved in mating, nesting, or foraging, so black metal combined with other elements to form patterns of interaction that eventually involved, among other things, arson and murder.

That music can be a powerful accompaniment to violent behaviour is undeniable, but the range of forms of musical expression capable of fulfilling such a role seems unlimited. (One thinks, for example, of 'Helter Skelter' among the Manson family, but also of Schubert in the Nazi death camps.) Conversely, there seems to be no hard evidence that any form of music is more closely associated with violent action than another. Black metal music was an important part of the lives of Norway's black metal arsonists and murderers, but neither black metal as a whole, nor the related forms of death and doom metal, have been shown to have a higher incidence of suicide, assault or murder among their performers or listeners than other forms of popular music. Still, one may ask, why do death, doom and black metal lyrics focus so often on gore, decay, corpses, and destruction? Why this pervasive fascination with death?

The answer, I believe, is that the lyrics are designed to evoke what the music seeks to create: the experience of the body without organs. In *Anti-Oedipus*, Deleuze and Guattari describe the body without organs as a decentred body that has ceased to function as a coherently regulated organism, one that is sensed as an ecstatic, catatonic, a-personal zero-degree of intensity that is in no way negative but has a positive existence. They argue that 'the body without organs is the model of death' (Deleuze and Guattari 1983: 329), by which they mean that the ecstatic trance-like state of this zero-degree of intensity is the experiential analogue of what is never truly experienced, at least as part of one's ongoing being, but is sensed only as the disappearing edge of existence. Hence the human fascination with death, so widespread and multifarious in its manifestations, may be seen from this vantage as an affirmation of a fundamental dimension of experience, that of the virtual, which is encountered as a paradoxical catatonic rush or immobile whir of differential speeds and intensive affects. But Deleuze and Guattari recognise as well that there are great risks and perils in the pursuit of a body without organs, and thus in *A Thousand Plateaus* they speak of both a suicidal and a cancerous body without organs, each with its specific dangers. Individuals produce a body without organs by becoming-other, by deterritorialising all the ossified, sedimented strata of regular codes and structures, but if 'you free [the body without organs] with too violent an action, if you blow apart the strata without taking precautions, then instead of drawing the plane [of consistency] you will be killed, plunged into a black hole, or even dragged toward catastrophe' (Deleuze and Guattari 1987: 161). In short, the fascination with the 'model of death', the body without organs, may become a fascination with real death, a suicidal dive into an all-absorbent black hole. The cancerous body without organs, by contrast, is produced not by an incautious, precipitous deterritorialisation of all coordinates, but by a fostering of partial, 'totalitarian' or 'fascist' deterritorialisations that are 'terrifying caricatures of the plane of consistency' (Deleuze and Guattari 1987: 163). The virtual is immanent and everywhere manifest within the real, and hence the plane of consistency, or the body without organs, is immanent within even the most rigid and oppressive of institutions. There is thus a 'BwO [body without organs] of money (inflation), but also a BwO of the State, army, factory, city, Party, etc.' (Deleuze and Guattari 1987: 163), and each of these bodies without organs may become an object of fascination for the individual, a kind of tumour that may proliferate and eventually take over. Deleuze and Guattari see the production of a body without organs as the only means of genuine creation, but they ask, 'How can we fabricate a BwO for ourselves without its being the cancerous BwO of a fascist inside us, or the empty BwO of a drug addict, paranoiac, or hypochondriac? How can we tell the three Bodies apart?' (Deleuze and Guattari 1987: 163).

Death, doom and black metal's fascination with death, one might say, is a fascination with the problem of the three bodies without organs, with the liminal areas where the three shade into one another. 'The BwO is desire,' say Deleuze and Guattari.

Even when it falls into the void of too-sudden destratification, or into the proliferation of a cancerous stratum, it is still desire. Desire stretches that far: desiring one's own annihilation, or desiring the power to annihilate. Money, army, police, and State desire, fascist desire, even fascism is desire.

And the problem is 'to distinguish the BwO from its doubles: empty vitreous bodies, cancerous bodies, totalitarian and fascist' (Deleuze and Guattari 1987: 165). The pursuit of an ecstatic, a-personal affective intensity can all too easily turn into a thirst for self-annihilation or a will to annihilate, and death, doom and black metal lyrics explore those moments when such desires interpenetrate.

Deleuze and Guattari also say that the body without organs may function as a 'war machine', and here especially we see highlighted the dangerous relation deterritorialisation may have with violence. Deleuze and Guattari posit a fundamental opposition between nomadic and sedentary modes of social life, to which correspond respectively the institutions of the war machine and the state apparatus. Commonly war is taken to be a state function, but Deleuze and Guattari argue that the informing principle of war, that of a mutative, chaotic force of transformation (and this is what they mean by the term 'war machine'), is antithetical to the state, and that the history of state-sponsored violence is one of an uneasy and perpetually unstable capture of this force of transformation. They note that in Indo-European mythology the warrior frequently is contrasted with such state figures as the king, lawgiver, or priest, the warrior often betraying social alliances and operating as an anarchic locus of unpredictable action. This mythic opposition of warrior versus king/lawgiver/priest they see as symptomatic of an opposition of two modes of existence, each with its own means of creating, inhabiting and propagating a specific 'space', one 'smooth', the other 'striated'. Smooth space is essentially fluid, heterogeneous, without centre or dimensional coordinates, whereas striated space is stable, homogeneous, and crisscrossed with organisational grids. The nomads' smooth habitat of shifting desert sands, for example, differs qualitatively from the striated fields of the sedentary state dwellers. Yet this contrast of smooth and striated spaces, though initially framed in geographic terms, Deleuze and Guattari extend in a number of ways, to include different artefacts (felt versus fabric), different kinds of time (unpulsed rhythm versus pulsed metre), different forms of thought (nomad science versus royal science, fractal geometry versus Euclidean geometry), different approaches to the arts (Egyptian, Gothic or Byzantine art versus Graeco-Roman art) and so on. Ultimately, the 'war machine' is simply a term for the metamorphic force of deterritorialisation and 'smooth space' the name of the body without organs, or plane of consistency, created and permeated by that metamorphic force. As Deleuze explains in an interview on *A Thousand Plateaus*:

> we define the 'war machine' as a linear assemblage which constructs itself on lines of flight. In this sense, the war machine does not at all have war as its object; it has as its object a very special space, smooth space, which it composes, occupies and propagates. Nomadism is precisely this combination 'war machine-smooth space'. We try to show how and in what case the war machine takes war for its object (when the apparatuses of the State appropriate the war machine which does not initially belong to them). A war machine tends to be revolutionary, or artistic, much more so than military. (Deleuze 1990: 50–1)

The war machine does not have war as its object, yet still it is called the war machine, and though its function is primarily revolutionary or artistic, its name is inseparable from a military domain. What Deleuze and Guattari reinforce through this term is the problematic relation between deterritorialising metamorphosis and violence, which, as we have seen, they also frame in terms of the body without organs and its dangerous doubles, the suicidal and cancerous bodies without organs. The dangers of constructing a body without organs are dangers of violence, risks that a creative, metamorphic war machine will turn into a veritable machine of war, a negative force bent solely on destruction. It is striking how frequently images of war, especially of an apocalyptic sort, appear in the lyrics of death and black metal (and occasionally doom as well). Often the persona in death and black metal songs adopts the pose of a warrior and espouses an ethos of unrestrained destruction. The warriors imagined in these songs, however, are not representatives of an organised military regime but embodiments of an anarchic force of chaos. They inhabit a space outside the regular order of any state apparatus and serve as mythic figures of a dimension of unrestrained social upheaval. What this recurring imagery of warriors, battlefields and Armageddon suggests, finally, is that the music of death, doom and black metal is a war machine ever becoming machine of war, a machine of war perpetually turning back into a war machine, a music focused on the perilous relation between ecstatic deterritorialisation and suicidal or fascistic annihilation.

Music 'is never tragic, music is joy', Deleuze and Guattari claim, yet there are times when music 'necessarily gives us a taste for death . . . Music has a thirst for destruction, every kind of destruction, extinction, breakage, dislocation. Is that not its potential "fascism"?' (Deleuze and

Guattari 1987: 299). This thirst for destruction Deleuze and Guattari tie to music's power as a deterritorialising force. Compared to painting, music 'seems to have a much stronger deterritorializing force, at once more intense and much more collective', which perhaps explains 'the collective fascination exerted by music, and even the potentiality of the "fascist" danger we mentioned a little earlier: music (drums, trumpets) draws people and armies into a race that can go all the way to the abyss' (Deleuze and Guattari 1987: 302). Music, one might say, is at once more abstract and more elemental than painting. As Deleuze remarks in *Francis Bacon: Logique de la Sensation*, music indeed 'deeply traverses our bodies, and puts an ear in our belly, in our lungs, etc.', but ultimately it 'rids bodies of their inertia, of the materiality of their presence. It disincarnates bodies' (Deleuze 1981: 38). In turn, through the manipulation of its sonic matter, it 'gives the most mental [*spirituelles*] entities a disincarnated, dematerialized body' (Deleuze 1981: 38). Music, in short, through its heightened and yet somehow dispersed, intangible sensuality, has the power of undoing the coordinates of the commonsense world and creating a sonic body of speeds and affective intensities, that sonic body traversing listeners and turning their organised, material bodies into dematerialised vectors spread out across an a-personal, trans-individual body without organs. But in music's great power as a deterritorialising force lies its danger. Its dissolution of codes, structures and conventions can expand, accelerate and form part of an undifferentiated will to annihilation and destruction. And its abstract, dematerialising affectivity can be channelled into any number of violent, repressive and reactionary circuits of power.

Like all forms of music, death, doom and black metal are modes of experimentation on the real. Their timbres, rhythms and textures are sonic analogues of the patterns and processes of contemporary electronic, industrial, machine culture. Their deterritorialisation of such extra-musical refrains, however, takes place within a musical deterritorialisation of popular music conventions, those conventions themselves functioning as refrains within the real. By deliberately adopting a limited musical idiom and pushing its elements to an extreme, death, doom and black metal develop inventive deformations of standard popular music practices, concentrating especially on timbre and rhythm rather than melody and harmony. Death metal seeks a music of intensity and speed, both a quantitative speed of emphatic rapid pulses and a qualitative speed of rushes and catatonic whirs. Doom pursues a music of atmospheric auras, at once immobile and yet heavily pulsed, whereas black combines elements of death and doom to fashion raw blocks of atmospheric speed.

The lyrics of death, doom and black metal intervene in the music, suggesting specific moods, emotions and attitudes as correlates of the broad and underdetermined affective dimension of the sounds. The lyrics in various ways evoke the experience of the body without organs, especially in its liminal forms in which the positive, creative body without organs merges with its violent suicidal or cancerous caricatures. The songs of death, doom and black metal are composed, performed, recorded, circulated and enjoyed within complex, multidimensional social situations, and those songs may or may not serve as refrains in counterpoint with extra-musical refrains involving violent action.

The final ethical measure of any music is its ability to create new possibilities for life, and such is the measure that must be applied to an assessment of the social practices within which death, doom and black metal music and lyrics are given concrete actualisation. Neither wholesale condemnation nor blanket approval of the sub-genres is called for, but instead a careful delineation of their musical, verbal and pragmatic methods and purposes, as well as an appraisal of their function within particular contexts. Deleuze and Guattari's concepts of the refrain, deterritorialisation and reterritorialisation, the body without organs, speeds and intensities, haecceities, and so on, provide us with significant tools for undertaking such an analysis.

References

Arnett, J. (1996), *Metalheads: Heavy Metal Music and Adolescent Alienation*, Boulder, CO: Westview Press.

Beckwith, K. (2002), ' "Black Metal Music is for White People": Constructs of Colour and Identity with the Extreme Metal Scene', *M/C Journal*, media-culture.org.au/0207/blackmetal.html

Berger, H. (1999), 'Death Metal Tonality and the Act of Listening', *Popular Music*, 18 (2): 161–76.

Bogue, R. (2003), *Deleuze on Music, Painting, and the Arts*, New York: Routledge.

Bogue, R. (2004), 'Becoming Metal, Becoming Death . . .', in *Deleuze's Wake: Tributes and Tributaries*, Albany: SUNY Press.

Deleuze, G. (1994), *Difference and Repetition*, trans. P. Patton, New York: Columbia University Press.

Deleuze, G. (1981), *Francis Bacon: Logique de la Sensation*, Paris: Éditions de la différence.

Deleuze, G. (1990), *Pourparlers*, Paris: Minuit.

Deleuze, G. and Guattari, F. (1983), *Anti-Oedipus: Capitalism and Schizophrenia I*, trans. R. Hurley, M. Seem and H. R. Lane, Minneapolis: University of Minnesota Press.

Deleuze, G. and Guattari, F. (1986), *Kafka: Toward a Minor Literature*, trans. D. Polan, Minneapolis: University of Minnesota Press.

Deleuze, G. and Guattari, F. (1987), *A Thousand Plateaus: Capitalism and Schizophrenia II*, trans. B. Massumi, Minneapolis: University of Minnesota Press.

Harrell, J. (1994), 'The Poetics of Destruction: Death Metal Rock', *Popular Music and Society* 18: 91–104.
Moynihan, M. and Søderlind, S. (1998), *Lords of Chaos: The Bloody Rise of the Satanic Metal Underground*, Venice, CA: Feral House.
Samuel, C. (1976), *Conversations with Olivier Messiaen*, trans. F. Aprahamian, London: Steiner and Bell.
Shapiro, M. (1993), 'The Birth of Death: A Speed Demonology', *Guitar Presents: Speed Demons of Metal*: 6–9, 23, 110–12.
Walser, R. (1993), *Running with the Devil Power, Gender, and Madness in Heavy Metal Music*, Hanover: Wesleyan University Press.
Weinstein, D. (1991), *Heavy Metal: A Cultural Sociology*, New York: Lexington.

Notes

1. For a detailed discussion of Deleuze's approach to music, see Bogue 2003: 13–76.
2. Messiaen's remarks on birdsong and their function in his music may be found in Samuel 1976, especially pp. 62 and 75.
3. The best introduction to heavy metal music as a whole is Walser 1993. Weinstein (1991) also provides useful information about heavy metal culture, but her sociological analysis pays little heed to the music per se. Neither Walser nor Weinstein explicitly discusses the sub-genres of death, doom and black metal. The portraits of heavy metal listeners in Arnett 1996 are of limited interest, especially since only one of his subjects listens to music that might be remotely classified as death, doom or black metal.
4. The categories of death, doom and black are somewhat fluid, and classification of individual groups within these categories is often disputed by listeners. Nor are these the only divisions of heavy metal music that might be brought to bear on a study of the three sub-genres, thrash, grindcore, stoner rock, and speed metal, for example, being other classifications often invoked in heavy metal discussions. Assessments of the popularity of death, doom and black metal are difficult to make. The sub-genres receive virtually no television or radio airplay. CDs are produced and distributed not by major manufacturers but by a number of small labels in various countries, and in many instances by the groups themselves. Communication about the music is carried on among musicians and listeners through a few glossy publications, numerous 'fanzines' produced by enthusiasts of the sub-genres, several websites devoted to the music, and personal correspondence among band members and their audiences. Especially useful websites include Dark Legions Archive (www.anus.com/metal), Doom-metal.com, www.doom-metal.com), American Black Metal List (www.usbmlist.cjb.net) and DarkLyrics.com (www.darklyrics.com). Perhaps some rough measure of the popularity of the sub-genres may be gathered from the following data: Doom-metal.com offers detailed profiles and discographies of 291 doom metal groups, over 200 of which are currently active; the American Black Metal List includes entries for 490 black metal groups from the United States alone; and DarkLyrics archives lyrics by over 1,100 bands, at least 60 per cent of which are death, doom or black metal bands.
5. I discuss death metal music at some length in 'Becoming Metal, Becoming Death . . .', in *Deleuze's Wake: Tributes and Tributaries*. Other helpful treatments of death metal music include Harrell 1994 and Berger 1999.
6. For more on Messiaen's distinction between metre and rhythm, see Bogue 2003, p. 25.
7. There is some question among doom listeners as to whether some forms of so-called 'atmospheric doom', less 'heavy' than the norm, even qualify as genuine

doom. John Del Russi of Heirophant, when asked to define doom, comments: 'I stand firmly in my resolution that doom should always maintain the earth-shattering heaviness the likes of diSEMBOWELMENT, Evoken, Thergothon etc. While there are those who strive to achieve a more "serene" form of doom, attempting to express purely the sorrowful side, I find it most lacking in power in the absence of the pulverizing heaviness of the afore-mentioned pioneers of doom . . . While I have no qualms with "calmer" moments throughout the journey of doom, which genuinely add to the atmospheres of doom, I believe there should be a quality of "brutality" to its composition' (Doom-metal.com/Information/What Is Doom/What Is Doom According Too . . .).

8. All music, of course, creates some sort of atmosphere, but doom (and black) metal exploit specific techniques of late-Romantic chromatic programme music and tone poems that have heavily influenced film scores and become standard elements of suspense and horror movies. The atmospheres they evoke are hence those typically associated with cinematic images of foggy landscapes, dark, mysterious spaces, graveyards, haunted houses, and so on, all conveyed musically through passages with relatively little temporal drive.

9. I am not able to address here the question of Norwegian black metal's connection to Nazism. Since his incarceration in 1994, Varg Vikernes ('Count Grishnackh') has issued statements of an increasingly racist, white-supremacist nature that have led some to associate Norwegian black metal and black metal as a whole with Nazism. In the liner notes to their 1995 release, *Panzerfaust*, Darkthrone felt compelled to add a postscript that 'Darkthrone is certainly not a Nazi-band nor a political band'. Although black metal bands with Nazi leanings do exist, they are relatively few, and many black metal fans resent the assumption among some critics that the music has an inherent tie to Nazism. For a critique of black metal as a racist form of music (an attack based largely on Vikernes's remarks in Moynihan and Søderlind, it should be noted), see Beckwith 2002.

Chapter 6

Becoming-Music: The Rhizomatic Moment of Improvisation

Jeremy Gilbert

> To improvise is to join with the world, or meld with it.
> (Deleuze and Guattari 1987: 311)

Improvisations: Hearing Rhizomes in the 1990s

A sawdust room in the back of a small North London public house. Half a dozen musicians, all well known to each other, sit scattered around the room. Spidery, jagged, incomprehensible sounds seem to leap from their instruments into a blank space of non-music, never quite intersecting, never quite emerging into anything like forms. They could each still be tuning their individual instruments, oblivious to the presence of the others, for all that the uninitiated can hear music in this room. But there are no uninitiated: no-one is there to act as an audience. Well, no-one but me . . .

An East London 'night club' of dubious legality (it will soon be condemned and never reopened, redeveloped or adequately demolished: its abandoned terrace garden looking ever-more haunted as the years and the Dalston traffic roll by). The place is packed with bodies of numerous shades and wildly varying ages, pressed and merging together in the medium of sweat. The music is a furious amalgam of beats, noise, snatches of scratched melody, propulsive lines and percussive figures spinning laterally in all directions. No-one knows who's playing it: maybe we all are. Maybe it's just playing itself. Maybe it's playing us.

As different as they were, these were the definitive musical experiences of my first year living in London, at the beginning of the 1990s: a typical 'improv' (free improvisation) gig organised by the London Musicians' Collective; a rave during the golden age of "ardkore" (hardcore techno music). As different as they were, both also represented styles of music-making which commentators during that decade would come to describe using the conceptual vocabularies of Gilles Deleuze and Félix Guattari.

Simon Reynolds, a unique figure in English language music writing for his combination of journalism and cultural theory, was only the most populist of a range of commentators who, during the 1990s, made use of terminologies drawn from *Capitalism and Schizophrenia* (1987) to describe the rave as a 'desiring-machine' aimed at the collective articulation of a 'body without organs' (Jordan 1995; Reynolds 1998: 411; Poschardt 1998: 328, 381–3; Eshun 1998; Gilbert and Pearson 1999: 118; Hemment 2000). Intriguingly, Reynolds, has also described the psychedelic jazz-rock music of Can and Miles Davis from the early 1970s as sharing a certain 'rhizomatic' quality with techno:

> The [image of the] rhizome – meaning a network of stems, like grass or ferns, that are laterally connected, as opposed to 'hierarchical' root systems like trees – is used by Deleuze and Guattari to evoke a kind of polymorphous perversity of the body politic. 'Rhizomatic' music might include the fractal, flow-motion funk of Can and early seventies Miles Davis (based around the 'nobody solos and everybody solos' principle), dub reggae (with its dismantling of the normal ranking of instruments in the mix), and the cut'n'splice mixology of hip-hop, house and jungle Djs'. (Reynolds 1998: 388)

> Deleuze and Guattari suggest that 'the fabric of the rhizome is the conjunction "and . . . and . . . and . . ."'. Can's extended jam sessions anticipated the 'sampler-delic' aesthetic of today's rave music; techno Djs construct a kinetic cut'n'mix collage that's potentially infinite . . .

> Manuel DeLanda, a writer who attempts to build theoretical bridges between Deleuze and Guattari and chaos theory, believes that the frontier between order and chaos is where 'magic' happens. This would seem to be true in music, judging by the combination of groove and improvisation, repetition and randomness, in Can, Miles Davis and techno. (Reynolds and Press 1995: 199–200)

Significantly, Reynolds goes on to compare the 'psychedelic' music of 'Can, Eno, the Aphex Twin' with the minimalist drone work of La Monte Young, the American composer commended by Deleuze and Guattari for achieving that 'becoming-cosmic' to which they believe modern music should aspire (Deleuze and Guattari 1987: 250).

Reynolds draws on Deleuze and Guattari in making a specific distinction between such 'rhizomatic' music and the avant-garde purism of free jazz, assaulting the listener with its 'sadistic' barrage of extreme noise, so it is interesting that John Corbett praises the militantly avant-garde work of free-jazz drummer Milton Graves and improvising saxophonist Evan

Parker in explicitly Deleuzian terms. Referring to the astonishing circular-breathing technique whereby Parker produces multiple musical lines simultaneously, Corbett remarks that:

> [T]here is no longer a single player per se. In its place stands the figure of an assemblage, creating not a fugue (where voices *follow* one another) but music that – in its construction of various strata, to borrow a phrase from Deleuze and Guattari – 'invents a kind of diagonal running between the harmonic vertical and the melodic horizon'. In Parker's music this diagonal, this pseudo-polyphony, serves as a musical critique of the inherent connection between technique and intentionality. (Corbett 1994: 84)

How can such different types of music-making be accommodated by the same frame of reference, especially when both are so radically different from any of the types of music which Deleuze and Guattari themselves discussed? What does this tell us about the capacities or limitations of a Deleuzian cartography of music? In trying to answer these questions, it seems logical to focus on the one obvious point of connection between the different styles of music under discussion: both Corbett's examples and most of Reynolds and Press's are characterised by large amounts of extended improvisation on the parts of musical performers. The apparent exception here would be what Reynolds calls 'techno' (meaning house, techno and their various offshoots): digitally produced music recorded on vinyl which is then played to a crowd by a DJ would hardly seem to be characterised by the same spontaneous musicianship which is the stamp of free jazz or the improvised psychedelic jazz-rock of Can or Davis. It's here, however, that we see how a uniquely Deleuzian perspective allows Reynolds, and us, to discern connections between apparently disparate forms of musical practice. For while the technicalities of musical production may differ in these instances, in all cases a similar set of structures is destabilised, similar lines of flight are plotted, and a similar exercise in desiring-production is enabled. In each of these cases musics are produced according to processes which defy ordinary notions of intention: no-one can say who is truly the 'author' of a DJ-mix, of a Can improvisation, even of one of Parker's pseudo-polyphonic solos. The lines between composers, producers, performers and audiences are all deliberately blurred in these contexts, and the relationship between authorial intention and sonic product is radically destabilised. Corbett cites Deleuze and Parnet in his rejection of any notion of improvised music as the product of a spontaneous outpouring of personal emotion, stressing that, by contrast, 'desire only exists when assembled or machined', and that Parker's need for the quasi-arbitrary frameworks which he sets up for his improvisations illustrates this fact perfectly. In each of these cases a continuous experience of trans-personal intensity – a body without organs – is generated by the deliberate subversion of any simple process of composition, expression and interpretation.

Given Deleuze's general philosophical concerns, it's easy to see why such musics should be understood as sharing an affinity with his project, which might itself be characterised as the perpetual search for terms of reference not bound by conventional assumptions as to the nature of meaning and individuality. Musics which operate apparently outside of any framework of signification, generating flows of intensity and subverting the rules of artistic propriety which cordon off composers, performers and audiences from each other, might be thought inevitably Deleuzian. Such a view, however, quickly runs into some problems. Most notably, Deleuze and Guattari, who wrote in great detail about music, did not seem to think about music in these terms at all. Indeed, the most obvious institutional hierarchy which typifies hegemonic musical practices in the West, and which is directly challenged by improvisatory practices, is one which they themselves seem happy to perpetuate. This is the ordering which places composition clearly above performance in term of importance to the process of music-making, implicitly maintaining a rigid separation between the two: a product of the capitalist division of labour virtually unknown prior to the advent of European modernity and still quite alien to many living traditions of musical practice. Clearly, 'improvisation' – real-time composition-in-performance – is a practice which simply upsets that distinction altogether. Improvised music does not have 'composers' and 'performers': it is composed and de-composed as it is performed, even when it takes place within pre-arranged parameters. Nonetheless, Deleuze and Guattari generally write in such a way that the terms 'music' and 'composition' can be read as entirely synonymous. When writing about 'music', they almost invariably write about composers: music, it is implied, is something that composers do. This is the case even when comparing birds, which clearly compose only as they perform, with human musicians, by which they mean composers (e.g. Messiaen). Indeed, this elision is reproduced even in recent commentaries on Deleuze's work. Ronald Bogue's remarkably lucid and reliable exposition of Deleuze and Guattari's ideas on music similarly reproduces the notion that in human terms, 'music' is something done by composers (Bogue 2003: 13–76). This is no fault of Bogue's: it is merely an accurate rendition of Deleuze and Guattari's writing on this topic.

It might be objected at this stage that my distinction between music which is 'composed' and music which is 'improvised' is itself deeply problematic from a Deleuzian perspective. As has already been suggested, a Deleuzian approach to music will understand it first and foremost in terms of the affects which it makes possible, the bodies which it vibrates in particular ways, and not in terms of the literal configuration of bodies involved in its production. Does it matter if a piece of music is generated by a group of 'improvising' musicians or by an orchestra 'interpreting' a score? Is it not the flows of force, the modes of becoming, which are generated by the sonic interventions in question which really matter? This is an important point to take on board, but it is one to which a response can be made. This response is to recognise that musics from many periods and many places are characterised by a high level of collective and/or individual improvisation on the part of their performers, and that despite their differences, all of these musics share certain affective similarities. This suggests that the specific arrangement of force – the 'assemblage', in Deleuzian terms – which generates them does in fact have some bearing on the forms of affect which they can generate. As Deleuze and Guattari themselves put it 'orchestration – instrumentation brings sound forces together or separates them, gathers or disperses them' (Deleuze and Guattari 1987: 341). What's more, the affective similarities between different types of improvised music are ones which should be more apparent from a Deleuzian perspective than from any other, as they lend all such musics qualities which Deleuze and Guattari appear to find desirable in music in general, and in particular in that music which they term 'modern'. Deleuze and Guattari argue that within 'modern' music 'by placing all its components in continuous variation, music itself becomes a superlinear system, a rhizome instead of a tree, and enters the service of a virtual cosmic continuum of which even holes, silences, ruptures and breaks are a part' (Deleuze and Guattari 1987: 95).

The Ecstasy of Complexity[1]

So what are the sonic-affective qualities typical of highly improvised musics? Let us return to Reynolds's key examples of improvised music as both 'cosmic' and 'rhizomatic'. In the amalgam of sources and sounds which Miles Davis brought together on albums like *Bitches' Brew* and *On the Corner*, a dynamic of disciplined looseness animates a soundscape of startling fluidity. In introducing electric instrumentation into jazz – not just electric guitars but electrified trumpet and so on, deterritorialising electrified sound, liberating it from its role as a mere conduit for brute sonic force and opening up a new musical assemblage, a new field of cross-generic techno-sonic possibilities, altogether – Davis inaugurated the genre whose very name could be a byword for rhizomatic creativity: 'fusion'(this contradicts Reynolds's assertion that a rhizomatic aesthetic is 'fissile' in nature, but that's a debate for another time). While jazz purists of the time regarded these first forays into fusion as heretical, the series of albums Davis produced from 1969 and into the early 1970s now have an unparalleled canonical status across a range of generic and inter-generic fields. Jazz, house, 'chill-out', ambient, post-rock, drum'n'bass all hear themselves pre-echoed in the beats, flows, textures and sonic intersections of these albums. If other recordings which bore the 'fusion' tag (for example records by Weather Report, Mahavishnu Orchestra, and so on) lacked both the sobriety and the range of connections to live up to its promise, it should hardly surprise. Davis assembled large groups of the most technically proficient jazz musicians of their time for his recordings, who then recorded in a supremely democratic manner, with overt displays of solo virtuosity rarely disturbing the miasmic interplay of rhythms and refrains in a process of constant deterritorialisation. Who could hope to imitate such a practice? Their stature having grown exponentially in recent years, it may still prove that the impact of these most perfectly rhizomatic of records on the wider field of music has yet to be felt.

There is another feature of these albums which places them ahead of their time. While the practice of improvisation can easily give rise to a naive ideology of spontaneous immediacy, a metaphysics of presence (Derrida 1974: 3–26) which would abjure the act of recording as an act of falsification, these Davis albums were in several cases heavily treated by producer Teo Macero, who edited, tape-spliced and rearranged sections from the original recordings to create collages of sound which bore at times only tangential relationships to what anyone had actually played. Like his contemporaries in the dub studios of Jamaica, Macero was engaged in a deliberately craftsman-like process which would dispel the last vestiges of Romanticism in undermining any notion of singular authorship, even collective authorship being dislocated and multiplied in terms of its temporality and location. While Romantic ideology maintains that art must be the original product of a singular genius, be it that of a Great Man or a homogeneous 'people', this production process entirely undermines any such possibility. As Deleuze and Guattari remark, 'To be an artisan and no longer an artist, creator or founder, is the only way to become Cosmic' (Deleuze and Guattari 1987: 345).

An entirely similar process constituted the practice of the other great psychedelic improvisers of the early 1970s: Can. Led by a renegade student of Stockhausen, inspired by The Velvet Underground, the German figureheads of the quasi-genre known in the Anglophone world as 'Krautrock' proceeded in much the same way as the Davis groups, improvising for hours at a time and editing the resulting tapes heavily. A smaller group with an agenda more informed by mimimalist and Modernist aesthetics, Can's forays are frequently described by Simon Reynolds as exemplary of his category of 'Oceanic Rock' (Reynolds and Press 1995: 191–210). Like the Miles Davis albums of the same period, Can's albums have acquired a pan-generic canonicity in recent years, the subject of reissues and remix projects, book-length surveys and much critical acclaim. (Freeman and Freeman 1996; Can *Sacrilege*). Given what Deleuze and Guattari repeatedly ask of a music which is truly 'modern' and positively rhizomatic in character, it seems fitting that the German name for 'Krautrock' was 'Kosmische Music': Cosmic Music.

So it's not hard to see why Reynolds hears a resonance between the thought of Deleuze and Guattari and the music of the Davis groups and Can. Music made through a non-hierarchal process of lateral connections between sounds, genres and musicians, which aims always to open onto a cosmic space, must be archetypically modern and rhizomatic in Deleuze's terms. The refusal of individualised modes of self-expression and ideologies of spontaneous purity which characterises their recording processes as 'artisanal' reinforces this connection. What's more, such as observation draws our attention to the fact that this anti-Romantic impulse is almost always present in improvised musics, putting to work as it does a wholly different set of relationships between performers, composers, audiences, and the traditions within which they operate from those typical of European concert music. Central to the methods of music-making which Romanticism inaugurated is the role of the conductor as representative of the composer – Pope as representative of God – by contrast to which improvisation involves the ceaseless subversion of any such singular authority by a process at once mysterious and thoroughly material: mystical yet irreducibly social. Collective improvisation always involves a non-signifying communication of energies, a complex dissemination of forces between the performers in an ensemble. If the sociality of the orchestra, the relationality of its component members, is mediated entirely by the subject in the form of the conductor/composer and the sign in the form of the score, then the sociality of improvising musicians is always constituted by transversal relations which cannot be understood in terms of any logic of signification. In Deleuze and Guattari's terms, the improvising collective is a perfect example of a *Dividual* (Deleuze and Guattari 1987: 341), a collectivity which cannot be reduced to the individuality of its members or to some leviathan meta-subject which encompasses them all in a perfect unity. It's surely here, in its realised experience of a sociality which is truly rhizomatic in its transversality and undecidable complexity, that the power of such improvised music lies. In the impure spontaneity of real-time composition/performance there is necessarily a moment of becoming-music at which the boundaries between performer and performed, between audience and compositions, between musician and instrument, between musicians and each other are all blurred: this is the moment of the opening onto 'the Cosmic' which is also an experience of sociality as such. If all music is characterised by this inherent sociality (Shepherd 1993: 145; Toynbee 2000: 42–6), this inherent capacity to break down the distinctions between inside and outside which guarantee the stability of individual subjectivity, then no element of music makes more vivid this dimension than the irreducibly social moment of improvisation.

One of the sonic characteristics of all of the musics under discussion here is melodic and rhythmic complexity produced by a small number of instruments: an energetic, democratic, socialistic desiring-production quite outside the 'enterprise of anti-production' (Deleuze and Guattari 1983: 235) delimited by the capitalist laws of harmony and the orchestra. Like the state and corporate machinery of capitalist societies, these mechanisms are designed first to generate lack (the desire for tonal resolution which the symphony first produces and then defers) then to fulfil it in a spectacular yet ultimately superficial and alienated manner: by generating the most simple, unilinear affects possible with the largest number of instruments. The Romantic orchestra works to generate the most sonic power possible and to contain it the most rigidly: the whole orchestra tied to the univocity of a single theme, all labouring for the generation of sonic surplus-value. By contrast the complexity and indeterminacy of improvised musics produce a proliferation of affects, none of which operates according to the law of lack, deferral and simple gratification.

The effect of this improvisational complexity on the listener (and, indeed, the performer) might be understood in terms of certain a/sexual morphology. Various writers in recent times have argued for a feminist and queer musicology which sees the Romantic symphony, like the classic 'cock rock' performance, as an expression of 'phallogocentric' power, a refusal of the cyclical plurality (hence femininity) of earlier and non-Western forms of music (McClary 1991; Gilbert 1999; Gilbert and Pearson 1999: 54–109). One of the simplest, but still most useful, contributions to this line of thought remains Richard Dyer's classic 1979 essay 'In Defence of Disco', in which he argues that the poly-

rhythmic drive, chromatic range and multi-timbral soundscapes of the
best Disco music offer the listener/dancer an experience of 'all-body
eroticism', a polymorphously perverse tactility quite different from the
regulated pelvis-thrusting phallocentrism of the rock sound-dance apparatus (Dyer 1990). Just the same argument might be made about the
ecstasy of complexity engendered by those intense 'peak' moments which
characterise most improvisatory musics, from traditional American banjo
music to the guitar-playing of the Grateful Dead's Jerry Garcia, moments
which may not be characterised by great speed or volume or extremes of
pitch, but almost always by a momentary affect of notes colliding in a
space too small to contain them, bursting out onto some new, smoother
space (Deleuze and Guattari 1987: 474–500) with photons bouncing in
unimagined directions and in and out of existence altogether. In these
moments when the affective morphology of sound takes shapes not easily
comprehensible in terms such as 'masculine' or feminine', 'order' or
'chaos', a becoming-music is enacted which draws a line of flight away
from the physical-ideological constraints of the gendered body or fixed
musical genres: a body without organs; a smooth, cosmic space. This
would in particular involve an escape from a specifically phallocratic
physical economy: 'the reconstruction of the body as a Body without
Organs, the anorganism of the body, is inseparable from a becoming-
woman, or the production of a molecular woman . . . all becomings begin
with and pass through becoming-woman' (Deleuze and Guattari 1987:
276–7). Once again here, we see the sonic-affective similarities between
recent dance musics and improvised musics, despite their superficially
different production processes, and we also see how radically they differ
from the qualities and processes of those hegemonic musics of Western
culture: the Classical-Romantic concert tradition and the late twentieth-
century white Rock formation (cf. Grossberg 1992; Gilbert and Pearson
1999). Clearly, to further the project of a Deleuzian cartography/histor-
iography of music, the issue of improvisation must be taken seriously,
something Deleuze and Guattari themselves do not appear to take very
seriously at all.

Taking Improvisation Seriously

What such 'taking seriously' should mean is a partial revision of Deleuze
and Guattari's history of 'music', a revision which takes into account the
geo-historical specificity of the European concert tradition to which they
confine their attention and which considers the extent to which the
qualities which they attribute to 'modern' music may actually be found

in many other places, and indeed may have come *to* 'modern' music from those other places. The very notion of 'improvisation' as a definable, circumscribable element of musical practice, rather than as a tautologous synonym for musicianship as such, is in fact the product of a specific history whereby improvisation was rendered marginal to hegemonic musical practices in Northern Europe. This history is not one easily accommodated by Deleuze and Guattari's quasi-dialectical history of 'music' passing through the simple phases of Classicism, Romanticism and Modernism, or by the conventional musical historiography on which that narrative draws. What we must do now, therefore, is consider the alternative perspectives offered by writers who have questioned such conventional historiography precisely by taking seriously the issue of 'improvisation'.

For example, it's with the clear aim of disturbing the established economy of creativity within Western music without simply reversing its terms that Jacques Attali names a practice of music-making which upsets the distinctions between composer, performer and audience in-scribed by both the regimes of the composer–conductor–orchestra axis and the technics of the music industry 'composition':

> [T]o improvise, to compose, is thus related to the idea of the assumption of differences, of the rediscovering and blossoming of the body. 'Something that lets me find my own rhythm between the measures' (Stockhausen). Composition ties music to gesture, whose natural support it is; it plugs music into noises of life and the body, whose movement it fuels. It is thus laden with risk, disquieting, an unstable challenging, an anarchic and ominous festival, like a Carnival with an unpredictable outcome. (Attali 1985: 143)

For Attali, the stratified hierarchy of the orchestra is a metaphor for a hierarchically stratified society (Attali 1985: 64). The emergence of the conductor and the composer as the key figures at the pinnacle of this pyramid prefigures and typifies the emergence of a society dominated by the bourgeois as individual, as entrepreneur, as social authority, as leader. Advocates of improvised music decry the sedimented nineteenth-century ideal of the musician as a mere neutral channel for the creative will of the composer, mediated by the individual authority of the conductor (Bailey 1992: 20), and tend to see certain tendencies of the twentieth-century music industry, such as the emergence of a star system, and the general processes of the alienation of audiences and performers from composers and from each other, as to some extent rooted in the deep individualisation of power and expression which this hierarchy enforces (Attali 1985;

Gilbert and Pearson 1999: 146; Toynbee 2000: 160–2). By the same token, the re-emergence of 'free' improvisation in music is seen as a gesture with which to refuse the whole system of meanings and affects which these mechanisms reproduce.

Consider Canetti's remarks on the function of the conductor, referred to directly by Derek Bailey in his famous study *Improvisation: Its Nature and Practice in Music* (Bailey 1992: 20):

> There is no more obvious expression of power than the performance of a conductor ... The immobility of the audience is as much part of the conductor's design as the obedience of the orchestra. They are under a compulsion to keep still . . . During a concert, and for the people gathered together in the hall, the conductor is a leader . . . His eyes hold the whole orchestra. Every player feels that the conductor sees him personally, and, still more, hears him . . . He is the living embodiment of law, both positive and negative . . .

Thus for the orchestra the conductor literally embodies the work they are playing, the simultaneity of the sounds as well as their sequence; and since, during the performance, nothing is supposed to exist except this work, for so long is the conductor the ruler of the world' (Canetti 1962: 394–6).

The orchestral concert, then, is in Deleuze and Guattari's terms, an arborescent assemblage, (arguably a mixed despotic-passional regime of signs, with the conductor its point of subjectification: see Deleuze and Guattari 1987: 119–35). Hierarchical, linear, static: its function is to regulate the energy of all its parts, to channel their collective desiring-production into the simple linearity of the harmonically stratified, mono-phonic melodic line of the symphony. Capitalism's division of labour and its roots in the division between mental and physical labour (Marx and Engels 1970: 51–2) is nowhere more manifest than in the divisions between composer and performer, so impermeable that it requires a third specialist – the conductor – invested with absolute authority to mediate between them. The same can be said of the whole branching hierarchy of the orchestra, the specialisation of types of musician and instrument (the 'parts' of the orchestra), and the gulf separating the audience from all of them. In fact, the composer, the symphony, the orchestra, the conductor and the audience all operate in conjunction with the concert hall itself for the purpose of generating a very specific set of affects and for marginalising the possibility of other such affects being generated at all. Even coughing, let alone verbalising any more dynamic physical response, is kept as far as possible at bay as the audience sits still in the dark and the materiality of music, the corporeality of sounds, is subl(im)ated into an experience of music as pure transcendence, of delayed gratification, until the singular and individual moment of climax: the crashing symphonic finale.

Historically, the moment when this configuration of elements came together was precisely that of high Romanticism at the end of the eighteenth century: the figure whose work, life and public biography embody the new image of the composer as Great Man of Sublime Genius and the symphony as his Magnum Opus is Beethoven. Of course, it is important always to bear in mind that the affective power of music can never be fully contained by such an apparatus, as Deleuze and Guattari themselves remind us:

> The romantic hero, the voice of the romantic hero, acts as a subject, a subjectified individual with 'feelings'; but this subjective vocal element is reflected in an orchestral and instrumental whole that on the contrary mobilizes nonsubjective 'affects' and that reaches its height in romanticism. (Deleuze and Guattari 1987: 341)

Nonetheless, it's clearly in just this moment that the orchestra-concert as arborescent assemblage is fully articulated, and it's at precisely this moment that improvisation is banished from the concert hall. As is now fairly well known, even scored music of pre-Romantic times was not informed by that paranoid desire of the composer to communicate a full and perfect intention to an audience via the transparent medium of orchestra-and-conductor which informs the symphony-machine. The 'score' was in general far more suggestive than prescriptive, and included long passages during which the performers were expected to extemporise within fairly minimal guidelines offered by the composer. Derek Bailey discusses the status of these passages and the accepted ways of filling them in the performance of Baroque music in the late twentieth century and elucidates the extent to which classical music discourse/practice today forecloses the creative possibilities inherent in these indeterminate scores (Bailey 1992: 26–8), concluding that improvisation, once the life-blood of European concert music, is now strictly controlled within its confines.

The Modernity of *Raga*

As telling as this observation is, it's when we consider the status of musics from outside Europe altogether that we come right up against the limits of Deleuze and Guattari's history of music, for in fact Deleuze and Guattari's descriptions of the musical 'Modern' would all seem to apply at least as accurately to that form of music with which Bailey begins his global survey of improvisation: the centuries-old classical tradition of Northern India.

> If there is a modern age, it is of course the age of the cosmic . . . This is the postromantic turning point: the essential thing is no longer to forms and matters, or themes, but forces, densities, intensities . . . Varèse's procedure, at the dawn of this age, is exemplary: a musical machine of consistency, a *sound machine* (not a machine for reproducing sounds), which molecularizes and atomizes, ionizes sound matter, harnesses a cosmic energy. If this machine must have an assemblage, it is the synthesiser. By assembling modules, source elements and elements for treating sound (oscillators, generators and transformers) by arranging microintervals, the synthesiser makes audible the sound process itself . . . (Deleuze and Guattari 1987: 343)

The synthesiser? Of course Deleuze and Guattari are right. Bear in mind, though, how much of this description could already apply to the traditional instrumentation of India. To those familiar with the instrumentation of the Western concert tradition, the idea of instruments created in the search for a certain molecular materiality of sound, for the exploration of microtonality, may seem novel: the instrumentation of that tradition (for example the pianoforte) has been developed in the search for a purity of tone designed to create the illusion of immateriality and in the quest for precision in the division of pitches. The classical Indian instruments, however, have been informed by quite different priorities. The most famous Indian instrument, the sitar, is a machinic assemblage precisely for the non-limitable production of mircrotones. The characteristic drone of the tamboura and the tactility of the tabla's percussion seem as close as can be imagined to an instrumentation of pure sound as 'cosmic energy'. Indeed the microtonal drones of this tradition were in fact the direct inspiration for some of the music of the twentieth century which Deleuze and Guattari themselves praise when they assert that 'It is clear that what is necessary to make sound travel, and to travel around sound, is very pure and simple sound, an emission or wave without harmonics (La Monte Young has been successful at this)' (Deleuze and Guattari 1987: 344). Not only could this be a perfect description of Indian as opposed to 'Western' music, devoid as it is of any harmonic theory in its quest for wave-pure melody, but La Monte Young was himself directly inspired by his study of Indian music. Indeed, he has been known since the 1950s as an expert on and teacher of Indian music. It seems almost incredible that at this point that Deleuze and Guattari make no mention at all of Indian music, despite their, earlier reference to 'Hindu rhythms' (Deleuze and Guattari 1987: 312) (we should be clear at this point that North Indian classical music is emphatically not 'Hindu' as such, being practised to the highest level by Moslems and by Sikhs), and the fact is testament to the extent to which their thought on music remains trapped in the Western concert tradition even while so evidently struggling to escape it.

In certain senses it would be difficult to imagine a music more diametrically opposed to that of the Classical-Romantic concert tradition than North Indian classical music. Here, harmony is of no importance, and composition in the European sense was simply not known prior to the twentieth century: to produce this kind of music is to improvise, to the point where Indian musicians may find it difficult to discuss 'improvisation' as a discrete practice somehow distinguishable from composition, interpretation and performance (Bailey 1992: 1–11). Most concerts involve the performance of *ragas*. A *raga* is a set of partially variable notes, pitch relationships and/or melodic phrases which are the basis for extended improvisation. The exact status of a *raga* – traditional melody?, scale?, mode?, key? – is not directly translatable into Western musicological terms, any more than are the other terms defining the elements of Indian music: tala (metre?, time-signature?), *laya* (pulse?, drive?, funk?) (Bailey 1999: 2–5; Bor 1992: 1–8) and so on, and this somewhat mirrors the ambiguous status of the improvisation-frameworks offered by Irish 'tunes' and 'reels' and by Spanish flamenco. Such vocabularies amount to technologies for the enablement of solo and small-group improvisation plus, in each case, the maintenance of a tradition within which musical knowledge can be produced, reproduced and retained.

The working of such technologies would seem to illustrate perfectly the ambivalent status of what Deleuze and Guattari call 'the refrain': that territorialising organisation of elements which music is always on its way to escaping in the process of its own becoming. The *raga* is a refrain precisely insofar as it is at once the precise set of limits which bounds the performance (yet which can never be exactly specified), and that which itself is never played: it is only ever extended, extemporised and escaped. The *raga* cannot even be played and rehearsed in the manner of a Western scale or mode: it exists only virtually, on the point of becoming-music, on the very brink between ordered territoriality and becoming-cosmic. Deleuze and Guattari write that 'a musician requires a *first type* of refrain, a territorial or assemblage refrain, in order to transform it from within, deterritorialized, producing a refrain of the *second type* as the final end of music: the cosmic refrain of a sound machine' (Deleuze and

Guattari 1987: 349). If the drawing of a line of flight away from the territoriality of the first type of refrain, towards the cosmic openness of the second, is precisely what constitutes musicality as such, then it would not be going too far to say that in Deleuzian terms Indian classical music – which is *nothing but* a perpetual plotting of such lines – is quite possibly 'more musical', and certainly more 'modern', than any music of the concert tradition.

While traditional Indian music does contain elements which – like Greek modes, the basis of European music – are associated with certain geographical territories, what it is notable about classical ragas is that they are not so much associated with the regions from which they originate as with the specific time of day and season of the year at which they are to be played. This exemplifies a quite different configuration of element, place and plane in Indian music from that which Deleuze and Guattari understand as typical of the European concert tradition, one which in their terms only 'modern' music comes close to. For an Indian performance is always unique in a way which a performance of composed music can never be, and yet it is bounded by rules which would be entirely alien to those of the Classical-Romantic tradition, of which the rule of seasonal and daily timing is the most obvious. Ultimately the prescription of these external rules can be understood only in terms of the drive towards a certain consistency: on one level, the affective aim of each performance is identical, hence the need to alter the musical parameters according to the one variable which is entirely outside the control of the performer, insofar as it cannot be reversed: time. To accommodate this element of the experience, the other elements of the performance must be manipulated in order to maintain the consistency which is sought. And in what does this consistency consist? Clearly, in Deleuze and Guattrai's terms, in 'an opening onto the Cosmos' (Deleuze and Guattari 1987: 333). While every *raga* has its distinctive *rasa* (flavour), there is no performance of Indian classical music which is secular, which is not a kind of musical prayer: more accurately, a continuous *nirguna* (formless, non-referential) *mantra* invoking the infinite, the cosmos, the ultimate plane of consistency. Therefore, we might say that the 'refrains' of Indian music are quite unlike those of the concert tradition – but like those of Celtic dance music, or flamenco, or jazz – in that they do not organise the territoriality of a musical event in the name of the laws of harmony, or of a composer's Subjective authority, or in the name of a posited divine order (Classicism) or a 'People' (Romanticism) (Deleuze and Guattari 1987: 338–9) but contain within themselves deliberately open spaces for the insertion of 'cutting edges': the machinic interventions of the performers and their instruments are enabled, eased, welcomed and intensified by the always already becoming-machine of the musical assemblages into which they intervene. This is quite unlike the Western concert-assemblage, whose entire function is to limit the movement and the expression of the performers and the audience, bending all to the will of the composer/conductor (Canetti 1962: 394–6). Opening onto a plane of consistency which might be the meditative bliss of yoga or the multiple body without organs of the dance (Deleuze and Guattari 1987: 149–66), the process of producing these 'traditional' improvised musics, like that of the beat-matched DJ mix, is always unique while the objective is always the same.

Indian music therefore constitutes a striking example of a rhizomatic musical culture which has developed along quite contrary lines to that of Western modernity, acquiring and refining a whole conceptual framework and technical vocabulary, as well as a system of training, designed to enable the transmission of a growing and developing body of knowledge and tradition of skilled practice which, despite its traditionality, retains improvisation at its core. It's interesting to note, then, that all of the musics with which we began our discussion have been affected and informed by the classical music of Northern India. La Monte Young (http://melafoundation.org/lmy.htm) taught John Cale, who brought the electric drone to The Velvet Underground, who passed it on to Can. The modal jazz of Miles Davis was not only directly informed by Indian music-making practices, but his groups often featured Indian instruments (most notably on *On the Corner*). The free and modal jazz experiments of Ornette Coleman, Joe Harriott and John Coltrane which inspired free players such as Evan Parker also drew directly and indirectly on Indian music. One can even say with confidence that Indian music was in some ways catalytic in the formation of the entire milieu of psychedelic culture during the 1960s,[2] the millieu of which 'dance culture' as we know it was itself initially a deterritorialisation, beginning with David Mancuso's legendary New York 'loft' parties. Inspired by a combination of committed audiophilia, a love of rhythmic music and psychedelic mysticism, Mancuso's regular parties became the template for the entire Disco movement (Lawrence 2003). They retained (unlike Can or Miles Davis) psychedelic jazz-rock's early commitment to sustained social dancing, a commitment itself inherited from very ancient traditions of improvisation and beaten out of psychedelic rock – including Jimi Hendrix, Pink Floyd, The Grateful Dead, MC5, The Velvet Underground – by the refusal of record companies to release music that hadn't been reterritorialised by the voice, insisting on songs instead of the improv-jams for which all of those musicians had been known. The loft parties created a desiring multitude from the machinic elements of bodies, records, sounds and sensations which stands to this day as a utopian model of polysexual, polycultural egalitarianism: a collective body without organs which remains the ideal of dance-floor democracy striven for by 'underground' discos, clubs, parties and raves ever since.

Even where, as in the case of Mancuso's musical presentations, there is no overt DJ-technique deployed, the 'dialogue', the affective flow, between dancers and DJ, between dancers and each other, between DJs and producers, between dancers and producers, between producers and each other, which came during the 1970s to constitute the sonic field of dance music, is surely akin to the rhizomatic energy of a dividual improvising group-subject. The sheer proliferation of dance musics in the 1990s and the relative paucity of 'stars' that their culture has generated in comparison to the number of unique sonic events (tracks, mixes, parties) is testament to this fact. It's no accident, then, that much of the most dynamic dance music of our time – deep house, drum'n'bass – is informed so heavily by the improvised legacy of jazz. While drum 'n' bass, the most formally radical music ever to be created in the UK, is generally described as a descendent of dub reggae and hiphop (for example, Reynolds 1998: 243–54), surely its polyrhythmic complexity and abrupt atonal tendencies owe as much to bop and free jazz: can we really imagine A Guy Called Gerald using his *Black Secret Technology* the way he does if Max Roach had never drummed? So-called 'deep house', the most direct descendant of the music of 'underground' New York, is characterised as much as anything as by the presence of live, often improvised instrumental segments and by the frequent use of the epithet 'jazzy' to describe its distinctive qualities. The ecstasy of complexity is heard nowhere in contemporary music as in a deep house cut like La Gente Urbana's *Osanyin*, where the flute playing of Munch Manship flies out from and back into a four-square house beat like a skylark flying into space and back; or in a free party drum'n'bass mix, so polyrhythmic that the pulse is only a microscopic point, endlessly tunnelling through the centre of a nebulous density of drums. It's no wonder that musicians drawing on the Indian tradition have at times been attached by the propulsive energy of drum'n'bass (Sharma and Hutnyk 1996): there's an obvious affinity with the disciplined freedom of tabla.

Dancing with Lyotard:
Improvisionality and the Deleuzian Postmodern

It's here, then, at the start of the twenty-first century, that we can feel the energy of improvisation still buzzing: creating, flowing, producing, now. The bodies of the participants may be distributed differently, but it's in the nurturing frenzy of a house bacchanal like London's Underdog (it's no accident that Underdog has the most socially diverse crowd that this writer has seen in over a decade of dancing in London) or San Francisco's Imperial Dub parties that a musical multitude is produced by dancers, DJs, producers, musicians, according to rhizomatic flows which echo those of the live jazz band, the Indian devotional performance, the Grateful Dead gig or the ceilidh. That's not to say that 'live' music is redundant, or to ignore the importance of those bands who fuse rock with jazz via the medium of electronica in new and productive ways (Fridge, Tortoise, Supernumeri and so on) or pursue new forms of cosmic free improvisation (for example, The Necks), only to say that the distinction between 'live' and 'recorded' is not what is at stake when assessing the 'improvisationality' of a musical event.

It is this concept of 'improvisationality' which seems to emerge from our discussion of improvisation. All musics possess an improvisational dimension, which is to say a rhizomatic moment at which connections are made between musics, subjects, and non-musical machines and at which a certain opening onto a 'cosmic' space of infinite possibility occurs: a moment of the musician-composer's becoming-music. However, some forms of music-making, and some examples of those forms, would seem to foreground this moment more than others, enabling it to proliferate and self-multiply without collapsing into a mere chaos of white noise, what Deleuze and Guattari would call a 'black hole' (Deleuze and Guattari 1987: 342–4) of too-rapid deterritorialisation and a loss of that 'sobriety' which a true becoming-cosmic demands. It is just these musics which seem to enable an opening to the 'machinic phylum' (that is, the endlessly productive continuum of materiality) (Deleuze and Guattari 1987: 409–10) of sound – in a way more stratified musics, locked into a logic of intention and signification, cannot – possessing the very characteristics which Deleuze and Guattari attribute to 'the modern'.

Does this mean that Deleuze and Guattari are wrong? No. Nothing that they say about music is contradicted by these observations, which could not have been made without them saying what they do. However, they may indicate the desirability of adding to and problematising

Deleuze and Guattari's historical narrative. If the music of La Monte Young, for Deleuze and Guattari, achieves that opening onto the cosmic for which 'the modern' only strives, then perhaps his music ought not to be labelled 'modern' at all, but postmodern. 'Postmodern' is a much abused and over-used term, but here I want to use it in the precise way designated by J. F. Lyotard. For Lyotard, postmodern art is characterised by a distinctive relationship towards that dimension of experience – called, following Kant, 'the sublime' – which escapes or exceeds the possibility of representation: something very like Deleuze and Guattari's 'opening onto the Cosmos'. Whereas, for Lyotard, modern art and literature regrets the sublime as something which they experience nostalgically, as always already lost, the postmodern (for example, the writing of James Joyce)[3] 'puts forward the unpresentable in presentation itself' (Lyotard 1984: 81). We could connect this observation to a Deleuzian perspective by suggesting that Modernism, like psychoanalysis, posits the sublime/cosmic as lack, the BwO as the lost, unrecoverable bliss of the pre-Oedipal state (for example, Kristeva 1980) whereas the postmodern by contrast posits these as dimensions of experience which can be actively accessed and positively produced, even if they cannot be signified. Where the music of Debussy, like the post-Oedipal subject, is haunted by the longing for pre-Oedipal *jouissance*, the Indo-minimalism of La Monte Young tries to open onto the cosmic directly, producing a BwO of its own.

Crucially for our discussion, Lyotard argues that the postmodern is not simply a moment which succeeds the modern in a dialectical unfolding of successive moments, but a dimension of aesthetic experience which in some sense precedes, inhabits and makes possible the modern. This is not simply a matter of some archaic, pre-modern or non-Western 'truth' being rediscovered, but of a dimension of experience being foreclosed as always-already-lost by the projects of Western modernity – including its musical projects – yet always retaining the potential to be activated in new ways at different times. The musics of the Hindustani tradition, flamenco, Baroque and pre-Baroque European musics, Celtic dance musics, jazz, the post-jazz of Evan Parker and Derek Bailey, the improvised psychedelic rock which characterised the live work of bands as diverse as Pink Floyd, The Velvet Underground, the MC5 and The Grateful Dead, the music of Miles Davis and Can, the DJ mixing at a contemporary club night: all might be said to occupy this fourth category beyond (yet before) the Classical, Romantic and Modern, a category which would be historical but not-historical, a category which subverts the implicit dialectic of Deleuze and Guattari's history of music – a Deleuzian-Lyotardian postmodern. It's this new category which Deleuze and Guattari's thought on music can be said to add to itself by way of a detour through the very moment which it appears at first glance to occlude, but whose thinking it makes possible: the rhizomatic moment of improvisation.[4]

References

Attali, J. (1985), *Noise: The Political Economy of Music*, trans. B. Massumi, Minneapolis: University of Minnesota Press.

Bailey, D. (1992), *Improvisation: Its Nature and Practice in Music*, Cambridge: Da Capo Press.

Bogue, R. (2003), *Deleuze on Music, Painting and the Arts*, New York: Routledge.

Bor, Joseph (ed.) (1999), *The Raga Guide*, London: Nimbus Records.

Buchanan, I. (2000), *Deleuzism: A Metacommentary*, Edinburgh: Edinburgh University Press.

Canetti, E. (1962), *Crowds and Power*, trans. C. Stewart, London: Phoenix Press.

Corbett, J. (1994), *Extended Play: Sounding Off from John Cage to Dr Funkenstein*, Durham: Duke University Press.

Deleuze, G. and Guattari, F. (1983), *Anti-Oedipus*, trans. R. Hurley, M. Seem and H. R. Lane, Minneapolis: University of Minnesota Press.

Deleuze, G. and Guattari, F. (1987), *A Thousand Plateaus: Capitalism and Schizophrenia* trans. B. Massumi, Minneapolis: University of Minnesota Press.

Derrida, J. (1974), *Of Grammatology*, trans. G. Spivak, Baltimore: Johns Hopkins University Press.

Dyer, R. (1990), 'In Defence of Disco', in S. Frith and A. Goodwin (eds), *On Record: Rock Pop and the Written Word*, London: Routledge.

Eshun, K. (1998), *More Brilliant than the Sun: Adventures in Sonic Fiction*, London: Quartet Books.

Freeman, A. and Freeman, S. (1996), *The Crack in the Cosmic Egg: Encyclopaedia of Krautrock, Kosmische Musik*, Leicester: Audio.

Gilbert, J. and Pearson, P. (1999), *Discographies: Dance Music, Culture and the Politics of Sound*, London: Routledge.

Gilbert, J. (1999), 'White Light/White Heat: *Jouissance* beyond Gender in The Velvet Underground', in A. Blake (ed.), *Living Through Pop*, London: Routledge.

Grossberg, L. (1992), *We Gotta Get Out of This Place*, New York: Routledge.

Hemment, D. (2000), *Microgroove: Simulation/Amplification/Intoxication* (unpuplished PhD thesis).

Jordan, T. (1995), 'Collective Bodies: Raving and the Politics of Gilles Deleuze and Félix Guattari', *Body and Society* 1 (1): 125–44.

Kristeva, J. (1980), *Desire in Language*, trans. T. Gora, L. Sl. Roudiez and A. Jardine, New York: Columbia University Press.

Lawrence, T. (2003), *Love Saves the Day: A History of American Dance Music Culture (1970–1979)*, Durham: Duke University Press.

Lyotard, J-F. (1984), *The Postmodern Condition: A Report on Knowledge*, trans. B. Massumi and G. Bennington, Manchester: Manchester University Press.

Marx, K. and Engels, F. (1970), *The German Ideology*, ed. C. J. Arthur, London: Lawrence and Wishart.

McClary, S. (1991), *Feminine Endings*, Minneapolis: University of Minnesota Press.

Perlongo, R. (1964), Liner notes to Ravi Shankar and Ali Akbar Kahn *The Master Musicians of India*, Prestige Recordings.

Poschardt, Ulf (1998), *DJ Culture*, London: Quartet.

Reynolds, S. and Press, J. (1995), *The Sex Revolts: Gender, Rebellion and Rock'n'Roll*, London: Serpent's Tail.

Reynolds, Simon (1998), *Energy Flash: A Journey through Rave Music and Dance Culture*, London: Picador.

Sharma, A. and Hutnyk, J. (eds) (1996), *Dis-Orienting Rhythms: The Politics of the New Asian Dance Music*, London: Zed Books.

Shepherd, J. (1993), 'Music as Cultural Text' in J. Paynter, J. Howell and R. Orton (eds), *A Companion to Contemporary Musical Thought*, New York and London: Routledge.

Toynbee, P. (2000), *Making Popular Music*, London: Arnold.

Discography

A Guy called Gerald (1997), *Black Secret Technology*, Juicebox.

Can (1973), *Future Days*, Spoon.

Can (1997), *Sacrilege*, Spoon.

Bailey, D. and Bennink, H. (2000), *Company Volume 3*, Spectrum.

Parker, E. (1995), *Saxophone Solos*, Chronoscope.

Fridge (2001), *Ceefax*. Output.

Hendrix, J. (1989), *Hendrix Concerts*, Castle Communications.

Coltrane, J. (1964), *A Love Supreme*, Impulse.

La Gente Urbana (2000), 'Osanyin (flutestrumental dub)', Rainy City.

Roach, M. and Shepp, A. (1994), *The Long March Part One*, Hat Art.

MC5 (1994), *Power Trip*, Total Energy.

Davis, M. (1968), *In a Silent Way*, Columbia.

Davis, M. (1969), *Bitches' Brew*, Columbia.

Davis, M. (1972), *On the Corner*, Columbia.

Pink Floyd (1967), *The Piper at the Gates of Dawn*, EMI.

Shankar, R. and Akbar-Kahn, A. (1964), *The Master Musicians of India*, Prestige.

Supernumeri (2003), *Great Aviaries*, Ninja Tune.

The Grateful Dead (1993), *Dick's Picks Volume One: Tampa Florida 12/19/73*, Grateful Dead records.

The Joe Harriott double quintet under the direction of John May (1966), *Indo-Jazz Suite*, Atlantic.

The Necks (2002), *Aether*, ReR Megacorp.

The Velvet Underground (1995), *Peel Slowly and See*, Polydor.

Tortoise (1966), *Millions Now Living Will Never Die*, City Slang.

Various Artists (1997), *Anokha: Sounds of the Asian Underground*, Omni.

Various Artists (1999), *David Mancuso Presents The Loft*, Nuphonic.

Various Artists (2000), *Lazy Dog Volume One*, Virgin, 2000.

Various Artists (2000), *Ohm: The Pioneers of Electronic Music*, Ellipsis Arts.

Notes

1. I'd like to thank Roger Drew for this suggestive phrase.
2. The first reference to psychedelic culture on a record sleeve appears in Robert Perlongo's liner notes to Ravi Shankar and Ali Akbar-Kahn (1964), *The Master Musicians of India*.

3. Deleuze and Guattari themselves seem to think that Joyce ultimately fails in achieving a true opening onto the cosmic, in his striving to create a self-contained 'cosmos-book' (Deleuze and Guattari 1987: 127), but that debate need not detain us here.
4. Of course, this might well be understood as a fully dialectical manoeuvre (cf. Buchanan 2000: 192–7).

Chapter 7

Rhythm: Assemblage and Event

Phil Turetsky

Introduction

Rhythm inserts time into ethics. The haka of the Maori exhibits the way rhythms perform temporal syntheses assembling bodies and distributing intensities. In *Crowds and Power*, Elias Canetti turns to the haka to exemplify the rhythmic composition of crowds (Canetti 1984: 31–4). He writes of rhythmic crowds to demonstrate how their composition gives rise to their main attributes of equality and density.

When walking the feet never strike the ground with the same force, and as a result they create rhythms. The rhythm of the feet repeated and multiplied while remaining in place produces growth and density. Rhythmic repetition attracts more participants so the mass tends to grow and condense. In addition to, and often in place of, an increase in number comes an increase in intensity. In a haka, the dancers' stamp of the foot marks the beat and the harder and more rhythmically they stamp the more a haka's intensity increases. It seems that participants in a haka enter its body without regard to gender, age, rank or social status (Polack 1838).[1] But Canetti extends his attribution of equality to the bodies of the dancers who all do the same thing, in the same way, and at the same time. He notes that this 'equivalence of the dancers becomes, and ramifies as, the equivalence of their limbs. Every part of a man which can move gains a life of its own and acts as if independent, but the movements are all parallel, the limbs superimposed on each other . . .' (Canetti 1984: 31–4). Each body part links with others of its kind constructing an aggregate which moves independently in accord with its own rhythm. A haka comes to act as a single individual 'as if the whole body of performers were actuated by *one* impulse' directed towards a single goal (Canetti 1984: 31–4).

We must build on Canetti's insights with caution, however. For he too readily subsumes haka under the metaphor of an organism 'a single creature dancing, a creature with fifty heads and a hundred legs and arms, all performing in exactly the same way and with the same purpose' (Canetti 1984: 31–4). While it is certainly true that a haka forms an individual, its individuality does not arise from the imposition of an organic unity, nor is it defined by its goal. A haka's goal will vary with the occasion. Hakas operate to welcome strangers, perform rites of passages, warn enemies and heighten courage in preparation for war, and perform many other functions. Moreover, in its rhythmic impeccability, a haka produces a unity that is able to protect itself from internal dissolution. But this unity is that of an individual and, rather than being imposed by some external order, it is produced – assembled – from within. A haka is assembled by the linkage of body parts through their rhythmic distribution. Of course, a haka distributes parts of bodies in both space and time. But it is the temporal distribution of the aggregates of arms and legs, fingers and toes, tongues and eyes, and their rhythmic connections that organise their spatial distribution and give them their parallel movements – what Canetti calls 'equality'. The individuality of a haka is entirely defined by relations of movement and rest, relations between different speeds with different affects.[2] A haka is an event, and so it has the sort of individuality belonging to a season, a walk, or a wound. The bodies of the dancers become disassembled and the haka's rhythms reassemble their parts under new relations of movement and rest. It is an assemblage that aggregates the parts of bodies so that they stand in relations of movement and rest, are defined by differential speeds and constituted by rhythmic syntheses.

Rhythmic syntheses bring bodies together under relations of movement and rest and also individuate a haka as an event. A haka is structured in this double articulation: aggregated as a mass of reorganised parts of bodies and individuated as an event happening with a certain duration. In the process of composing this doubly articulated individual, rhythms also operate to augment the intensity of a haka's power, increasing its many capacities: its capacity to give independence to a set of limbs, eyes, and tongues, its capacity to draw the dancers together making them feel as one, its capacity to manifest the invincibility of this unity tending to resist dissolution from within, its capacity to attract increasing numbers eventually drawing even strangers or potential enemies into its body, its capacity to increase the dancers' degree of excitement, its capacity to heighten certain feelings appropriate to the function of a particular haka (feelings of joy, courage, or aggression, for example), its capacity to propel the dancers toward an irresistible climax to the point when only sheer exhaustion can stop them, and its capacity to facilitate passages to new stages of life (Canetti 1984: 31–4).[3] Intensities increase internally with the fineness in a haka's execution – with the precision and grace of the dancers – and externally with the approval and affective inclusion of the onlookers and, in the case of the war dance (the peruperu), with the degree of threat posed by the enemy.

Ethics

To understand the ethical import of such an assemblage requires a general approach to ethics which diverges from most traditional approaches.

Ethics takes the body and what it can do – a mode of existence – as its model. Bodies are composed as assemblages, aggregates of parts constituted by distinctive relations. Depending on their composition, these assemblages correspond to different degrees of power insofar as an assemblage may be affected in various ways and exercise various powers. The model of the body allows for the comparison of such powers. When bodies encounter one another, they may combine to create more powerful assemblages, they may fail to combine, or one may decompose the other as a whole or in part. So, as a result of such encounters an assemblage's power may increase or decrease. These differences make it possible to evaluate modes of existence by criteria immanent to those modes. Ethics seeks to describe actual modes of existence and to evaluate them in terms of their immanent differences. From the perspective of a particular body its encounters are to be evaluated according to whether the combinations into which it enters increase or decrease its power. Moreover, a mode of existence is to be evaluated by the proportion of its capacities which it exercises through its own activity in comparison with the proportion of its capacities which are occupied in reacting to exterior forces. As Spinoza says, each individual has as much right as it actually exercises power (Spinoza 1951: 292). Ethics favours joyful passions experienced when something affects a body so as to make it pass from a lesser to a greater degree of power. Facilitating and cultivating passages from lesser to greater degrees of power tends to promote the exercise of a body's own capacities preparing an individual to come into its own power and experience active joys.

There are three positive tasks for ethical inquiry.[4] The initial task is to analyse the composition of modes of existence, that is, to analyse the passive syntheses by which actual assemblages come to be produced and individuated. The analysis of rhythm and its performance of the passive syntheses of time pertain first and foremost to this first task. The second task is to evaluate the ways a mode of existence comes to exercise its capacities to affect and to be affected. This evaluation of an assemblage's degrees of power criticises whatever interferes with a body exercising its own capacities – with a body coming into possession of its power. A mode of existence betters itself by intensifying and increasing its capacity to affect and to be affected. Passages in intensity, increases and decreases in power, comprise the temporal aspects of this second ethical task. The third task of ethics is that of coming to understand the various ways modes of existence transform themselves, creating new modes, and also of coming to understand the conditions for their creation. Assemblages are becomings by their very nature; they are individuated as events. New assemblages, new modes of existence, can arise only when an assemblage becomes capable of affecting itself. Ethics studies such *askesis*. Becomings are singular and actual; they are individual events rather than general types or mere possibilities.

Rhythm and Synthesis

Rhythms group heterogeneous material elements together. In music such elements include pitch, volume, timbre, and other aspects of sound, but rhythms may take up a great variety of other material having a great variety of different forms. In the haka, for example, rhythms deploy parts of human bodies, their various motions, and objects such as weapons as elements, arranging them along continuously varying lines. Rhythms both organise these heterogeneous materials by distributing them over time and also arise from differences within and among these materials and from their complex interactions.[5] Tensions, contrasts, and interplay between elements provide differential inflections that can articulate temporal intervals. Rhythms themselves, however, are ways purely temporal intervals become grouped together by distributing accented and unaccented moments regardless of the specific nature of the material elements deployed. The same rhythm may be realised in almost any diverse materials, and the same materials may instantiate almost any rhythmic organisation. Yet, while material elements and their differences consolidate in the form of a complex body, this body expresses its coherence in the production of rhythms formed by the distribution of accented and unaccented points which determines a contour of abstract temporal intervals. In this way, there are two sides to every rhythm: on one side, a complex connection of formed matters, on the other, the expression of a distribution of accents marking off an abstract organisation of temporal intervals.

This double articulation comprises an assemblage individuated and constituted by its rhythmic organisation. This rhythmic organisation combines, that is, synthesizes, the formed matters into a single body, the groups of abstract intervals into a single event, in a single assemblage in which the two become articulated together. This combination requires the coincidence of three passive syntheses. In experience, combinations of elements may appear as a result of the activity of representation or of consciousness, or they may be given already combined – presupposed by the acts of representation or by the acts of consciousness. The latter combinations require syntheses that occur passively.[6] Each of the passive syntheses of time correlates with one mode of time, present, past, and future constituting time in terms of its respective correlate.[7]

I shall now explicate each of these syntheses, and show how they operate in rhythmic assemblages. In doing so, it will be apparent how a rhythmic assemblage, such as a Maori haka, can perform the tasks appropriate to the sort of ethics outlined above.

The Synthesis of the Living Present

Rhythm organises time and the ways a great variety of material elements occur in time. Elements that get organised in a rhythmic assemblage usually occur independently of one another until they become rhythmically organised. There need be no particular material or causal connections inherent in these elements so long as they become coincident. In a highly regular rhythmic assemblage like a haka, where strict time is kept, parallels of movement and rest occur predominantly because of their temporal coincidence which happens when earlier and later occurring elements become connected by correspondent temporal intervals: where the intervals of one sequence of movement and rest come to stand in some definite relation to, and to resonate with, other sequences which may occur within the same duration. The rates of passage of movement and rest will continue in their correspondence so long as an assemblage can maintain the connections between earlier and later moments. Achieving connections between successive moments produces a centre around which chaotic elements may become stabilised, the beginnings of order may crystallise, and from which the growing assemblage may be given a direction.

Understanding how such connections come about is tantamount to an analysis of the first passive synthesis of time, and so goes part way toward executing our first ethical task. This first synthesis operates on successive independent moments contracting them together with one another to constitute a living present. This contraction retains preceding moments connecting them to the present moment as its past. The contraction also anticipates succeeding moments connecting them to the present moment as its future. Each past is a former present and each future an expected present. The contraction of these moments imparts a direction to the passage of time, since each present moment succeeds a particular past, but can only anticipate its future in general. These past and future moments combine as dimensions of an extended or living present constituted by the contraction of moments which connects them.[8]

The implementation of habits passively performs this synthesis by producing contractions, acting as passive subjects, for which time passes in a living present (Deleuze 1994: 71ff).[9] Habits establish associations between body parts, their movements and rests, so that they can be produced at definite intervals and become ordered in time. Young Maori, for example, would become prepared for their place in haka by incorporating the postures and rhythms of their elders, learning to quiver their fingers, protrude their tongues and eyes, and stamp in unison, thus developing habits enabling them to join in the composition of haka upon reaching the appropriate age (Hiroa and Buck 1966: 357–8).

Such habits take shape, then, by drawing materials from their external milieus and associating them by the repetition of 'gestures which develop before organised bodies' (Deleuze 1994: 10). We might call these habitual lines and complexes of bodies 'kinecepts' – belonging to the kinaesthesia of bodies as concepts belong to the formulations of thought and percepts to the organisation of sensation. Kinecepts can be found in the postures and movements of dance, sport, martial arts, and rituals and other bodily practices. They can be invented, acquired, and shared, but cannot be reduced to concepts, percepts, or affects. While they have a sort of generality insofar as they may be instantiated in different bodies, they may function representationally only incidentally. While no kinecept occurs without generating various sensations, they are not associated with particular sense organs; and while they often occur along with and often engender affects, they are not themselves felt but belong to bodies as habitual gestures.

As important as the shapes of habitual contractions is their capacity for entrainment – a phenomenon pervasive in natural systems capable of oscillation. Entrainment is the tendency for an oscillating body to synchronise or lock into phase with other oscillating bodies. Entrainment is a pervasive phenomenon, appearing in physical, biological, psychological, and sociological systems. This capacity embodies the dual aspect of rhythms as organising while being organised by the material elements that actualise them, for it demonstrates the potential for rhythms abstracted from particular bodies to transfer to, suffuse, and organise other complex bodies. With entrainment order emerges. If kinecepts embody habits of rhythmic contraction, then entrainment expresses the implementation of such habits.

Habits, and rhythmic habits in particular arise from but also give rise to repetition – both repetition of movements and rests and repetition of relations of accented and unaccented abstract moments. We experience a pulse when a series of regular equivalent elements repeat, marking off equal temporal intervals. Pulse always involves the repetition of abstract equivalent instants. We only experience pulse insofar as habitual contractions already operate on the repetition of abstract equivalent instants. Moreover, this repetition of instants disposes them to group together, 'whence the natural tendency of passive synthesis' to generate rhythmic accents "to experience tick-tick as tick-tock" (Deleuze 1994: 72). The phenomenon of pulse requires that, in experience, successive moments or groups must appear as factors which repeat. This points to a difference which lies between the passive synthesis of habit and the active synthesis of representation. Different factors contracted by habit become, in active synthesis, repetitions of something which is the same in both instances, while passive synthesis contracts and thereby repeats differences. The appearance of phenomena of pulse in active synthesis, then, presupposes the contractions of passive synthesis. Still, habit in contracting the repeating instances must draw a difference from them. It is in this sense that habit acts as a passive subject; it carries out a contemplation of the instances it contracts by drawing a difference from them. Since the instances contemplated do not change, there can only be a repetition if something changes in that which contemplates them, that is, if a habit is formed (Deleuze 1994: 74–6). This as Deleuze points out echoes Hume's claim that 'repetition changes nothing in the object repeated, but does change something in the mind which contemplates it'[11] (Deleuze 1994: 70).

As we have seen, the synthesis of habit operates on independent presentations. It contracts them so they become dimensions of a single living present. Although the first synthesis of time constitutes it as a living present, that does not mean that it constitutes time. The contractions produced by habit can only extend so far before fatigue sets in and they begin to unravel. The exercise of a habit is always subject to and limited by a point where its exhaustion sets in. Repetition of the haka, for example, often continues until the participants 'exhaust themselves in excessive fatigue' (Karetu 1993: 33).[10] Fatigue limits the interval of time that can be contracted into the living present; so it is physically impossible for the living present to be coextensive with time (Deleuze 1994: 77). Moreover, while the first synthesis of time contracts independent moments, that does not render them simultaneous. Within the living present the present passes, one moment must disappear for the next to arise. But, while this synthesis constitutes time as a living present, the present cannot pass in the same time as it constitutes. Since the living present is, in these ways, intratemporal there must be another time in which the present passes, and there must be a second synthesis of time.

The Synthesis of the *A Priori* Past

Experiencing periodic accented and unaccented moments is insufficient for rhythm. Rhythm requires memory, the having been experienced of that periodic articulation as given in representation (Abraham 1995: 68). If in the first synthesis rhythm connects bodies, produces repetition, and constitutes a living present, in the second synthesis rhythm individuates bodies, makes them expressive, and constitutes an *a priori* past. While the first synthesis establishes time in the present through habit, the second grounds time in the past as a condition of memory. The first synthesis retains moments that have just passed. Memory, in contrast, reproduces the past in representation. Memory depends on habit, but habit is not sufficient to constitute it. Memory operates according to the laws of association on former presents contiguous with and resembling the present one. Furthermore, memory must not only represent the past, it must represent that past along with its present present, and along with those representations it must represent its own act of representation. For to count as a memory an act must situate its past, as past, relative to its own act of reproduction, and situate it as such an act. The act of memory takes place in a present, which therefore must contain an extra reflective dimension in which it represents itself and a former present. Memory, then, performs an active synthesis combining acts of reproduction, reflection, and recognition (Deleuze 1994: 79–81).

In this context, the former present is not the past. Rather the past is the medium in which memory focuses on a particular former present. The past is never itself represented, but rather is a condition of representation giving it an extra dimension in which reflection may occur. Each living present becomes a particular relative to a past that is general. This past is general because it includes different moments as repetitions of the same forms by means of their resonance, so that the active synthesis of memory embeds each former present in the medium of the past in general. As a synthesis, memory, then, must itself be grounded as a consequence in yet another synthesis, one that passively constitutes the being of the past in which memory operates, and which is also the medium in which the present passes.

The passing of the present is paradoxical; but the paradoxes here are not failures in our understanding, rather they are positive aspects of time productive of a second time, the past in general.[11] The second synthesis operates through a set of constitutive paradoxes. For the former present to pass it cannot merely be replaced by the present present. The first paradox, then, is that the former present must pass at the same time as it is present, that is, that the past is contemporaneous with itself as present. Hence, each present passes in favour of a new present. This first paradox requires a second, that the whole of the past coexist with each present. For, if the past is contemporaneous with the present it was, then the past does not itself pass, it does not belong to the former present any more than it does to the present one. The past in general, then, is not a dimension of time, but is rather the synthesis of the whole of time which contains the present and future as dimensions. Such a past is always virtual and never actual; it is 'real without being actual, ideal without being abstract' as Proust says of states of resonance (Proust in Deleuze 1994: 208).[12] The past is time in-itself, a virtual coexistence of the whole of time. But, if the past does not belong to any present, a third paradox results, that rather than developing after the passing present the past pre-exists. The past was never present; it is *a priori*, presupposed by and coexisting with the passing present yet conserved in itself.

The past is a virtual multiplicity which is also dynamic; it is continuously becoming actual, becoming present. Bergson pictured this continous actualisation in the metaphor of the cone in which the whole of the past coexists with itself at different levels of relaxation and contraction. Here contraction does not mean the bringing together of successive moments as in the first synthesis. But instead, the whole of the past becomes more concentrated, contracting into the present, becoming actualised, passing to the limit, and making the present pass. Actualisation amounts to a fourth paradox. For, as the most contracted level of the past, each successive present actualizes different levels of the past. Each present repeats the past as a whole but at different levels. This multiplicity of levels, as Deleuze puts it, 'implies between successive presents non-localizable connections, actions at a distance, systems of replay, resonance and echoes, objective chances, signs, signals and roles which transcend spatial locations and temporal successions' (Deleuze 1994: 83).

The importance of invariant repetition in many rituals attests to the virtual multiplicity of the pure past. It has often been observed that practitioners of ritual performances require that the ritual acts be performed exactly the same way each time. In the haka, for example, any mistake was viewed as a sign of misfortune (Best 1979: 111). In particular, participants must maintain the rhythm of the haka to guarantee that its message is heard (Karetu 1993: 31). The invariance requirement is often accompanied by the claim that the ritual renews a great event of the past. In such cases, the ritual performance may, paradoxically, not act merely as a memorial but as a reactualisation, an intensification, of that event.[13]

Performances of such rituals inherit their sense from their resonance, replay, and non-localisable connections with a distant past which is reactualised in the present. This sense may be symbolic, as when the quivering of the hands in the haka recalls the dance of Tane-rore, the goddess who appears in the trembling air of hot summer days. But such symbols act effectively in the actualisation of the dance in the living present. The effective reality of the symbol is not its representational content but its differential structure.

The effective reality of the virtual, its differential elements and relations point to the way rhythm effectuates the second passive synthesis. Rhythms cannot be reduced to either mechanical production or to aspects of perception (Abraham 1995: 73). Even though a rhythm may appear in manifold embodiments, it is always embodied somehow. But rhythms also always exceed their embodiment because of their differentiated polyvalence. Rhythmic motifs, with their own relations of accented and unaccented structures, function as actualisations of diverse (even incongruous) larger structures (Cooper and Meyer 1960: 2). Each embodied rhythm stands in virtual states of resonance with a multiplicity of architectonic levels of other rhythmic structures. A new motif cannot emerge without a continuous modulation of its entire preceding structure; so the emergence of every motif is already retrospectively incorporated into and unified with preceding structures. Moreover, even the accidental and discordant are already virtually implicit in this complex structure. What seems divergent and accidental on one level becomes integrated and necessary on another. Complex architectonic rhythmic structures coexist, continuously varying yet contemporaneous with and already implicit in each passing rhythm, thus effectuating the passive synthesis of the past.

In effectuating this second passive synthesis, rhythm becomes expressive. Certain aspects of rhythms become selected and relatively stable producing rhythmic motifs. Through the coalescence of virtual rhythmic motifs assemblages acquire certain qualitative characters. Rhythmic motifs express relations of joy and sadness. A rhythm becomes pounding, graceful, solemn, that is, it takes on certain affective tonalities or resonances. In doing so it forms an expressive organisation that marks out and individuates an assemblage of bodies. Such expressive marks are not subjective states but articulate configurations of complex bodies (Deleuze and Guattari 1987: 317).[14] Different qualities index different assemblages. Rhythmic motifs select and appropriate a complex body's movements and rests, making it possible for them to function in various ways. Haka, for example, may express joy, anger, mourning, defiance, or contempt. As Timoti Karetu says, 'Haka run the whole gamut of human experience' (Karetu 1993: 33). Rhythmic motifs will differ with different expressions, and different expressions make it possible for various haka to perform different functions, to welcome guests, prepare for war, insult transgressors, perform funerals, or act as a means of divination. A mistake in rhythm would dissolve the expressive motifs, dissipating the assemblage, reducing it to chaos, and making the performance of its functions impossible.

Insofar as the second synthesis of the past individuates assemblages, its analysis, like that of the first synthesis, belongs to the first ethical task. It goes part way toward an understanding of the production of assemblages, in this case as a selection and actualisation of rhythmic motifs, of affective resonances. Every assemblage has two sides: one side the actual present organisation of bodies, the other the virtual past expressing potential – what a body can do. The passing present is a becoming or actualisation of what that body can do. The intensity of such passages may increase or decrease and is experienced as affections of joy and sadness respectively. The Maori have no doubt about the evaluative import of the haka as expressive of relations of joy and sadness (McLean 1996: 46). In certain rituals of welcome, for example, the haka (whakatu waewae) is described as a war party of joy (Karetu 1993: 39–40). In addition to affections of joy and sorrow, the haka expresses grace, competence, and well regulated action. The Maori closely scrutinise performances for any flaw in the execution of their rhythms and for their intensity, their fire and energy (Best 1979: 290). Such scrutiny, evaluating passages in intensity actualising the powers of the assemblage executes, in part, the second ethical task.

The Synthesis of the Future

That each assemblage has two sides, one constituted by the organisation of bodies and the other by the actualisation of their powers entails a doubling of the present. Habit constituting a living present which passes, on one side; and memory constituting a pure past grounding this passage as its consequence, on the other. The present itself, then, must have two sides, the most contracted virtual point insisting in the passing of the living present. This passing present and the virtual relation of resonating differential elements appear in representation as a field of problems and questions. Which level of the past is to become actualised in the present? But neither the habits which constitute the living present, nor the resonances of the *a priori* past can resolve these problems or make this selection.[15] They can only be resolved by a third moment of time, by a synthesis of the future, by an original inception. The two sides of the present, the virtual and the actual, are cleaved by an abstract line of becoming, a differential line of continuous passage of the present opening each present onto a future. This line constitutes a third synthesis of time. The future it produces can no longer be repeated by the continuation of a habit, for nothing guarantees the future will repeat the same act or event so long as the present's articulation with the past remains problematic. Nor can it be a repetition of an *a priori* past which for all it makes each present resonate with the whole of the past, that past can never itself be actually present, and so cannot act to produce a future. The first two syntheses are conditions for the production of the future, but are themselves excluded from it. What is repeated in habit and resonates in the past only appears for itself in the third synthesis, in the production of something new.

The third synthesis, as a line of passage, is first of all a purely formal line. Its form is the static, unchanging form of change, that of a caesura (that is, a break or interruption) which asymmetrically distributes a before and after, and hence continuously unfolds in an eccentric, con-stantly decentered circle. The caesura characterises the whole of time as a single event divided into two unequal parts, drawing that which comes before the change together with that which comes after. Just such a formal line of passage defines every rhythmic term. Rhythmic groupings, or terms, would be impossible without a distinction between their elements; this requires an asymmetry between accented and unaccented beats. Rhythmic terms constitute dynamic vectorial distributions of accented and unaccented beats around a caesura.[16] The difference between accented and unaccented beats, the caesura, is the focal point of the rhythm. The forward motion of rhythmic assemblages characterise a line of increasing tension oriented toward a release yet to come. Tension and release are unequally distributed around the caesura which constitutes the differential moment that continuously distributes and redistributes the tension in time. There is no material element, nor any prior rhythmic term that determines the distribution of accents. While some difference must set what is accented off from what is unaccented, there need be neither an element occupying the accented moment nor any contour nor regularity creating the accent. Accent is basic to the experience of rhythm but is neither a product of habit nor determined by resonance with preceding forms.[17]

Secondly, the line of passage is an intensive rather than an extensive line. An intensive line extends an inequality without resolving that inequality or cancelling it out. A quantitative inequality continues from each member of an intensive series to the next in any series of differences. This also establishes a positive ordinal distance between one member of an intensive series and another. Each member of an intensive series envelops lesser intensities, so that any given member may both envelop a lesser intensity and be enveloped by a greater. An intensive line establishes distances between heterogeneous members of a series. Intensive quantities, then, cannot be divided, and an intensive line cannot be continued without changing in nature. It is this last feature of the intensive line of passage that makes it capable of producing something new, and which bears on the third ethical task.

The intensity in rhythmic assemblages appears first in the distinction between rhythm and metre and then in the difference between two types of rhythm. Metre is an extensive quantity. Like any extensive quantity, metre can be measured by comparison between a magnitude and its divisions. Metre measures the number of pulses between regularly repeating accents. The equal intervals between pulses serve as a common measure making metre an extensive quantity – it can be divided without changing in nature. But rhythms can occur independent of any metre and even independent of a regular pulse; for an accented beat may group together with unaccented beats without the accent recurring regularly or in such a way that the rhythm can be divided into units of equal duration or pulses. Rhythmic patterns may even conflict with an established metre. For example, unaccented beats may be displaced closer to the accent than a regular pulse would dictate, as in *tempo rubato*. Resonance with the past dissolves in such intensive agogic rhythms.[18] Of course, many rhythmic assemblages, such as haka, will incorporate metre and pulse as well, but this incorporation merely clothes an intensive rhythm in an extensive one; covering non-pulsed intensive rhythmic lines expressing tonic or tensional rhythms with pulsed extensive rhythmic lines and cadence rhythms. Cadence rhythms comprise isochronic repetitions of identical elements, but these only arise because already at their core lie intensive tonic accents creating distinctive instants continuously displaced in an eccentric series. A cadence repetition, repetition of the same, is only the outward appearance or abstract effect enveloping and produced by another repetition, a repetition of difference, dissymmetrical and rhythmic, tonic and intensive.[19]

Rhythmic intensity is essential to the haka, and is a primary criterion in a haka's evaluation. The stamping of the foot controls the beat with each movement timed to the stamping of the right foot while the left foot remains in place. If the foot is not stamped properly the beat can be lost. Even the Maori words for the beat refer to the stamping of the foot.[20] While hakas usually keep a strict metre, tempos sometimes increase as the excitement mounts. Evaluation of a haka considers not only its passion and excitement, but, fundamentally, its intensity – the performers give their all. Karetu comments that 'to perform haka with élan and panache one must give one's all – there are no half measures. If one is still able to speak after a performance, one has not given one's all' (Karetu 1993: 44).[21] Haka masters tend to scorn exaggerated movements as too overt, preferring more subtle movements performed with greater intensity. They claim that being 'in full cry and giving their all' generates mutual attraction between the performers (Karetu 1993: 16).[22] In our terms, the haka's rhythmic intensity generates an assemblage.

Lastly, the empty intensive line of passage exceeds past and present. It is a synthesis of the future through the production of something new. Through habitual action the first synthesis of the living present constituted its past in retention and its future in anticipation. Through resonance of moments subordinating differences to similarities the second synthesis contained a present and future as dimensions included within the *a priori* past. The third synthesis, however, consigns both of these to its past – a before of an assemblage's metamorphosis – using them, but leaving them behind as incapable of producing a new assemblage. To produce something new an assemblage must become capable of dislodging the agency of habit, changing and disrupting its cycle. Moreover, what is created must become something other than a mere repetition of the same assemblage subordinated to the condition of memory. For something new to emerge, then, it must happen in a present belonging to the third synthesis. The caesura constitutes this present – a becoming or actualisation in which a differential inequality makes an assemblage capable of exceeding both its agent and its condition. This becoming constitutes the event in which the assemblage becomes capable of changing, when it comes into its power of acting. This moment is precarious, always in danger of collapsing into incoherence or falling back into its past, into the same old forms. While its variations do not come from outside, the coherence of a new assemblage belongs only to the future, to a moment after its transformation. Relative to past forms, the synthesis creates something formless, a difference which is extreme and excessive. It prolongs an intensive line that, as such, can continue only by changing its nature.

Rhythmic variation is capable of exceeding the form and content of an assemblage. Surprising moments may radically alter whole rhythmic organisations (Abraham 1995: 59, 75–8, 87).[23] Even constrained by periodic repetition rhythms may have the effect of producing a dissymmetrical difference radically altering an existing rhythmic organisation, regrouping the forces operating in an assemblage. Firstly, rhythms may become expressed in an assemblage shifting the relations between accented and unaccented beats, for example by changes in the dynamic intensification of a beat, that is, by changes in stress.[24] Secondly, rhythms may also pass between heterogeneous assemblages by effecting changes in direction. While a metrical assemblage like a haka may be divided into rhythmic groupings sharing a common measure, other assemblages may change rhythms without regard to a common measure and are irreducible to the divisions of a larger rhythmic whole. The *waiata* or songs of the Maori proceed by the changing vectors of such additive rather than divisive rhythms. Additive rhythms may even intervene in the regular metre of a haka.[25] Finally, one rhythmic assemblage may incorporate new elements through a caesura operating between the assemblage and the elements of the external milieu.

In this last way rhythmic passage effects an assemblage's growth if not in size at least in intensity, as in Canetti's analysis.[26] Such rhythmic passage prevents an assemblage collapsing into chaos. When dancers enter into a haka their bodies become reorganised so that parts are taken over by different rhythms. A new assemblage, the haka, with its own organisation and nature incorporates what had been other assemblages, the previously individuated bodies of the dancers. The haka itself also becomes capable of producing new assemblages. Karetu tells us that 'No Maori ceremony is complete without haka. It is as fundamental to our rites of passage as the language . . .' (Karetu 1993: 13–14). In the welcoming ceremony, the haka plays a crucial role in the transformation of the identities of the participants. Even today there is at first a competitive relation between guests and host, where the guests test the power and competence of their hosts.[27] The welcoming ceremony is a complex ritual of encounter in which the visitors are at first treated as hostile intruders who are also wary of their hosts. In pre-*pakeha* times (before the British settlement of New Zealand) these attitudes were not mere formalities, there was a real potential that the ritual could break down and turn into war. Salmond describes one encounter as follows:

> [T]he encounter began with a firing-off of muskets on both sides, then the local warriors stripped naked and armed, started up the wardance (*haka*). The visitors followed with a *haka* of their own, and knelt down facing their hosts. A challenger came running out toward them . . . he . . . was chased by the visitors in a body, and as they approached the local people the sham fight began . . . The sham fight was a dangerous part of the ritual, because fighting could easily break out in earnest, but if it ended peacefully both sides joined in the *haka*, then pressed noses and wailed for the dead . . . . (Salmond 1975: 127)[28]

The metric forms of two hakas are precariously connected by a few bodies breaking off from the metric assemblage in intense movements that take the assemblages to their limits. There is a point where the intensification is taken to its extreme limits, a point of caesura where the organisation can fall back into the situation before the encounter, break down into chaos and war, or become a new assemblage with new affections of its own. The example of the haka in the welcoming ritual illustrates how rhythm performs the third synthesis of time going to its limit to create something new, helping to fulfil our third ethical task. To some degree we have come to understanding how a rhythmic assemblage, a mode of existence, may transform itself.

References

Abraham, N. (1995), *Rhythms: On the Work, Translation, and Psychoanalysis*, trans. B. Thigpen and N. T. Rand, Stanford CA: Stanford University Press.

Barlow, C. (1991), *Tikanga Whakaaro: Key Concepts in Maori Culture*, Auckland: Oxford University Press.

Best, E. (1979), *The Maori*, New York: AMS Press.

Boulez, P. (1976), *Pierre Boulez: Conversations with Célestin Deliège*, London: Eulenburg Books.

Canetti, E. (1984), *Crowds and Power*, trans. Carol Stewart, New York and London: Penguin.

Cooper, G. and Meyer L. B. (1960), *The Rhythmic Structure of Music*, Chicago: The University of Chicago Press.

156   Phil Turetsky

Deleuze, G. (2000), *Proust and Signs*, New York: George Braziller, Inc.
Deleuze, G. (1988), 'Spinoza and Us' in, *Spinoza: Practical Philosophy*, trans. R. Hurley, New York: City Lights Books.
Deleuze, G. (1994), *Difference and Repetition*, trans. P. Patton, New York: Columbia University Press.
Deleuze, G. (1989), *The Logic of Sense*, trans. M. Lester with C. Stivale, New York: Columbia University Press.
Deleuze, G. and Guattari, F. (1987), *A Thousand Plateaus: Capitalism and Schizophrenia*, trans. B. Massumi, Minneapolis: University of Minnesota Press.
Hiroa, T. R. and Buck, P. (1966), *The Coming of the Maori*, 2nd edn, Wellington: Whitcombe and Tombs.
Husserl, E. (1973), *Analyses zur Passiven Synthesis: Aus Vorlesungs-und Forschungsmanuskripten 1918–1926*, vol. XIII, ed. M. Fleischer, The Hague: Martinus Nijhoff, Husserliana.
Husserl, E. (1991), *On the Phenomenology of the Consciousness of Internal Time 1893–1917*, trans. John Barnett Brough, Kluwer Academic Publishers.
Karetu, T. (1993), *Haka! Te Tohu O Te Whenua Rangatira: The Dance of a Noble People*, Wellington: Reed Books.
McLean, M. (1996), *Maori Music*, Auckland: Auckland University Press.
Polack, J. S. (1838), *New Zealand, Being a Narrative of Travels and Adventures During a Residence in That Country Between the Years 1831 and 1837*, vol. 1, London: Bentley.
Rappaport, R. A. (1976), 'The Obvious Aspects of Ritual' in *Ecology, Meaning, and Religion*, Berkeley, CA: North Atlantic Books.
Salmond, A. (1975), *Hui: A Study of Maori Ceremonial Gatherings*, Wellington: Reed Books.
Smith, D. (1998), 'The Place of Ethics in Deleuze's Philosophy: Three Questions of Immanence', in E. Kaufman and K. J. Heller (eds) (1998), *Deleuze and Guattari: New Mappings in Politics, Philosophy, and Culture*, Minneapolis: University of Minnesota Press, pp. 251–69.
Williams, R. G. and Boyd, J. W. (1993), *Ritual Art and Knowledge: Aesthetic Theory and Zoroastrian Ritual*, Columbia, SC: University of South Carolina Press.

Notes

1. The appropriate part of the text is quoted in Polack, cited in Canetti 1984: 36–7.
2. Deleuze and Guattari, following Duns Scotus, call this sort of individuality a 'haecceity' (Deleuze and Guattari 1987: 260–5).
3. On the importance of haka in Maori rites of passage see Karetu 1993: 13–14.
4. Deleuze 1988: 122–130. These tasks are also explicated in 'The Place of Ethics in Deleuze's Philosophy: Three Questions of Immanence' by Daniel Smith, cf. Kaufman and Heller 1998: 251–9.
5. See Cooper, Grosvenor and Meyer 1960: 1–2. See also Abraham 1995: 71–2.
6. Passive syntheses have a major role to play in phenomenological description (see Husserl 1973). At this point we may characterise passive syntheses both in terms of representation (see Deleuze 1994), as well as in terms of consciousness. A phenomenological approach treats consciousness as a nexus of intentionalities and denies that this nexus is representational. Deleuze's critique of phenomenology's approach to the *a priori* requires a less restricted approach.
7. For the three syntheses of time see Deleuze 1994: 70–96.

8. Deleuze describes the constitution of the living present by contraction (Deleuze 1994). The characterisation of the living present as the synthesis of anticipation, impression, and retention is attested to by phenomenological description, see Husserl 1991, especially pp. 21–75.
9. See also Abraham 1995: 75ff. and passim.
10. See also Polack, cited in Canetti 1984, as quoted above (see Note 1).
11. Deleuze discusses the productive nature of paradox (Deleuze 1994: 81–4).
12. See Deleuze 1994: 60.
13. Deleuze remarks on this point that festivals repeat something unrepeatable, that festivals 'do not add a second and a third time to the first but carry the first time to the "nth" power'. Roy A. Rappaport notes the invariance of ritual performances in 'The Obvious Aspects of ritual' (Rappaport 1976: 173–221). A discussion of the insistence on exact invariant repetition in Zoroastrian Ritual can be found in Williams and Boyd 1993, pp. 68–78.
14. Deleuze and Guattari make clear that in cultures such as that of the Maori semiotic systems are thoroughly corporeal. They say, 'If we consider primitive societies, we see that . . . their semiotic is nonsignifying, nonsubjective, essentially collective, polyvocal, and corporeal, playing on very diverse forms and substances. This polyvocality operates through bodies, their volumes, their internal cavities, their variable exterior connections and coordinates . . .' (Deleuze and Guattari 1987: 175–6).
15. These questions cannot be resolved by appeal to desire either, at least insofar as desire requires the continuation of the desiring agent which presupposes the passive synthesis of habit. On this point see Deleuze 1994: 85ff.
16. The word 'caesura' refers to a break, interval or interruption– a formal break or stop. In Greek and Latin prosody it indicates the division of a metrical foot between two words especially near the middle of a line. In English prosody it indicates a pause or breathing place near the middle of a metrical line, generally indicated by a pause in sense. In our usage, the caesura will be connected to rhythm regardless of whether that rhythm is also metrical.
17. On the dynamic nature of rhythmic terms see Abraham 1995: 79–80. On the problem of the causation of accents and their primacy see Cooper and Meyer 1960: 7–8.
18. See Abraham 1995: 84. For the distinction between pulsed and non-pulsed time see Boulez 1976: 68–71, and also comments in Deleuze and Guattari 1987: 296–7.
19. On cadence rhythms and tonic rhythms see Deleuze 1994: 20–1. On the two sorts of repetition see p. 24ff. and throughout.
20. On the foot stamp see Karetu 1993: 76, McLean 1996: 251, 254, and Buck 1966: 292.
21. On this point see also the comments by haka masters in Karetu 1993, Chapter 7 and his discussion of the evaluation of haka competitions in Chapter 8.
22. Karetu 1993. See also the critique of contemporary performances on p. 87 'the minimum of movement with the maximum of expression is becoming difficult for the majority of the groups to achieve'.
23. Abraham (1995) notes how surprises may enter rhythms at any time and transform whole rhythmic organisations.
24. Cooper and Meyer distinguish stress from accent (Cooper and Meyer 1960: 8). Stress placed on a weak beat will not make it accented. Stress, however, can change the grouping of the beats and so change the rhythm.
25. On additive rhythms see McLean 1996: 250–2, and on additive rhythms in the haka see McLean 1996: 254. On *waiata* see McLean and also see Barlow 1991: 150–1.

26. Canetti notes that even a stagnant crowd has a rhythm and that this rhythm is one of increased intensity, see Canetti 1984: 34–5.
27. Karetu claims that it is on these occasions that the haka is at its most intense (Karetu 1993: 85).
28. The precariousness of the resolution of the haka was also attested to by the earliest observers (Buck 1966: 103).

Chapter 8

What I Hear is Thinking Too: The Deleuze Tribute Recordings[1]

Timothy S. Murphy

Following Gilles Deleuze's suicide in November 1995, two record labels released memorial CDs in his honor. The first, *Folds and Rhizomes for Gilles Deleuze* (hereafter abbreviated *FR*), had been prepared by the Belgian label Sub Rosa prior to his death but did not reach the shelf until afterwards.[2] In the liner notes to that disc, label founder Guy Marc Hinant writes:

> '*L'Anti-Oedipe* was written by the two of us, and since each of us was several, we were already quite a crowd.' It is on the basis of this sentence, the first in *Mille Plateaux*, that we conceived of Sub Rosa. From the beginning, we wanted to be more than a label; a machine perhaps, composed of rhizomes, of peaks and troughs, of tranquility and doubt . . . Obviously, this is not an official tribute to this great figure, one of the foremost of our time. It is only the fraternal salute of a few young people who admire him deeply, and who, better still, were one day helped in their lives and in their creations by his writings.

The disc contains tracks by five bands or artists, four of whom also contributed tracks to the second memorial project, a two-disc, twenty-seven-track set entitled *In Memoriam Gilles Deleuze* (hereafter *IM*), from the Mille Plateaux label in Frankfurt, Germany. Founder Achim Szepanski describes the work of the artists on his label as 'Becoming, so that the music goes beyond itself; this is the search for the forces of the minoritarian that the label Mille Plateaux is part of. In a letter Gilles Deleuze welcomed the existence of such a label' (*IM*: 5, translation modified).

Both of these labels are independents, unaffiliated with the large multinational music corporations that dominate the international recording market. They are also 'alternative' labels, in the sense that the music they circulate is not designed to compete directly with the 'mainstream' music of the multinationals. In addition to the Deleuze tribute discs, Sub Rosa has also released recordings of sound experiments by William S. Burroughs, Antonin Artaud, Bill Laswell and Richard Pinhas, among others, while Mille Plateaux specialises in dense techno dance/trance mixes and electronica.[3] What they have in common is a focus on musicians who have been profoundly affected by the most recent computer revolution in music – the one that broke the monopoly of large, limited-access mainframe machines (and their bureaucratic administrators) over sound synthesis.[4] The proliferation of personal computers through the 1980s and 1990s spawned an entire generation of musicians (and listeners) for whom sound is practically a tactile substance, digitally reproducible, malleable and storable, and consequently for whom traditional musical forms and notation have become increasingly irrelevant.[5] Their music is pop, not in the Adornian sense of commodity music produced by corporate professionals and intended to impose a false universality upon consumers, but in a sense much closer to the old meaning of 'popular': an amateur, *bricolage* music arising from people's everyday activities. In this regard at least, the contemporary cultural situation is similar to those that gave rise to the blues, or to the American counter-culture of the 1960s and the Italian one of the 1970s. Today, everyday activities for many people depend upon advanced digital technology, and the music that arises from, or mixes with, those activities constitutes an index of political potentialities that have yet to coalesce.[6]

What use were Deleuze and Guattari's concepts to these musicians who were seeking new categories and forms for musical creation and social intervention? To determine this, we must now attempt to discern the ways in which certain musicians have detached concepts from, or grafted elements onto, Deleuze and Guattari's philosophical rhizome for use in their own creative activities. To do so, we must make a little machinic assemblage, a refrain or temporary musical territory, of our own: we must select a few tracks, passing over others in silence, and resequence them in order to make the breaks fall, not between the two memorial discs, but between our particular line of enquiry and other virtual lines. Our choice of line should be construed neither as an essentially privileged account of these recordings nor as a devaluation of other approaches to them, but simply as one stem of a rhizome. We do what we can with them, and leave it to other listeners to do otherwise.

The clearest line for our enquiry goes back to Deleuze and Guattari's basic concepts, but viewed from the less systematic, more pragmatic and selective perspective of these musicians. Music is made of percepts, intensive sensory complexes which 'are no longer perceptions; they are independent of a state of those who experience them . . . Sensations, percepts, and affects are *beings* whose validity lies in themselves and exceeds anything lived' (Deleuze and Guattari 1994: 164, translation modified). But before the elements of music can be percepts, they must become perceptible. This becoming-perceptible complements or complicates the becoming-imperceptible of movement which Bergson described:

> If movement is imperceptible by nature, it is always so in relation to a given threshold of perception, which is by nature relative and thus plays the role of a mediation on the plane that effects the distribution of thresholds and percepts and makes forms perceivable to perceiving subjects. It is the plane of organization and development, the plane of transcendence, that renders perceptible without itself being perceived, without being capable of being perceived. (Deleuze and Guattari 1987: 281)

This threshold of perception must be crossed for music to arise, and the work of the musician is directed toward making perceptible what is as yet imperceptible.

The crossing of the threshold is the object of two tracks on *IM*, Jim O'Rourke's 'As In' (disc 2, track 1) and DJ Spooky's 'Invisual Ocean' (disc 2, track 8). O'Rourke's track takes almost three minutes to fade slowly into perceptibility, and as it does it gradually assembles a smooth continuum of modulated sound (to which we will return in a moment). This track assembles itself as a perceptible continuum, however, only through the accumulation and superimposition of myriad instantaneous 'little perceptions'. It is like the murmuring of Leibniz's ocean:[7]

> [W]e say that the little perceptions are themselves distinct and obscure (not clear): distinct because they grasp differential relations and singularities; obscure because they are not yet 'distinguished,' not yet differenciated. These singularities then condense to determine a threshold of consciousness in relation to our bodies, a threshold of differenciation on the basis of which the little perceptions are actualised, but actualised in an apperception which in turn is only clear and confused; clear because it is distinguished or differenciated, and confused because it is clear. (Deleuze 1994: 213)

As the little perceptions accumulate, their differences become audibly distinct from one another (to the perceiving subject), and in so doing they define a large-scale perception of the ocean. The perception of the ocean is clear because the little perceptions from which it is assembled are audibly distinct, but because the little perceptions are not fully individualised, this clear perception remains dynamically confused. DJ Spooky's track assembles such an audible ocean, which remains 'Invisual' (invisible or infra-visual, imperceptible to vision?), out of non-maritime sound elements in precisely this way. This ocean is part of the larger sonorous and social territory that defines all his work: 'I wanted to create music that would reflect the extreme density of the urban landscape and the way its geometric regularity contours and configures perception . . . The sounds of the ultra futuristic streetsoul of the urban jungle shimmering at the edge of perception' (DJ Spooky 1996: 7–8).[8]

Once the threshold of perceptibility has been crossed, the assemblage of sound begins to actualise its space-time, its imperceptible plane of organisation. Such a plane actualises itself in terms of its breaks and cuts, or rather its resistance to them. A smooth, sonorously continuous space-time unfolds, as in O'Rourke's 'As In': *glissandi*, continuous lines or gradients of sound that modulate from tone to tone without discontinuous jumps across the sonorous spectrum. The tracks by the German group Oval, 'You Are * Here 0.9 B' (*IM*disc 2, track 2) and 'SD II Audio Template' (*FR*: track 3), also embody this smooth construction, at least temporarily. The Oval tracks also intentionally dramatise the process by which smooth space-time becomes striated and vice versa. 'Oval is a very strict and limited approach,' claims principal musician Markus Popp, 'in order to make some new distinctions clear – and, in a way, to go beyond the music concept, the music metaphors underlying the concepts used in the digital instruments involved' (quoted in Weidenbaum 1996). In 'SD II Audio Template,' the continuously modulating tones are abruptly interrupted by punctual percussive events that sound like scratches on the surface of an LP. These interruptions obviously allude to the dialectic of tone and noise, consonance and dissonance that has defined modern music from Schoenberg to Cage, but they also have a more novel function. Despite their metric irregularity, these events introduce something like a rhythm or striation into the smooth plane. As Deleuze and Guattari point out, 'Meter, whether regular or not, assumes a coded form whose unit of measure may vary . . . whereas rhythm is the Unequal or the Incommensurable'; it is this unequal element that is the imperceptible 'difference that is rhythmic, not the repetition' of perceptible metre (Deleuze and Guattari 1987: 313–14). These irregular striations are digitally 'looped' to form a repeating metric phrase that constitutes the striated space-time of the Oval track. Thus metric irregularity at short intervals becomes rhythmic regularity at longer intervals or higher levels of scale.

Conversely, the striations can also reconstruct a smooth space/time through acceleration and accumulation; in 'SD II Audio Template' this happens when the metric striations occur at shorter and shorter intervals until they begin to overlap, either in actuality or simply in the perception of the listener. As they do so, their differenciated or striated features begin to merge, to return to a smooth continuity or indistinguishability at a higher frequency. The track passes through a circular progression, from smooth sonorous continuity to striation and then back to smoothness via increasing striation. As a result of these exemplary transformations, this track by Oval can stand, as its title implies, as an 'audio template' or abstract map because it reveals that all audio assemblages are in fact what Deleuze and Guattari call multiplicities: 'A multiplicity has neither subject nor object, only determinations, magnitudes, and dimensions that cannot increase in number without the multiplicity changing in nature.' Thus when the tempo of striation, the number of one of the track's sonorous dimensions, increases, not only the speed of the piece but also its sound quality changes. 'When Glenn Gould speeds up the performance of a piece, he is not just displaying virtuosity, he is transforming the musical points into lines, he is making the whole piece proliferate' (Deleuze and Guattari 1987: 8). Just as acceleration changes the nature of the piece, so does deceleration. Obviously, deceleration of a sound lowers its pitch and thus alters its tone quality, but it also alters all its other relationships and reveals qualitatively new features in them; if you slow down a passage of *pizzicato* strings, for example, you will find the continuous hum of a motor. To a certain extent, the Blue Byte track 'Can't Be Still' (*IM*: disc 1, track 12) and the Bleed track 'Pâtent' (*IM*: disc 2, track 5) also embody this principle of audio multiplicity via acceleration and deceleration.[9]

Another way that smoothness emerges from striation – in fact the most common method employed on the Deleuze memorial discs – is via the superimposition of a number of distinct metric patterns of striation. These superimposed patterns intersect at a variety of singular inflection points, creating indirect harmonies and virtual melodies. Deleuze and Guattari describe it this way:

> Certain modern musicians oppose the transcendent plan(e) of organiza-
> tion, which is said to have dominated all of Western classical music, to the
> immanent sound plane, which is always given along with that to which it
> gives rise, brings the imperceptible to perception and carries only differ-
> ential speeds and slownesses in a kind of molecular lapping. (Deleuze and
> Guattari 1987: 267)

In this molecular (over)lapping the perceiving subject 'hears' virtual sounds that have not actually been played and 'counts' virtual beats that have not actually been measured. The amplified ensemble music of

Philip Glass is the most well-known example of this method of super-imposition; the track 'The Grid' from his soundtrack for the film *Koyaanisqatsi* is representative. On the Deleuze memorial discs, the tracks contributed by Mouse on Mars, 'Subnubus' (*FR*: track 1) and '1001' (*IM*: disc 2, track 3), provide examples of generative superimposition in techno music.[10]

Within the mutating smooth/striated space-time of the musical multiplicity, other concepts drawn from Deleuze and Guattari's work also become productive. In his piece 'Unidirections/Continuum' (*IM*: disc 1, track 6, Christophe Charles makes use of the techniques of *musique concrète* pioneered by Pierre Schaeffer to construct a decentred sonorous rhizome according to principles of connection and heterogeneity. *Musique concrète* assembles not only pure sounds produced by wave generators but also everyday sounds not normally considered to be musical: the creaking of a hinge, a sigh. This heterogeneity follows from the musician's recognition that all sonorous materials are available for use on this plane of development. The musician makes music by assembling 'semiotic chains':

> [S]emiotic chains of every nature are connected to very diverse modes of coding (biological, political, economic, etc.) that bring into play not only different regimes of signs but also states of things of differing status . . . A rhizome ceaselessly establishes connections between semiotic chains, organizations of power, and circumstances relative to the arts, sciences, and social struggles. A semiotic chain is like a tuber agglomerating very diverse acts, not only linguistic, but also perceptive, mimetic, gestural, and cognitive . . . (Deleuze and Guattari 1987: 7)

Charles's semiotic chains range from the unearthly mechanical purity of oscillator and wave generator tones to the entropic crackle of broadcast static and recording surface noise. Between the extremes, we hear pitched and unpitched percussion, sirens, the delicate movement of water and sounds of flight in field recordings; the heterogeneity of connected elements leads the listener across vast distances of sonorous intensity.[11]

The final element of these memorials to which we must turn seems at first glance to be more intimate but is actually just as distancing as static: the voice. Up to this point we have focused on elements of Deleuze and Guattari's philosophy of music that have no clear correlatives in popular music criticism, but with the voice we move onto critical terrain that is currently dominated by methods and categories drawn from psychoanalysis, an interpretive strategy on which Deleuze and Guattari declared war in *Anti-Oedipus*. Our purpose here is not to rehearse that all-out assault, nor to intervene concretely in the ongoing musicological debates over the voice, but merely to identify the general limits of a psycho-analytic representational approach to pop music as a way of highlighting the originality of Deleuze and Guattari's productivist perspective.

In psychoanalysis and the criticism derived from it, the voice functions like the gaze to address and thus subjectify individuals, to interpellate them as the subjects of a symbolic order whose structure their psyches reflect imperfectly.[12] Thus the recorded voice forms an 'acoustic mirror' in which the subject (mis)recognises him- or herself, and the activity of listening to that voice becomes an unavoidably narcissistic enterprise.[13] Deleuze and Guattari accept the validity of this model as far as it goes, but they propose a more broadly based alternative that also opens up new territories and structures for music.[14] The narcissistic model of listening, they claim, is a fundamentally retrospective and representational one that cannot account for the production of novelty or innovation in music. Everything new gets cut down to fit the Procrustean bed of universal Oedipal triangulation ('papa–mama–me') and the endless deferral of desire conceived as lack; every action is separated from its practical efficacy to become a pure dramatic signifier of the interminable desire for desire. The psychoanalytic unconscious is a Victorian theatre of familial narcissism, a model of dialectical negativity that is incapable of escaping its own constitutive impasses, so Deleuze and Guattari propose instead a productivist uncon-scious that exceeds the representational model on all sides.[15] This affirma-tive model enables the prospective temporality of subjective improvisation as well as the negative abyss of psychoanalysis's repetition compulsion.

The voice provides a good example of the interpretive consequences that this broader model entails. In much pop music, the voice is the fixed point of thematic reterritorialisation around which the sounds tempora-rily deterritorialise (through distortion, feedback, overdubbing, and so on). '[A]s long as the voice is song, its main role is to "hold" sound, it functions as a constant circumscribed on a note and *accompanied* by the instrument' (Deleuze and Guattari 1987: 96). Since the listener's attention to the voice as a carrier of discursive content or meaning usually effaces its impact as sound or intensity, the voice most often functions to delimit and preserve the pre-established territories of the piece, both harmonically and conceptually. The voice tells us what the song is about, and it does this while doubling or harmonising with its accompanying instrumental melody and reproducing the more or less regular metre. The voice, especially the 'good' or 'trained' voice in pop music, addresses the listener, demands (mis)recognition and interpellates her or him as a docile subject precisely because of the power it gains by this process of harmonic/

thematic reduplication or reterritorialisation. This can be true even (and especially) when the voice sings or speaks of escape, of lines of flight out of its territorial constraints; think for example of the vicious irony of 'I'm Free' from the Who's *Tommy* ('I'm free/I'm free/And I'm waiting for you to follow me . . .'), which reterritorialises the newly-claimed freedom of the 'I' in its control of the second person, the 'you'). So far, Deleuze and Guattari would agree with Adorno, Althusser and the psychoanalytic tradition.

Such is not the case, however, with respect to Scanner's track 'Without End' (*IM*: disc 2, track 7). Here a hoarse voice whispers of events or haecceities, saying, 'it is dawn eternally, time of prophecy,' while the process of sound assembly creates an unexpected auditory space-time that does not double or reflect the sonic contour of that voice. The slow, diffuse metric pulse of human breathing provides a foundation for the piece, a foundation upon which are laid layers of indistinct vocal sounds, ungraspable fragments of speech and angular melodic cells that constitute an unstable soundscape. The listener does not (mis)recognise her- or himself in the vocal/harmonic pattern here, but rather must wait for some pattern to emerge, only to see it subside again into the constantly mutating mix. A similar procedure of discontinuous assemblage, though often without the intelligible lead vocal that provides thematic continuity and territorialisation here, underlies all of Scanner's work, including his piece on *FR*, 'Control: Phantom Signals with Active Bandwidth' (track 4). Robin Rimbaud took the name 'Scanner' from his primary enabling musical machine, the broadband scanner that intercepts the transmissions of radios, cellular telephones, and other broadcast machinery. His method itself is formally subversive and deterritorialising, in that he is transforming a surveillance technology – originally devised to allow police to monitor broadcast communications and intervene in that medium – into a generator of aesthetic affects and percepts. But it is also a new territorialisation, as he has said:

> A good way of putting it with the scanner stuff is *mapping the city* . . . it's like mapping the movements of people during different periods of the day. It's fairly predictable [during the day] . . . Then in the evening, that's where the riot happens. That's when it gets really exciting because all hell gets let loose. The phone rates go down and people have the most surreal conversations. I've always been interested in the spaces in these conversations . . . It amazed me with these mobile phones, which are much more expensive than standard phones – you get these enormous gaps happening. They're the points that really interest me. What's happening in there. (Rimbaud quoted in Toop 1995: 35)

In deterritorialising the technology, he generates a new refrain and hence new spatio-temporal territory: a perceptual map of the city and the day. From his recordings of human voices snatched from these broadcast bands, Scanner often selects the least intelligible statements, those that are so unconventional and decontextualised that they carry no direct meaning even when they can be understood clearly; he also selects voices that have been so distorted in transmission that they cannot be understood at all. These voices, and even the static-filled gaps in conversations, are used as concrete sound, as in *musique concrète*. In other words, he uses the scanner as a source of raw sonorous material and not generally as a source of subjectively referential information, as the police do; the demand for stable reference and command that informs police use of surveillance technology is much closer to the territoriality of the traditional pop song form (and to psychoanalytic criticism of it) than to Scanner's audio maps.

Scanner deterritorialises the voice by centring it in the mix but depriving it of its direct signifying capacity and its continuous harmonic intensification. In his piece 'Control', we hear voices speaking, but often we cannot understand what they are saying. The voices become elements of the sound, values of timbre, without the privilege (and limitation) of discursive meaning. 'Only when the voice is tied to timbre does it reveal a tessitura that renders it heterogeneous to itself and gives it a power of continuous variation: it is then no longer accompanied, but truly "machined"' (Deleuze and Guattari 1987: 96). The voice always has timbre, of course, but not all timbre is equally perceptible; indeed, the mark of the 'trained' or 'pure' singing voice is precisely its minimal noticeable timbre in comparison with the gruff, cracked or shrill vocal quality of blues or rock singers. By 'machined' Deleuze and Guattari mean that the timbrally distinctive voice ceases to be tied to a stable harmonic structure or its attendant subjective form as limiting territories, and is instead opened up to a process of sonorous production that exceeds the expression of an individual psyche. The voice becomes an inhuman sound, a noise, and is no longer personal, subjective, or most importantly, subjectifying (interpellating). Like Adorno, psychoanalytic critics treat this inhuman vocality as a source of anxiety that must inevitably be repressed, only to return as an uncanny recorded double of the fractured self.[16] Deleuze and Guattari, on the other hand, find in this inhumanity, so unexpectedly close at hand, an affirmative and convenient step out of the straightjacket of normative subjectivity.

The uncanny point of indiscernibility between human voice and inhuman sound can be reached in a number of ways. For example, it is what post-serial composers like Milton Babbitt and Luciano Berio have sought in their vocal and electronic works through the transformation of traditionally trained voices. Babbitt's *Philomel* for soprano, recorded soprano and synthesised sound (1963) dramatises the Greek myth of Philomel's metamorphosis into a nightingale by continuously manipulating the soprano's voice, sending it off down a line of flight toward one, then the other of the endpoints of its constant becoming: singing woman or synthesised bird. The sonic affirmation of flight from a constraining subjectivity counterbalances the mythic tragedy of Philomel's punishment. Berio's *Thema: Omaggio a Joyce* (1958) and *Visage* (1961),[17] both electronic manipulations of soprano Cathy Berberian's voice on tape, occupy the same point of transition between voice as discursive meaning and voice as inhuman sound. Of *Thema*, which actualises the virtual *fuga per canonem* in the 'Sirens' chapter of James Joyce's *Ulysses*, Berio has written in the liner notes:

> I was interested in developing new criteria of continuity between spoken language and music and in establishing continual metamorphoses of one into the other . . . [In *Thema*] it is no longer possible to make distinctions between word and sound, and between sound and noise; or between poetry and prose, and between poetry and music. We are thus forced to recognize the relative nature of these distinctions, and the expressive characters of their changing functions. (Berio 1998: 1)

Scanner's work uses different techniques and different vocal timbres, but it forces a similar recognition upon us as well, one that complements the political subversiveness of his chosen medium: there is a becoming-sound of the voice that can draw the subject into a parallel becoming-other of the self, one that is marked not by primal castration anxiety but by prospective affirmation.

Even so, the indiscernibility of voice and sound in Scanner's pieces often highlights, paradoxically, the subjectively expressive power of the voice even in the absence of intelligible meaning. The deterritorialising line of flight out of normative subjective structure may reterritorialise within something similar to the psychoanalytic paradigm. Even when we cannot understand the words or locate a melody in 'Control' or 'Without End', we can sometimes still extract some signifying value by grasping the mood or tone of the sounds.

This reterritorialising aspect has also been explored by post-serial composers, most significantly by György Ligeti in his pieces *Aventures* (1962) and *Nouvelles Aventures* (1962–5), for three singers and seven instrumentalists. In these pieces, Ligeti uses an invented language to demonstrate that: 'All the ritualized human emotions that are expressed colloquially, such as understanding and dissension, [and so on . . .] can be expressed exactly in the a-semantic emotional artificial language.' In singing this artificial language, the performers produce 'the opposite of what we were used to at the performance of an opera . . .: the stage and protagonists are evoked by the music – the music is not performed to accompany an opera, but an opera is performed within the music' (Ligeti 1985: 8–9). Here the accompaniment itself serves to interpellate the listening subject, even without direct address from the voice.

The *reductio ad absurdum* of this situation is surely The Residents's album *The Third Reich and Roll* (1979), which consists of two LP-side-long 'semi-phonetic interpretations of Top Forty hits from the Sixties' (Residents). On this album The Residents, perhaps the most important conceptual art band in pop, perform hit singles like the Rascals's 'Good Lovin' ', Lesley Gore's 'It's My Party' and ? [Question Mark] and The Mysterians's '96 Tears' as if they were being heard over a poor quality AM radio; the melodies and arrangements are largely intact, but the words are reduced to 'semi-phonetic' approximations at best, in acknowledgement of the historical and phenomenological experience of many actual listeners who would have encountered much of the most influential pop music of the twentieth century via low-fidelity AM radio.[18] The Residents' method also ironically acknowledges the fundamental irrelevance of stable discursive meaning to the world of pop, where pure sound intensity and affective projection should rule.

The imperative to deterritorialise the voice, to use it timbrally rather than harmonically or referentially, must include even the voice of the philosopher who articulates that imperative. There is a difference, however imperceptible it may be, between the randomly sampled voices used by Scanner, or the rigorously disciplined voices required for the performance of Babbitt's, Berio's and Ligeti's pieces, and the singular voice of Deleuze himself. It is the difference between the deterritorialised voice and the deterritorialising voice, between the listener hearing a voice become an inhuman sound and the listener actually becoming an inhuman sound via that voice. Deleuze once said:

> Some of us can be moved by certain voices in the cinema. Bogart's voice. What interests us is not Bogart as subject, but how does Bogart's voice function? What is the function of the voice in speaking him? . . . [I]t can't be said that this is an individualizing voice, even though it is that also . . . I deterritorialize myself on Bogart . . . [I]t's a kind of metallic voice . . . a horizontal voice, it's a boring voice – it's a kind of thread which sends out a sort of very very very special sonorous particles. It's a metallic thread

that unwinds, with a minimum of intonation; it's not at all the subjective voice. (Deleuze 1998: 215)

Deleuze's own voice was also such a non-subjective 'metallic voice' through which others deterritorialised themselves. At his death, his friends and colleagues uniformly evoked his familiar gruff voice, which Richard Pinhas described as 'difficult but beautiful' (Heldon 1973), and two of the artists on the memorial discs make use of that deterritorialising voice in their compositions. Hazan + Shea, in 'Rhizome: No Beginning No End' (*FR*: track 5), sample Deleuze's voice from the *Abécédaire de Gilles Deleuze* television broadcasts. In the first section, 'End', they use Deleuze's voice as pure timbre, setting its isolated phonemes against a synthesised ensemble of keyboards, strings and percussion; in the second section, 'Beginning', the voice re-emerges as a signifying instrument as the sentences broken down into timbral elements in section one are cited in their entirety. Hence the inversion of sequence: (no) end before (no) beginning. Wehowsky/Wollscheid's 'Happy Deterritorializations' (*IM* disc 1, track 2) 'reformulates . . . an auratic sound, once recorded by a French rock band accompanied by a reciting Gilles Deleuze [sampled from 'Le Voyageur' on Heldon 1973]. Pieces of this archetypal sound are projected onto different contemporary sound matrixes and merge with their sonic corpora' (Wollscheid in *IM*: 9). Wehowsky/Wollscheid enfold and unfold Deleuze's voice by sampling, resequencing and overdubbing his performance with Heldon to create a multiplied, polyphonic, deterritorialising/reterritorialising Deleuzian voice distanced from and in conversation with itself.

Richard Pinhas's latest recordings, released by Sub Rosa and Cuneiform, constitute a third memorial disc, though they are not billed as such, and they too are organised around Deleuze's words and voice. For this project Pinhas recruited the musicians (and science-fiction writers) Norman Spinrad and Maurice Dantec to form a unit called Schizotrope, subtitled 'The Richard Pinhas and Maurice Dantec Schizospheric Experience – French Readings of Gilles Deleuze's Philosophy with Metatronic Music and Vocal Processors' (Schizotrope 1999 and 2000). Much on these discs reprises Pinhas's earlier collaborations with Deleuze: either Deleuze's words, read by Dantec, are set to music, or Deleuze's voice itself is set. They differ in the form the musical setting takes. On the initial Heldon recording of 'Le Voyageur', the music is progressive rock, as bands like Heldon and King Crimson were inventing it in the early 1970s, music which we have described as 'bolero-like' in structure and sound. Schizotrope's music, however, is quite different from that. Instead of repeating metric and harmonic forms in regularly striated space-time, the new music is smooth and ambient. Drawing on experiments from his previous solo album *De l'Un et du Multiple* (1996), Pinhas has created a contemporary style that owes equal amounts to the 1990s explosion of sampled, computer-generated techno music and to the pioneering 1970s/80s 'Frippertronics' work of King Crimson founder Robert Fripp.[19] Eric Tamm defines Frippertronics as follows: it is

> the technological setup whereby two reel-to-reel tape recorders were connected together and to . . . electric guitar; [and it is also] the musical style, that is, the potential for creatively shaping ever-fluctuating masses of sound in real time, ordinarily upon a tonal, pandiatonic, modal or multi-modal basis; and the various uses of Frippertronics–as music performed solo, or as one timbral/structural element within a more conventional song, or as a 'thematic sound' used to unify a large musical collage . . . (Tamm 1990: 115)

By the 1990s the technological set-up had changed to include DAT recorders and digital signal control, but otherwise the description remains accurate (though, significantly, Fripp changed the name of the activity to the more territorial 'soundscapes'). The interconnected recorders produce cyclic loops of varying durations that grant a periodicity to even the most irregular metres. At the same time, the 'thematic sound' gradients of modulating tone and timbre establish smooth lines of sonorous continuity against which Deleuze's words and voice are set. Pinhas's work here is at once the most territorial of the pieces we have examined, in that Deleuze's concepts and the grain of his voice clearly function as continuous centring elements in the sound assemblage (see Deleuze and Guattari 1987: 96); and also perhaps the most conceptually radical in its extensive deployment of Deleuze's thought according to its own internal logic and rhythm. Instead of the repetitive interpellations of harmonic doubling, we find pure differences of sonorous intensity.

Coda: *Ad libitum*

Our analysis of the contemporary productive potential of Deleuze and Guattari's musical philosophy cannot be as complete as was our account of their borrowings from – and participation in – historical pop music,[20] in part because that potential is still in the process of being realised in diverse concrete forms, but also, more importantly, because its mass political threshold has yet to be crossed. At present there is no broad-based socio-political movement, comparable to the counter-cultures of the 1960s and 1970s, in which that potential can find smooth, open territory for large-scale experimentation and composition. So far it has found only small and temporary autonomous territories, hemmed in by the market or the state and sustained precariously by the local refrains of DJ Spooky, Richard Pinhas and other musicians. But the market and the state are themselves nothing more than temporary territories, legitimated by advertising jingles and national anthems, and yet ominously prone to mutation whenever enough people call a different tune. Plato recognised this instability in the *Republic* when he warned that '[t]he introduction of novel fashions in music is a thing to beware of as endangering the whole fabric of society, whose most important conventions are unsettled by any revolution in that quarter' (Plato 1941: 115). If for the moment such a revolution is effectively contained at the local level, its deterritorialising effects summarily reterritorialised in musical niche markets, the potential for its intensification and spread remains, awaiting the bigger and better assemblages that we will have to construct in order fully to realise it.

For now, though, we have the brief audio assemblages dedicated to Deleuze. They are not models to be imitated, but rather distinct cases of realisation for the conjoined potentials of sound and society. Guattari would call them molecular revolutions. We have scarcely begun to explore the richness of invention contained in these memorial discs and the related works of the musicians in question, but we hope that our analysis has at least sketched a provisional answer to our question: what use were Deleuze and Guattari's concepts to these musicians? In brief, the musicians extracted concepts like tools from the Deleuze–Guattari toolbox and used them to intensify or amplify their own thinking and performing in sound. This is not a matter of simply applying or illustrating philosophical ideas in another medium, but of thinking in and with what we play, what we sing, and what we hear. Atom Heart captures this idea neatly in 'Abstract Miniatures in memoriam Gilles Deleuze' (*IM*: disc 1, track 7): as the track opens, a deadpan, synthesised voice says, 'What I see is thinking. What I hear is thinking too.'

References

Adorno, T. W. (1990), 'The Curves of the Needle', trans. T. Y. Levin, *October 55* (Winter 1990): 49–56.
Althusser, L. (1971), *Lenin and Philosophy,* trans. B. Brewster, New York: Monthly Review Press.
Born, G. (1995), *Rationalizing Culture: IRCAM, Boulez and the Institutionalization of the Musical Avant-Garde*, Berkeley: University of California Press.
Burroughs, W. S. (1964), *Nova Express*, New York: Grove Press.

Cutler, C. (1993), *File Under Popular: Theoretical and Critical Writings on Music*, Brooklyn: Autonomedia.

Deleuze, G. (1990), *The Logic of Sense*, trans. M. Lester with C. Stivale, New York: Columbia University Press.

Deleuze, G. (1994), *Difference and Repetition* trans. Paul Patton, New York: Columbia University Press.

Deleuze, G. (1998), 'Vincennes Seminar Session of May 3, 1977: On Music', trans. T. S. Murphy, *Discourse: Journal for Theoretical Studies in Media and Culture* 20 (3) (Autumn): 205–18.

Deleuze, G. and Guattari, F. (1977), *Anti-Oedipus*, trans. R. Hurley, M. Seem and H. R. Lane, Minneapolis: University of Minnesota Press.

Deleuze, G. and Guattari, F. (1987), *A Thousand Plateaus*, trans. B. Massumi. Minneapolis: University of Minnesota Press.

Deleuze, G. and Guattari, F. (1994), *What is Philosophy?*, trans. H. Tomlinson and G. Burchell, New York: Columbia University Press.

Dunn, L. C. and Jones, N. A. (eds) (1994), *Embodied Voices: Representing Female Vocality in Western Culture*, Cambridge: Cambridge University Press.

Fitzgerald, J. (1998), 'An Assemblage of Desire, Drugs and Techno' *Angelaki: Journal of the Theoretical Humanities* 3 (2), *The Love of Music*: 41–57.

Hardt, Michael, and Antonio Negri (1994), *Labor of Dionysus: A Critique of the State-Form*, Minneapolis: University of Minnesota Press.

Leibniz, G. W. (1981), *New Essays on Human Understanding*, trans. P. Remnant and J. Bennett, New York: Cambridge University Press.

Murphy, Timothy S. (1999), 'Music *After* Joyce: The Post-Serial Composers', *Hypermedia Joyce Studies* at http://www.2street.com/hjs/murphy/index.html

Plato (1941), *Republic,* trans. F. M. Cornford, New York: Oxford University Press.

Silverman, K. (1988), *The Acoustic Mirror: The Female Voice in Psychoanalysis and Cinema*, Bloomington: Indiana University Press.

Tamm, E. (1990), *Robert Fripp: From King Crimson to Guitar Craft*, Boston: Faber & Faber.

Toop, D. (1995), *Ocean of Sound: Aether Talk, Ambient Sound and Imaginary Worlds*, New York: Serpent's Tail.

Weidenbaum, M. (1996), 'Popp Music: Oval, Microstoria, and the Man Behind their Curtains' at the online archive *Disquiet: Ambient/Electronica* (http://www.dnai.-com/~marc/popp.html). Originally published in *Tower Records Pulse!* Dec. 1996.

Discography

Babbitt, M. (1990), *Philomel* on *Electro Acoustic Music: Classics*, Neuma Records.

Berio, L. (1998), *Thema: Omaggio a Joyce* and *Visage* on *Many More Voices*, BMG.

DJ Spooky, That Subliminal Kid (1996), *Songs of a Dead Dreamer*, Asphodel.

Fripp, R. (1981), *Let the Power Fall*, Editions EG.

Fripp, R. (1995), *1995 Soundscapes Live*, Discipline Global Mobile.

Glass, P. (1983), *Koyaanisqatsi: Original Soundtrack from the Film*, Antilles Records.

Heldon (1973), *Electronique Guerilla*, Cuneiform Records.

Napalm Death (1988), *From Enslavement to Obliteration*, Earache Records.

Pinhas, Richard (1996), *De l'Un et du Multiple*, Spalax.

The Residents (1979), *The Third Reich and Roll*, Ralph Records.

Schizotrope (Pinhas, R. and Dantec, M.) (1999), *Le Plan*, Sub Rosa.

Schizotrope (Pinhas, R. and Dantec, M.) (2000), *The Life and Death of Marie Zorn: North American Tour 1999*, Cuneiform Records.

Various Artists (1995), *Folds and Rhizomes for Gilles Deleuze*, Sub Rosa.

Various Artists (1996), *In Memoriam Gilles Deleuze*, Mille Plateaux.
Various Artists (1996), *Double Articulation – Another Plateau*, Sub Rosa.
The Who (1969), *Tommy*, MCA Records.

Notes

1. This text is an excerpt from a much longer essay, co-written (in distinct sections) with Daniel W. Smith, entitled 'What I Hear is Thinking Too: Deleuze and Guattari Go Pop' that was published in the online journal *ECHO: A Music-Centered Journal* 3 (1) (2001) (http://www.echo.ucla.edu/Volume3–Issue1/smithmurphy/index.html). The editors of this volume and I would like to thank Dan and the editors of *ECHO* for their permission to republish this section of the essay.

2. A year later Sub Rosa released a second CD of tributes to Deleuze. *Double Articulation* consists of revisions of the tracks from *Folds and Rhizomes*: the artists involved swapped tapes and remixed each other's work. In order to keep our discussion of the musicians as focused as possible, we have chosen to examine the original mixes rather than the remixes.

3. For a Deleuze/Guattarian sociological analysis of the techno music scene with which these labels are associated, see Fitzgerald 1998.

4. On this significant transition, see Born 1995: 183–93, 207–10.

5. For example DJ Spooky, who is discussed below, writes, 'Based on the notion that all sonic material can be manipulated with the same ease that computers now generate composite images, the DJ combines the musical expression of other musicians with their [sic] own and in the process creates a seamless flow of music' (DJ Spooky, 'Flow My Blood the DJ Said', included as liner notes to his debut album *Songs of a Dead Dreamer* 1996: 8).

6. On the technologisation of everyday activity, see Hardt and Negri: 7–11.

7. See Leibniz 1981: 54: 'To hear this noise as we do, we must hear the parts which make up this whole, that is the noise of each wave, although each of these little noises makes itself known only when combined confusedly with all the others, and would not be noticed if the wave which made it were by itself.'

8. DJ Spooky That Subliminal Kid (the name refers to a character in the final chapter of William S. Burroughs' *Nova Express*, 'Pay Color' [129ff]) is, after Richard Pinhas, the musician whose work is most consistently and closely bound up with Deleuze and Guattari's philosophy. Unlike Pinhas, who comes out of the 1970s progressive rock/ambient music scene, DJ Spooky is associated with the 1990s hip hop and 'illbient' scene. See 'Flow My Blood the DJ Said,' pp. 7 and 14.

9. Something similar happens in the hyperkinetic form of punk rock known as 'grindcore': simple chords and rhythmic patterns are played so fast that they begin to form higher-level gradients of sonorous density and diffusion in which the original chord patterns are rendered imperceptible. The early work of Napalm Death, for example the album *From Enslavement to Obliteration*, is perhaps the most significant manifestation of this form of smoothness emerging from extremely rigid striation.

10. On this technique of overlapping or superposition in general, and Glass's music in particular, see Richard Pinhas's discussion with Deleuze in Deleuze 1998: 209–14.

11. Charles has collaborated with Oval on a CD entitled *Dok*, in which the German musicians use Charles' field recordings as material for electronic processing.

12. The classic statement of this is Louis Althusser's 'Ideology and Ideological State Apparatuses' in Althusser 1971: 170–83. Althusser's formulation draws explicitly on Lacan's reading of Freud.
13. This is a key element in Adorno's argument in Adorno 1990; see especially p. 54. For the most influential exposition of this model of the voice, see Silverman 1988.
14. See for example 'Twenty-seventh Series of Orality' in Deleuze 1990, especially pp. 193–5.
15. See Deleuze and Guattari 1977: ch. 2. Although they do not explicitly take Adorno as one of their targets in this critique, his model of pop music is clearly implicated in it; see the Adorno texts cited above.
16. See Engh in Dunn and Jones 1994: 130–1.
17. See Deleuze and Guattari's commentary on Berio's *Visage* in Deleuze and Guattari 1987: 96 and 546, Note 91. On *Thema*, see Murphy 1999.
18. Chris Cutler, who was close to The Residents and studied their techniques, describes the production of *The Third Reich and Roll* as follows: it was 'made by running the songs to be copied on one track and then playing along with them, adding part by part and finally erasing the original–then cutting and montaging the whole into a long single work. A tribute to/vicious parody of pop' (Cutler 1993: 84).
19. For examples of Fripp's work, see his albums *Let the Power Fall* (1981) and the trilogy *1995 Soundscapes Live* (1995).
20. In the full version of this essay, we examine Deleuze and Guattari's theory of music (sect. I) as well as their textual references to popular music and their involvement in popular music performance or production (sect. II).

Chapter 9

Music and the Socio-Historical Real: Rhythm, Series and Critique in Deleuze and O. Revault d'Allonnes

Jean-Godefroy Bidima
Translated by Janice Griffiths

Introduction

At least three difficulties arise when one attempts to study the status of Deleuze's music: first, the fact that he was not a musician, unlike a number of his contemporaries, such as Vladimir Jankélévitch or Theodor W. Adorno, and more importantly, that he had never written either a treatise on musical composition, or a monograph on a great musician. Invited by Pierre Boulez, along with Michel Foucault and Roland Barthes, to Institut de Recherche et Coordination Acoustique/Musique IRCAM in Paris in order to comment on five works chosen for them,[1] Deleuze, in a paper entitled 'Why Us, Non-musicians?',[2] maintains that what interests him while listening to these pieces is the musical tempo, which allows him to sketch both the 'particular profiles of the tempo' and to undertake a 'true cartography of the variables'.[3] Deleuze's specific intention is to surprise through music by demonstrating how the tempo is perpetually heterogeneous.[4] The difficulty resides in the fact that the temporality does not summarise the music in its entirety, and that the 'pick up' method, which consists of withholding here and there a few points of view of the music, can be a handicap. Why? Because 'Deleuze thought of music as an infinite discretion. Several references launched here and there, and more often a silence that opens large the doors of musical creation on a renewal that in the 80s was no longer expected' (Cohen-Levinas 1998: 141).

The second difficulty, raised by Rancière and relative to the particular status of Deleuze's discourse, questions what might be called 'Deleuze's aesthetic'. Rancière admits, 'It is not a question for me of situating a Deleuzian aesthetic within the general context of Deleuze's views. The reason is simple: Deleuze's views . . . I do not yet know what they are; I am searching. And the so-called aesthetic texts of Deleuze are a means of drawing nearer to these' (Rancière 1998: 525). How can one address the theme of music in Deleuze's work without first having clarified what his particular aesthetic is?

The third difficulty that arises concerns the problem of classification. When studying music, philosopher-aestheticians do so in two ways: either they adopt a philosophical approach or the theoretician, armed with a philosophy of history, samples elements in the musical corpus that confirm his or her own process. It is thus a musicological approach that studies in minute detail the content of musical text. As for Deleuze, we do not know very well where he stands, since although he spoke a great deal about painting, his remarks on music remain scarce. This is perhaps the reason why some – including Richard Pinhas, a former student of Deleuze – studied music with Deleuze by first taking a detour via Nietzsche (Pinhas 2001). Or, is it perhaps the reason why the musicologist, Cohen-Lévinas, in a somewhat enigmatic formula, entitled one of her articles 'Deleuze Musicien?'?

It is of little importance if Deleuze is a musician or not; what is important here is to compare his musical conception with that of a comrade, friend and contemporary, such as Oliver Revault d'Allonnes. François Châtelet, a colleague of Deleuze and of Lyotard at the University of Paris VIII, and to whom Foucault suggested the candidature of senior lecturer (Châtelet 1977: 89), cites among his comrades and friends at the Sorbonne – after the war and just before 1950 – Deleuze, and Olivier Revault d'Allonnes (Châtelet 1977: 89). Significant is his statement 'Gilles Deleuze, Félix Guattari, Jean-François Lyotard . . . are old and dear friends . . .' (Châtelet 1977: 89). Revault d'Allonnes and Deleuze, according to this statement, knew each other and above all frequented the Sorbonne during the same period. One of their professors, Maurice Patronnier de Gandillac, along with Alquié, Bachelard and Hyppolite, recollects his students between the years 1948 and 1949, mentioning names such as Althusser, Jean Deprun, François Dagognet, Deleuze and Revault d'Allonnes (Gandillac 1998: 292–5). How did these two thinkers, who knew the same educators and lived the same events marking twentieth-century France, conceive of music? How, for them, did music pose the problem of liberating the subject? To respond to this question, we shall first explore the place of music in relation to Deleuze's philosophical disposition, then examine the functioning of the relation between music and society for Revault d'Allonnes in order to evaluate finally the limits of Deleuze's views concerning the relationship between music and the critique of society. I will not undertake a comparative study here, but will follow each of these philosophers in his relation to music, and through these parallel itineraries will be in a position to formulate a critique of Deleuze on these precise points.

Music and Becoming in Deleuze

Deleuze speaks of music in his exploration of 'becoming' in *A Thousand Plateaus*, in particular when he examines the concept of the *ritornello*, or refrain. In order better to grasp the nuances of the connection between music, subjectivity, critique and society, we should try to understand the diverse constellations woven through his conception of music without taking into account the sequence of chronological variations.[5] This constellation will be composed of the relation between Baroque music, the necessary interconnection between composition of sense and composition of sound, the link between material and essence, the idea of music as a line and as a becoming and the refrain.

'Creased' music, 'folded' music: the infinite and the fold of Baroque

Deleuze defined Baroque as that which infinitely converges through folds. Baroque does not invent things, but folds them, unfolds them and refolds them: 'The Baroque refers . . . to an operative function, to a trait . . . The Baroque fold unfurls all the way to infinity, fold over fold, one upon the other, one upon the other. The Baroque fold unfurls all the way to infinity' (Deleuze 1993: 3). Deleuze adopts the notion of a fold only because it refers to the Multiple and the latter is only grasped in the shape of a labyrinth. 'A labyrinth is said, etymologically, to be multiple because it contains many folds' (Deleuze 1993: 3). These folds concern not only the material that is creased, but also the folds that are found 'in the soul' (Deleuze 1993: 14–26) and it is this which brought Deleuze to work on compossibility, individuality and freedom. But his point of view of music brings him back to the notion of the event, which itself refers to that of the meeting. It is in a particular type of meeting called the 'concert' that Deleuze describes the infinite dialogue of musical instruments, each one perceiving the sound of the other which perceives it in turn:

> Vibrations of sound disperse, periodic movements go through space with their harmonics or submultiples. The sounds have their inner qualities of height, intensity, and timbre. The sources of the sounds . . . are not content only to send sounds out: each one perceives its own, and perceives the others while perceiving its own . . .: 'First the solitary piano grieved, like a bird abandoned by its mate; the violin heard its wail and responded to it like a neighbouring tree . . .' (Deleuze 1993: 80)

This cooperation between instruments indicates that music is the domain of possibilities, of potentialities: 'And the notes of the scale are eternal objects, pure Virtualities that are actualized in the origin, but also pure Possibilities that are attained in vibrations or flux' (Deleuze 1993: 80). A fold is a labyrinth, and thus a musical sound is a fold, a flow, a source of possibility, and in consequence a labyrinth.

If the Baroque was, according to Deleuze, an attempt to reconstitute classical reason, in the 'neo-Baroque':

> with its unfurling of divergent series in the same world, comes the irruption of incompossibilities on the same stage . . . In its turn the harmony goes through a crisis that leads to a broadened chromatic scale, to an emancipation of the dissonance or unresolved accords . . . not brought back to a tonality. (Deleuze 1993: 82)

The musical model is the most apt at making the rise of harmony in the Baroque understood, and then the dissipation of the tonality in the neo-Baroque: from the harmonic closure to the opening into a polytonality, or as Boulez says, a 'polyphony of polyphonies' (Deleuze 1993: 82). Deleuze uses the musical model in a heuristic manner to rethink the Baroque; he accentuates only the music, in the way that it folds and unfolds, in the way that it wants to be the pure reserve of potentialities, opening outwards onto the infinite.

The haptic: the composition of the senses and the composition of sounds

Deleuze allows for both a haptic vision and a haptic act of listening. A haptic vision is that which, from the easel of the painter, summons not only the vision (the eye) but more importantly *the act of listening* (the ears) and *the touch*. Ordinarily, a painting arouses a look, but in the haptic optic, the sight or act of listening to a work of art should arouse, summon and reveal all the senses. The pictorial is thus musical, and it is this reversibility of the senses composing amongst themselves (the act of listening composes with the vision which itself composes with the tactile) that characterises the haptic vision. The composition of sounds that are music becomes a *composition of the senses;* in the act of listening, it is the sight and the touch that are at play. Three reasons explain this bias for the haptic aesthetic sensibility: the non-segregation of the senses, the notion of excess and an acquaintance with Pierre Boulez. Firstly, art should lead the subject to an experience of multi-sensoriality, meaning that one should not partition the senses. Secondly music is addressed both to the ear and to sight and this leads Deleuze to demand of art that it exceeds, that overflows the smaller transfers. The act of listening must *overflow its own region* to reach vision, and the latter should produce *a line of flight* to join the tactile. Art can be respectable only by denying its own territory. Thirdly, Deleuze draws this idea from Pierre Boulez, who believes that music is made with sounds, with the writing of gestures and concepts (Boulez 1981: 443). Through the de-compartmentalisation of the senses and the notion of excess and overflowing, Deleuze challenges the ancient conception of the Fine Arts. He wants to bring them nearer, not to make a homogeneous merger of arts, but to underline their heterogeneity. And when we speak of art as a system (in the expression systems of fine-arts), it refers to art as a total system, and it is exactly this idea of totality that Deleuze challenges, 'In no way do we believe in a fine-arts system; we believe in very diverse problems whose solutions are found in heterogeneous arts. To us, Art is a false concept, a solely nominal concept . . .' (Deleuze and Guattari 1987: 300–1). Art as a concept subsumes particular forms of art leading to a consideration of the work of art as that 'in itself', an autonomous sphere, an end in itself functioning through its own demands.

Deleuze objects to such an autonomisation of the work of art, because for him, 'art is never an end in itself; it is only a tool for blazing life lines' (Deleuze 1987: 186). Art is only a means of setting in motion within us our becoming. Thus one must not close the system.

Music between difference and repetition: the material and the essence

In his book *Proust and Signs*, Deleuze defines the mission of a work of art, within which he studies the notions of essence and material style. For Deleuze, by way of Proust, the work of art helps us to discover time, a time that reveals a primordial complication, 'There is only the work of art that lets us regain time: the work of art is "the only means of regaining time lost". It bears the highest signs, whose meaning is situated in a primordial complication' (Deleuze 2000: 46). Deleuze uses the term 'complication' in its neo-Platonist sense, which would have that the original state preceding all development is a complication that 'envelops the many in the One and affirms the unity of the multiple' (Deleuze 2000: 45). Once art has allowed us to access time, Deleuze brings us to the notion of essence. The latter is not based on identity of self to self, but rather 'is always a birth of the world' (Deleuze 2000: 48); it is a metamorphosis. The essence 'which is ultimate difference' should thus be incarnated in its style. If 'essence is always a birth', then 'style is that continuous and refracted birth . . . in substances [*matières*] . . . Style is not the man, style is essence itself' (Deleuze 2000: 48). If the essence is difference, repetition and complication, how is it incarnated? The essence incarnates itself in a material and in art; 'the substances are spiritualized' (Deleuze 2000: 50). Art is 'a veritable transmutation of substance' (Deleuze 2000: 47) the reason for which the true theme of a work of art as a piece of music 'is therefore not the subject the words designate, but the unconscious themes, the involuntary archetypes in which the words, but also the colours and the sounds, assume their meaning and life' (Deleuze 2000: 47). It is this metamorphosis that situates all of artistic creation, and it is probably this that makes the production of artistic signs already a means of thinking. The sign (pictorial or musical) is the subject of an encounter into which it is contingently inscribed. The musical sign is therefore that which, somehow, guarantees us an encounter with contingency.

Music and the diagonal

Deleuze establishes a sort of analogy between musical representation and pictorial representation: 'musical representation . . . draws a horizontal, melodic line . . . On the other hand, it draws a vertical, harmonic line or plane . . . Pictorial representation has an analogous form . . . not only because the painting has a vertical and a horizontal . . .' (Deleuze and Guattari 1987: 295). But what is important in these lines is to trace *the diagonal* – and to do so he contrasts the *punctual system* in which '[T]he line and the diagonal remain entirely subordinated to the point because they serve as coordinates for a point' – and the *linear system* – from which we can '[F]ree the line, free the diagonal' (Deleuze and Guattari 1987: 295). Neither musician nor painter has this intention. Deleuze and Guattari find in Boulez this process of tracing the diagonals, 'When Boulez casts himself in the role of historian of music, he does so in order to show how a great musician . . . invents a diagonal running between the harmonic vertical and the melodic horizon' (Deleuze and Guattari 1987: 296). The relationship of music with time then becomes quite distinctive, a diagonal performing a de-territorialisation by abandoning the points. The line is that which frees the point, from its origin, leaving only streams of becoming. This 'non-pulsed' time is in the pure becoming and hates chronological history with its past, its present and its future: 'the musician can say *par excellence* "I hate the faculty of memories, I hate memories". And this because he or she affirms the power of becoming' (Deleuze and Guattari 1987: 296–7). Music becomes in this way a block of expression through diagonals, and it is by way of music that we have access to joy, to destruction and to death, 'Music is never tragic; music is joy . . . But there are times it necessarily gives us a taste for death . . . Music has a thirst for destruction'. (Deleuze and Guattari 1987: 299). It is what brings us to say that music contains within it the refrain. '[T]he refrain is properly musical content' (Deleuze and Guattari 1987: 299). Music is therefore a process of transformation of oneself and of other, but society and its classes here remain rather quiet.

Music and History for Revault d'Allonnes

Rebetiko: popular music and reification

Revault d'Allonnes begins with the rehabilitation of the Subject in art. The subject as we see it is not only the individual subject who creates, or the author who receives both praise and disapproval. In musical creation, there can be a sort of 'collective subject' that creates, which Revault d'Allonnes believes he sees in the music of Greek Rebetiko:

> We have up until now studied only works of art produced by a well-known individual creator. But it would be an error and an illegitimate limitation to believe that the study and the rehabilitation of the Subject in artistic creation is necessarily that of the individual Subject, of the famous personality . . . who frees himself or herself from the mass. (d'Allonnes 1973: 143)

How does a 'collective subjectivity' (d'Allonnes 1973: 143) produce a musical work and what is its relationship to society? To respond to this question, Revault d'Allonnes takes the example of Rebetiko, a popular music form appearing around the year 1922 on the banks of the Aegean Sea and in 1950s Greece – as the ferment *par excellence* of social critique. Revault d'Allonnes enumerates several reasons for the choice of this form of music. Firstly, it is a negative music that objects and, in doing so, creates. It creates a form of 'elective affinity' (Goethe) between the members who practise it, promoting in this way the dawning of a form of subjectivity that establishes itself only in inter-subjectivity and in a co-affiliation to the same space of values, 'Rebetiko is an art in which individuals communicate at the level of smiles and half-words, in other words through a mutual recognition of their semi-clandestine affiliation to the group' (d'Allonnes 1973: 144). The question that seems funda-mental here (and which Revault d'Allonnes does not raise) is that of knowing how to construct 'orders of recognition' (Ricoeur 1995: 200–1) within the inter-subjectivity of artistic creation. Rebetiko was a music damned by the good-thinking people of Greek society. As a form of art, it was not recognised; in terms of its social criteria, '[R]ebetiko became an exterior sign which sufficed for police oppression to rain down on a specific social milieu' (d'Allonnes 1973: 144). And as a form of subjectivity, Rebetiko was 'refused both by popular classes who accused it of debauchery, and by the supposedly revolutionary apparatus who were afraid of its romantic and anarchistic tendencies' (d'Allonnes 1973: 144). According to Revault d'Allonnes, we can define Rebetiko by four criteria. Firstly, the 'morphological criterion': impoverishment of vocabulary, elements of slang referring to 'milieu': 'primitive style; rigorous rhythm . . . simple orchestration on two instruments (bouzouki and baglamas)' (d'Allonnes 1973: 146). Next, he counts the 'criterion of creation': appearance amongst the poorest social stratum and the least educated of urban sub-proletariat; 'bad-boy' music (*rebet* in Turkish means 'outside the law'); but the creator is always an 'individual' even though the place of composition was most often 'the local gathering place . . . such as the tavern' (d'Allonnes 1973: 146). We should also note what Revault d'Allonnes calls the 'criterion of diffusion . . . this diffusion is always oral . . .' (d'Allonnes 1973: 146), and the 'functional criterion . . . [characterising] rebetiko as an art consciously created "against the world"' (d'Allones 1973: 146).

Through rebetiko music, Revault d'Allonnes wants to return the notion of negation to the work of art; he is simply borrowing this idea from Adorno to nourish his own viewpoint, 'To accept culture as a whole is to deprive it of the ferment which is its very truth: its negation' (Adorno 1967: 28). In order to understand the continuation of Revault d'Allonnes's views and above all the essential place that he gives to negation, we might refer to an article he wrote on Adorno where he maintains that:

> in short, the immanence of negation has two consequences, which are the immanence of conflict, and that of its solutions. Negative thought renounces any aspiration for external freedom, through the same movement that forbids it from despairing over what appears to be the most hopeless of situations. (d'Allonnes 1975: 146)

Rebetiko is therefore that music which maintains the promise of happiness within an immanence worn away by reification. This relationship between musical creation and social critique is found once again in Revault d'Allonnes's treatment of the music of Beethoven.

From Beethoven to Xenakis

Revault d'Allonnes begins his commentary on Beethoven with a sequence that indicates his own philosophy, first the incomprehensibility of works of art as a condition for comprehension, and next utopia as a condition for action. 'If Beethoven so powerfully attracts the written, if he solicits each of us to better understand, it is precisely because he is incomprehensible – and in some respects, he puts us on the edge of comprehension. On the edge: with the risk of falling in . . .' (d'Allones 1982: 11). Incomprehensibility is a situation that reveals a *threshold*. The threshold divides, connects and only introduces so as to exclude. The threshold is therefore the region *par excellence* of possibilities and of the incomprehensibility of the work of art, making the latter the ultimate threshold, a swarming of possibilities. Taking up Adorno once again and his work in *Aesthetic Theory*, Revault d'Allonnes asks about the relation of the work of art to time and to action:

> Theodor Adorno says that the greatest of works are waiting. To be understood? But perhaps they have several meanings . . . To be forgotten? . . . If it is true that a work of art is utopian, that it searches to prefigure in the world of appearance what should be in that of reality . . . The great works are waiting to become true, because they are already, but they are waiting for their truth to be fulfilled. (d'Allonnes 1982: 11)

It is thus by way of utopia and social transformation that Revault d'Allonnes addresses Beethoven. D'Allonnes speaks first of the pleasure he has in listening to the Seventh Symphony and establishes an equivalence between *listening* and *existing*. Existing is to leave oneself – it is the meaning of the prefix *ex* – and to have a taste for the outside, for the unexpected and for the event. Like existence, the act of listening has its sense of outside which each time shakes up the inside, 'I heard on an old record . . . *the Seventh Symphony* . . . Since then, I listen, in other words I no longer exist except through my ears, through that sense of outside and that sense of happening . . . each time this outside stirs up the inside' (d'Allonnes 1982: 61). But the act of listening itself refers to an immanence that makes the music of Beethoven both the prelude to a utopia and a sort of 'transcendence into the immanence' (to borrow a term that is dear to Ernst Bloch). Revault d'Allonnes concludes:

> one of the hypotheses that passes through these pages is that the music of Beethoven, because it is a search for imaginary powers, escapes social determinisms . . . This same dimension that has made music something that outlives its time and its place of arrival is found in its current power not to allow itself to be absorbed by commercial and technical methods. (d'Allonnes 1982: 33)

For Revault d'Allonnes, music carries this utopia, which consists of outliving and transcending social determinisms to suggest something

else. Here social transformation is important. In an article entitled
'Xenakis and Modernity', he examines the alliance that Xenakis makes
between science and art. What he admires in the latter is the freedom that
Xenakis gives to the polyphonic tradition in adding, next to the *collective*
privilege, the notion of *singularity*. For him, the Western tradition treats
orchestral series in large blocks:

> the quartet of the orchestra constitutes the nucleus in relation to which the
> brass instruments, the woodwind section and the percussion decide and
> define themselves . . . But in each sub-series, the instruments play in unison.
> The result is an overall effect that makes up the allure . . . of a military
> march, where all the *spahis* in their proper content, are marching in step . . .
> without any of the itineraries being individual. (d'Allonnes 1979: 21)

From this dictatorship of the group over the individual, Xenakis, according to Revault d'Allonnes, would like to analyse the mass phenomenon so
as to extract individual sounds which are no longer directed by the
dictatorship of the series. By doing so, it is the privilege of the singular
that d'Allonnes celebrates here. Xenakis

> treats acoustic phenomena with the help of conceptual instruments and
> calculation processes that mathematics . . . puts at his disposal . . .
> Musically speaking, we obtain the effects of mass rigorously laid out,
> which push forward the inter-dependence of the series and the component.
> (d'Allonnes 1979: 21)

For Revault d'Allonnes, the music of Xenakis permits us to go beyond the
antagonism between the all and the part in order to underline their
reciprocal determinisms. This interaction is similar to the problem of
difference. 'Each of us in this society, are we not like an instrumentalist in
Xenakis' orchestra, soloist and yet in one's place, in accordance with the
series and different from all others, and all the same knowing and wanting
freedom?' (d'Allonnes 1979: 26).

Revault d'Allonnes is here closer to Adorno than to Deleuze when he
affirms the power of the singular in each of us, indicating in *Minima
Moralia* 'the Whole is the false' (Adorno 1981: 50).

Around the 'Polytopes' of Xenakis: Revault d'Allonnes and the Constellations Method

To break the hegemony of certain forms and certain sounds in perception
and audition, and to counter with a form of syntactic exposition where
everything is subordinated to a pivot, Adorno advocates always considering a work of art in a paratactic manner; in other words broken up

into constellations around a central theme that does not drive the others. The refusal of hierarchy is a rule here, because the parataxis is the other face of the trial. The latter does not constitute 'a continuum of operations, the thinking does not advance in an unequivocal manner, but on the contrary, moments are weaved together as in a carpet' (Adorno 1992: 56–60, translation modified). Adorno is neither in favour of linearity nor of harmony which he always considers as violence:

> The harmony of the logical work is misinformed by the antagonistic nature of that on which it was clad . . . in defining the concepts, one in relation to the other, in terms of their function in the strong parallelogram of things, it refuses to bend itself to this superior concept to which all must be subordinated. (1992: 45, translation modified)

Revault d'Allonnes takes up this method of Adorno's and applies it to the exposition of the 'Polytopes' of Xenakis. In displaying the work of the musician, d'Allonnes maintains that:

> the order of documents, texts, dates, and ideas were voluntarily deconstructed by us so that each one would be obliged to reconstruct itself and in its own way. 'Polytopic' works, in other words dispersed but united, multiple but homogenous, made from variation and from imagination . . . As he does in his works, you will yourself find or create the unity, your unity, from this diversity. (d'Allonnes 1975: 9)

In the aesthetic conceptions of Xenakis, Revault d'Allonnes notes a reversal between *time* and *space*. 'Polytopes', as their name indicates, refer to space, but the works are events situated in time. Xenakis, by formalising music using computers, removes its acoustic characteristics so as to conserve only the curves and the figures that constitute its spatiality; polytopes are thus a form of music 'outside-sound'. This does not mean that they are 'outside-time', the time of polytopes is consistent with space. This reversal of space and time refers us once again to a *haptic* aesthetic vision as defined by Deleuze. D'Allonnes believes he has deciphered in Xenakis a tendency to break the borders of artistic disciplines, and an opening of senses to a multiplicity of sensations. The hearing becomes seeing and the sight becomes listening. Revault d'Allonnes summarises this reversal of 'Polytopes' in the following way:

> Polytopes are key-works of this new art of space and time, where time governs and submits to space, where space is ordered so as to emphasize time . . . the distinction between architecture and music, and even the division of work between architects and musicians, is perceived by Xenakis as a constraint, or even as an oppression. (d'Allonnes 1975: 19)

Through this commentary on Xenakis, d'Allonnes establishes a link between an atomised conception of art and that which insists on auto-reflexivity as well as the interpenetration of the senses (hearing, becoming, seeing) as preludes to a break in social barriers. However, there is a danger which d'Allonnes underlines in the work of Xenakis. 'First danger: to pass for a false creator who forces oneself in front of a computer . . .' (d'Allonnes 1975: 48). D'Allonnes insists that the music of Xenakis must not be picked up by the cultural industry as an electronic gadget. This is a real danger, so much so that we are assured that:

> in terms of the conciliaiton between the absurd world and works that are not absurd, the bet is and can only be lost. Whoever seeks to find in Xenakis work the valorisation of the world or its gentle acceptance will not find them there . . . Xenakis is not the apologist for the world as it is, but the prophet of what it can become the day when men renounce both the nostalgia of a lost past and the fatalism of an ungovernable present, taking it in hand to lead it where they would like. (Xenakis 1979: 56–8)

The music of Xenakis thus makes one take responsibility outside of art by manufacturing a utopia through technique. We witness Xenakis's introduction of game theory in musical composition, that of the freedom to glimpse the unexpected, the possible. And in this aesthetic of Xenakis, the essential is no longer truly the notion of beauty in the way that it often accompanies the stakes of art, but that of *novelty*. The *Novum* demonstrates – as Ernst Bloch says – that reality has no more truth than the possible and that the *nondum* (the not-yet being) is one of the essential conditions for the advent of the work of art. And Xenakis concludes, 'I could not define beauty. I have had much deception in this area . . . [W]hat is that which is permanent? Is it the acceleration of the acquired, the difference between the point of departure and the point of arrival? In relation to something given, to do something new: here is what is interesting' (Xenakis 1979: 56–8). The new is therefore the major stake of a society that loves repetition, and above all detests everything that is dissonant.

Schoenberg and his Moses and Aaron: *Subject, reflection and freedom*

In the special edition of the *Review d'Esthétiques* dedicated to Adorno, Revault d'Allonnes undertakes the study of Schoenberg's *Moses and Aaron*. D'Allonnes, in contrast to what Adorno does in his *Quasi una Fantasia* (1992), does not interpret Schoenberg's piece in terms of the few important moments of the work, but according to the genetic method, which consists of 'reporting on most of the structures of the piece from origins more or less remote from the project' (d'Allonnes 1985: 47).

In 1928, Schoenberg wrote a drama in three acts entitled *der Biblische Weg* (the Biblical Way). In the first act, a certain Max Aruns, a Jewish man from Vienna, wants to found a Jewish state in Africa with the help of the Americans and an African emperor of Ammongea. The project falls through and the wise Asseino speaks to Aruns in a way that recalls *Moses and Aaron*, the opera that it would later become:

> Max Aruns, you want to be Moses and Aaron in one and the same person? Moses, to whom God concedes thought but to whom speech is lacking; and Aaron, who could not conceive of thought, but who was capable of expressing it . . . (d'Allonnes 1985: 49)

But for d'Allonnes, Schoenberg's *Moses and Aaron* reflects the drama of the complicated relationship between the subject, freedom, and the authority of the group. God, this dictatorial power, is obliged, in order to give the law to the Hebrew people, to negotiate with them through Moses, the *mediation* of God. This divine mediation meets *the mediation* of men, in other words Aaron. Aaron and Moses re-present – they are the 'place-holders' – and this representation plays out the destiny of multiple relations that exist between *the powers* (God), *the law* (the Ten Commandments), *the group* (the Hebrews), *the interpreters* of the law (Moses interprets that of God and Aaron that of the golden Lamb), *the contract* (the law is a contract between the Hebrews and their God) and *autonomy* (the people break the contract with God by manufacturing the golden Lamb). Revault d'Allonnes, through his reading of Schoenberg, links music and politics.

Critique and Dialectic

The 'Minor' Music

In an interview for the newspaper, *Libération*, dated 25 October 1989, and reprinted in *Negotiations 1972–1990* (Deleuze 1995), Deleuze maintains that the research movement of his time allowing university disciplines to meet, rather than remaining isolated, is an initiative to be encouraged. To this effect, he cites the work of Barthes, which runs from the syntactic to the pragmatic, then cites Sarraute who has philosophy and the novel coincide in her work, and finally he notes 'Labov's research in pragmatics, his opposition to Chomsky, and his relationship with the languages of ghettos and specific districts' (Deleuze 1995: 28). These languages produce zones of continuous variation and in doing so create an 'outside'. If Deleuze recognises, on a linguistic level, the importance of these ghetto languages, why did he not address the music of minorities and minority music? He justifies this of course by claiming that the minority is not comprehensible in quantity but through a process by which a language establishes from within a programme of deterritorialisation, of flight, tracing diagonal lines (Deleuze and Guattari 1986: 22–7). In other words, ' "minor" ' no longer qualifies certain literature, but the revolutionary conditions of all literature within that is called great' (Deleuze and Guattari 1986: 22–7, translation modified). In adapting this, we could say that major music, that which interests Deleuze, could find its revolutionary character within its 'minority', but it is nevertheless the case that Deleuze was not interested, at the time that he wrote these lines on the musical ritornello, in *Zouk*,[6] emerging at this time in France, or even in African music such as *Soukous*,[7] which had also made its breakthrough in France. These two forms of music offer an example of 'minor music' in the sense that Deleuze uses the term in literature. According to Deleuze and Guattari there are three characteristics of minor literature: that it uses language's ' "high co-efficient" of deterritorialisation, that it opens the individual onto the political, and that it operates through a collective assemblage of enunciation' (Deleuze and Guattari 1986: 16–17, translation modified). First, *Zouk* deterritorialises the French language through the revision of vocabulary and of syntax, next its existence is linked to the claiming of Caribbean identity within French society, and finally the lyrics of *Zouk* reflect the construction of a Caribbean subjectivity on a collective level. Why is it that Deleuze did not pay attention to the emergence of this music in the French cultural space in which he was an informed observer? The following question should be asked: how could Deleuze have passed by this music that was not of European culture, but existed in European space? To speak of dodecaphony, of atonality and of the constituent discontinuities of a music that traces lines of flight like that of Boulez, is to repeat the same: Western–Capitalist–Judeo–Christian civilisation!

Another question to be asked with regard to the Deleuzian musical aesthetic is that concerning *the dialectic appreciation of composers*. In addition to the notion of *mediation*, dialectic conception allows for an *overtaking*, of the old by the new, and yet this overtaking is a recapturing of the old. This means that an innovative music allows for – it goes without saying – old elements. A music that traces the lines of flight indeed escapes toward an elsewhere, but in all flight one carries on one's back provisions from the old existence. Deleuze, in his evaluation of Boulez, does not demonstrate how his very innovative style is also a suppression that is in fact a conservation of the old (in the Hegelian sense of *Aufhebung*!). With Deleuze there is a kind of dualist seizure of music: on the one hand, the old tonal, conservative school; and on the other, the new, atonal. How do the new and the old overlap to the point of producing a unity in diversity? While Deleuze insists upon the very important notion of *detail* in music, Adorno thinks that music which produces a variance like that of Mahler creates new from old; from the old material of the tonal closure he has manifested the other from this same. 'While drawing on the old compulsion for repetition, its objectivity [that of the symphonic music of Mahler] breaks with it at the same time through the continual production of novelty. From the timelessness of the same that repeats itself, Mahler allows historic time to appear' (Adorno 1996: 105, translation modified). Perhaps Deleuze does not perceive this dialectic because his musical analysis does not begin with the works of the refrain, but with the concepts. In fact, it is through the notions of lines of flight, diagonal and deterritorialisation that he grasps music. By starting from musical works, Deleuze could have avoided two sorts of abstraction that Adorno denounces in his aesthetic theory: philosophical abstraction and the fetishisation of the work. Philosophical abstraction is content with occurrences taken from the musical corpus in order to confirm the philosopher's approach, while fetishisation of the work is characteristic of certain musicologists who study the work in a literal way without revealing the 'restrained truth' (Adorno). To be concerned about the immanence here consists of beginning with the work so as to extract concepts. The work is an imperfect translation of history, but Deleuze does not like history; he is more concerned about becoming. For him, history evokes the past and the future, the origin and the advent; Deleuze likes the becoming and not the essence; he prefers 'the circumstances of the thing: in which case, where, when, and how, etc.?' (Deleuze 1995: 31). Neither does Deleuze like the term 'revolution'. He prefers that of 'involution', since the revolution refers to the interpretation and the notion of competence, while it is only with involution that we are faced with the decoded, the *a-subjective*, the *a-signifiant* and the informal that make the imperceptible the site of performance. The revolution is interpretation and the involution experimentation.

Deleuze: an anti-democrat?
The relationship between music and the transformation of society for Deleuze is subordinated to his conception of democracy. Deleuze does not believe – and in this he is loyal to Nietzsche – in democracy, human rights and the notion of public opinion.

On the question of the relationship between philosophy and the city, Deleuze does not believe in any kind of effectiveness on the part of philosophy in the city, and the latter shows through two arguments. First, with regard to 'the State of law', Deleuze responds ironically that 'it is not a great philosophical invention' (Deleuze 1995: 153), and then the role of the philosopher is reduced almost to clandestineness:

> I think there's a public for philosophy and ways of reaching it, but it's a clandestine sort of thinking, a sort of nomadic thinking. The only form of communication one can envisage as perfectly adapted to the modern world is Adorno's model of a message in a bottle, or the Nietzschean model of an arrow shot by one thinker and picked up by another. (Deleuze 1995: 154)

We find with Deleuze an aristocratic philosophy addressed only to his peers, looking down from above at all the actions or odd jobs of 'minor races' clogging up the public place. Deleuze's attitude is along the same lines as the diagnostic outlined by Hannah Arendt, that since the time of Plato, philosophy has set itself up against the city, and that the philosopher cannot feel as such unless (s)he wanders as far as possible from the political arena (Deleuze 1995: 138). This implies a desertion of the field of democratic discussion by the philosopher who does not want to compromise him or herself in opinion.

The notion of public opinion does not find any favour in the eyes of Deleuze either. For him, opinion is truly, as Plato believed, the mistress of errors, but the philosopher is there to lead a war against stupidity as Nietzsche said, a war that is inseparable from anger: 'it is true that philosophy cannot be separated from an anger against the era' (Deleuze 1995: 137). However, the nature of war led by philosophy is rather like that of guerrilla warfare, which is turned toward the interiority of the person:

> Philosophy can have internal battles (idealism – realism, etc.), but these are battles for fun. Not having any power, philosophy cannot engage in battles with powers, and rather leads a war without battles, a guerrilla war against powers. And it cannot speak with them; it has nothing to say to them, nothing to communicate, and leads only negotiations. Since powers are not content with being exterior, but also pass through each of us, it is each one of us who finds that we are continually in negotiations and guerrilla warfare with ourselves. (Deleuze 1995: 27, translation modified)

First point: philosophy has nothing to say to power because it is not a power. Second point: philosophy negotiates through individual interiority. These two arguments initiate topographically the desertion of the public space for individual interiority, in a purely private sphere. The epistemological consequence is that the philosopher fights; (s)he does not discuss. Thought negotiates with itself and is not in dialogue with otherness, 'there are truly people for whom thinking is "discussing a little". Of course it is an idiotic image, but even idiots have made themselves an image of thought' (Deleuze 1995: 148). The reason for which – 'the philosopher has very little taste for discussing. All philosophers flee when hearing the phrase: "we are going to discuss it a little"' (Deleuze 1995: 148). In sum, for Deleuze, philosophy, the creator of concepts *par excellence*, 'has a horror of discussions' (Deleuze and Guattari 1994: 29). Democracy for Deleuze is the reign of public opinion, and yet the latter is always from the area of the largest number, or the majority; it is opposed therefore to the power of the minority who are in essence inventive. Not only is the concept of democracy not new, but it also crushes the new. It conceals the strengths in tension within the social, and public opinion is only an artefact forged by the purveyors of domination. The reign of democracy is that of opinion fabricated by the media. Only the domain of the minor is creative; the majority flattens the becoming and is thus by essence conservative.

Conclusion

Deleuze's views have met with many objections, one of the most serious being that of Badiou which concerns ontology. For Badiou, Deleuze returns to Plato on two key points. Firstly, 'Deleuze's fundamental problem is most certainly not to liberate the multiple, but to submit thinking to a renewed concept of the One' (Badiou 2000: 11). Secondly, Badiou is highly apprehensive of the univocity of the virtual put forward by Deleuze as an eternal truth, 'the "descent" towards the One-true and the "reascent" toward the Multiple-false' (Badiou 2000: 59). It is not necessary to demonstrate the genesis of Badiou's critique of Deleuze, since it is here a matter of grasping the essentials of Badiou's questioning about Deleuze's doctrine of subjectivity. For Badiou, Deleuze's view of the eternal return is conceived of only in relation to that of 'chaos', or to what Deleuze – like Joyce – calls the 'chaosmos'. If Deleuze uses this term, it is to counter all Hellenic and pacific views of the 'cosmos' as being the well-ordered, immutable and sufficient One against the Multiple. Badiou's question to Deleuze in this case becomes pertinent; since the latter does not like dualisms and presents immanence as One, the question would be to know what the Deleuzian doctrine of the One-all-immanent discloses through the theme of 'chaosmos' authorised as definition of subject? One might have preferred that Badiou not economise on his analysis of Deleuze and Guattari's two volumes of *Capitalism and Schizophrenia*, in which Deleuze attempts to re-think the notion of subjectivity away from the Subject, a task with obvious difficulties. But beyond this critique, it is the manner of studying Deleuze that is called into question.

One should read Deleuze while avoiding two simplifications. Firstly, the tendency to paraphrase which consists of mechanically taking Deleuzian concepts and transporting them to another field in order to say that they function well; (we replay the same piece on another stage). Secondly, one can take up the concepts or the views of Deleuze and mechanically connect them to others, 'Deleuze and Kant, Deleuze's concept of "assemblage" and Lacan, etc., etc' (Badiou 2000: 59). These two readings often make Deleuze's views a reservoir of slogans, where one reproduces quotations and concepts by pasting them in a Dadaist manner: 'we proclaim ourselves to be of this or that orientation of the Master and we critique in the name of loyalty to the Master's words'.

What we have attempted to do here is not to interpret Deleuze – the latter so distrusts representative thought! – but (as he said himself) 'experiment'. But we could only experiment with Deleuze in bringing him face to face to an outside, with an *enlarged conception of the other in musical matters*. To do so, we have borrowed a mediation, namely Revault d'Allonnes, his old comrade, who also reflected on the modernity of music. What is revealed is that Deleuze's views, in contrast to those of d'Allonnes, remained very 'official' in musical matters. His assemblages, flows, intensities, deterritorialisations, and his haptic vision of art remained valuable in official music, tolerated, reproduced, and sold by the Western cultural industry. He did not, like d'Allonnes, see how peripheral music, non-tolerated and emanating from popular classes, could produce 'assemblages', 'flows', 'intensities', or 'deterritorializations'. Through an itinerary that takes him from Beethoven, through Xenakis and Schoenberg, up to the Greek Rebetiko, Revault d'Allonnes shows how music plays a major role in the transformation of the history of peoples, in the constitution of a critical subjectivity and in the edification of a public sphere of debate and of deliberation. Jacques Rancière explains:

> the understanding of a thinker is not coinciding with his/her centre. It is, on the contrary, to transport it, to carry it off on a trajectory where his/her articulations are put to use and leave them in play. And thus it is possible to disfigure this thought in order to refigure it otherwise, to escape the restraint of one's own words so as to utter in this foreign language. (Rancière 1998: 525)

In attempting to transport Deleuze, carrying his views outside of his centre – the Western–Capitalist universe of reference – and wanting it to attend to the foreign language of popular music (whether it be African, Chinese or Greek), we were only following Deleuze himself who wanted thought always to be 'experimented' in order to find its points of blockage. Deleuze remains, with the privilege that he gives to the sphere of Western representation, entangled in the Same, and his attempts to find an outside remain movements around and in the Same (European civilisation). His attitude reflects the very aristocratic distance often manifested by these thinker-writers, who are so generous when it comes to defending freedom in their own culture and who decree their valuable cause *a priori* for other cultures. As Deleuze himself says, 'In truth, it is not enough to say "Long live the multiple", difficult as it is to raise that cry. No typographical, lexical or even syntactical cleverness is enough to make it heard. The multiple must be made' (Deleuze and Guattari 1987: 6), and this can only be done if one opens up to other cultures and above all to non-official views that are haughtily ignored by the cautious propositions flowing from our academic pens, never short for arguments and never worried for their own existence. What is music worth, what is its place and its creating and liberating role when the existence of the Subject is threatened by violence? This is the true question that no 'deterritorialization' can bypass.

References

Adorno, T. (1967), *Prisms*, trans. S. Weber and S. Weber, London: Neville Spearman.

Adorno, T. (1981), *Minima Moralia: Essays on a Damaged Life*, trans. E. F. N. Jephcott, New York and London: Verso.

Adorno, T. (1992), *Notes to Literature*, two volumes, trans. S. Weber Nicholsen, New York: Columbia University Press.

Adorno, T. (1992), *Quasi una Fantasia*, trans. R. Livingstone, New York and London: Verso.

Adorno, T. (1996), *Mahler: A Musical Physiognomy*, trans. E. Jephcott, Chicago: University of Chicago Press.

Badiou, A. (2000), *Deleuze: The Clamor of Being*, trans. L. Burchell, Minneapolis: University of Minnesota Press.

Boulez, P. (1981), 'L'Écriture du Musicien, le Regard du Sourd?', *Critique* 408: 443–54.

Châtelet, F. (1977), *Chronique des Idées Perdues*, Paris: Stock.

Cohen-Levinas, D. (1998), 'Deleuze Musicien?', in *Gilles Deleuze Immanence et Vie*, Paris: Presses Universitaries de France, pp. 137–48.

Deleuze, G. (1993), *The Fold: Leibniz and the Baroque*, trans. T. Conley, Minneapolis: University of Minnesota Press.

Deleuze, G. (1995), *Negotiations 1972–1990*, trans. Martin Joughin, London: Continuum Publishing.

Deleuze, G. (2000), *Proust and Signs*, trans. R. Howard, New York and London: Continuum Publishing.

Deleuze, G. and Guattari, F. (1986), *Kafka: Towards a Minor Literature*, trans. D. Polan, Minneapolis: University of Minnesota Press.

Deleuze, G. and Guattari, F. (1987), *A Thousand Plateaus: Capitalism and Schizophrenia*, trans. B. Massumi, Minneapolis: University of Minnesota Press.

Deleuze, G. and Guattari, F. (1994), *What is Philosophy?*, trans. G. Burchell and H. Tomlinson, New York and London: Verso.

Gandillac, Maurice de (1998), *Le Siécle traversé*, Paris: Albin Michel.

Pinhas, R. (2001), *Les Larmes de Nietzsche, Deleuze et la Musique*, Paris: Flammarion.

Rancière, J. (1998), 'Existe-t-il une Esthétique Deleuzienne?', in *Gilles Deleuze, une Vie Philosophique*, ed. Eric Alliez, Paris: Institute Synthélabo, pp. 510–39.

Revault d'Allonnes, O. (1973), *La Création Artistique et les Promesses de la Liberté*, Paris: Klincksieck.

Revault d'Allonnes, O. (1972), 'Xenakis et la Modernité', *L'Arc* 51: 14–36.

Revault d'Allonnes, O. (1975), 'Adorno non Adorno', *Revue d'Esthétique* 1: 165–90.

Revault d'Allonnes, O. (1975), *Xenakis: Polytopes*, Paris: Balland.

Revault d'Allonnes, O. (1982), *Plaisir à Beethoven*, Paris: Christian Bourgois.

Revault d'Allonnes, O. (1985), 'Un Opéra Profane de Schönberg: *Moïse et Aaron*', *Revue d'Esthétique* 8: 40–9.

Ricoeur, P. (1995), *Le Juste*, Paris: Editions Esprit, 1995.

Xenakis, Iannis (1979), 'Changer l'homme' in *L'Arc*, special issue on Xenakis, pp. 56–8.

Notes

1. See IRCAM, work coordinated by Peter Szendy, ed. Centre G. Pompidou and IRCAM 1996: 149–54.
2. Ibid, p. 150.
3. Ibid, p. 150.
4. Ibid, p. 150.
5. Certain works subsequent to *A Thousand Plateaus* will be examined first. What is important here is to follow the relationship between music and certain notions of Deleuzian philosophy.
6. *Zouk* is a Creole word used in Martinique and Guadeloupe to describe evening dances at home using recorded music. *Zouk* is different from ballroom dances in that an orchestra plays at the latter. 'Zouk combines various influences including Haitian compas, Kadans-lypso from the Dominican Republic, Gwoka from Guadeloupe and Funk'. Siron, J. (2002), *Dictionnaire des Mots de la Musique*, Paris: Edition Outre-Mesure: 304.
7. As for *Soukous*, it originates from the Congo. Known since the 1950s, it is a mixture of traditional music and Congolese rumba.

Chapter 10

Cosmic Strategies:
The Electric Experiments of Miles Davis

Marcel Swiboda

> Between '68 and '75, Macero and Miles . . . turned effects into
> instruments . . . Effects are now acoustic prosthetics, audio extensions,
> sonic destratifiers.
>
> (Eshun 1998: 6)

> *CBS MEMORANDUM*
> *FROM: IRVING J. TOWNSEND – TO: TEO MACERO – DATE: 24*
> *OCTOBER 1968*
> *Miles Davis called . . . to tell me that would he like to purchase from*
> *Fender an electric piano, a guitar, bass and tom toms . . .*[1]

Gilles Deleuze, it has to be said, had many a strange idea when it came
to expounding his particular take on philosophy. This was especially the
case in the texts he co-authored with Félix Guattari. One need only list –
even in the most provisional fashion – some of the 'concepts' or
methodological 'tools' they collectively and separately created: bodies
without organs, faciality, the rhizome image of thought, nomadology,
desiring machines, war machines, in addition to many others. Most
notable amongst the work that these two writers produced with regard
to the proliferation of neologisms is without doubt, *A Thousand
Plateaus* (1987), by turns a fascinating, intoxicating and infuriating
brew of monstrous conceptual combinations. Two such combinations
will provide the main philosophical points of reference for this chapter:
the highly inventive and ostensibly rather insane agglomeration of
fragments from a variety of disciplines that forms the plateau entitled,
'10,000 BC: The Geology of Morals (Who Does the Earth Think It Is?)';
and the connections drawn together from a disparate array of sources in
the plateau entitled '1833: Of the Refrain'.[2] The idea is that each plateau
of the book interconnects with others whereby the affective response of
the reader is supposed to intensify as their subjectivity is implicated in

the concepts and ideas as these are gradually folded, refolded and unfolded.[3]

By the end of this piece, a wider array of connections will have been drawn between these two plateaus, and between numerous key concepts informing each: de-/stratification, the diagram, the body without organs, machinic assemblages of bodies and collective assemblages of enunciation, as well as the 'minor' – all key concepts in A Thousand Plateaus. The reason for these choices, which should become gradually clearer as the piece proceeds, is due to the specific case providing the point of departure for the aforementioned connections: the music produced by the African-American jazz performer, composer and band-leader Miles Davis during what has become known as his 'electric' period.[4]

There are a number of reasons why the case of 'electric Miles' forms a worthwhile 'mediator',[5] although it will not be possible to record them all in detail here. Instead it will be necessary to patch the lines of connection into the concepts of Deleuze and Guattari in an illustrative way; firstly, in order to address the criticism levelled at Deleuze by Alain Badiou in his book Deleuze: The Clamor of Being (2000), that his method at once relies on and yet simultaneously effaces his chosen 'cases'. Take for example Badiou's contention with regard to the Cinema books of Deleuze, in which the latter expounds his most sustained case-based analysis of philosophy in its relation to a 'non-philosophical' medium. Badiou claims that – in attempting to find the concepts unique to cinema – one inevitably ends up reverting to a philosophical mode of engagement that forfeits the integrity of the case: 'Let us understand that, under the constraint of the case of cinema, it is . . . always (Deleuze's) philosophy that begins anew and that accuses cinema to be there where it cannot, of itself, be' (Badiou 2000: 14).

For Badiou, Deleuze's philosophy of 'the multiple' is flawed because the latter refuses to relinquish his fundamental ontological claim to combine multiplicity with univocity: the 'One-all'. Badiou's claim is that Deleuze must choose one or the other, univocity or multiplicity, one or all, and thereby effectively accuses him of wanting to have his case-based-cake and eat it, and in so doing reverting to a Platonic privileging of the one rather than the multiple, against Deleuze's overriding claim to the multiple. As a result, the 'repetition of difference' or Deleuze's idea that thought should suspend a diversity of different ways of thinking without reverting to a transcendent reduction of this diversity is – for Badiou – more a repetition of Deleuze's conception of difference, rather than of a properly ontological difference. However, where it comes to the case, Badiou's choice of texts and concepts is somewhat selective and misses out some of the most important case-based instances in Deleuze's work, including those constituting the plateaus of *A Thousand Plateaus*. That is not to say that Badiou's claims do not pose a challenge to the materialist ontology in this work, and it is in part the challenge that Badiou's criticism poses that this piece seeks to address. Badiou's position might be considered strategic, in the sense that he makes a strategic selection from Deleuze's work, and in seeking to address the criticism it will be necessary to counter with a different idea of strategy.

Extensions and Expansions: 1967–75

Between the years 1967 and 1975, Davis and his constantly shifting and expanding band line-ups, not to mention the crucial post-production input of his producer of the time, Teo Macero, yielded an extensive and diverse array of recorded and live material whose overall sonic development was partially conditioned by the advent of the new technologies of the time. This technological watershed came in 1967 with the first inclusion of the Fender Rhodes piano, appearing on a track called 'Water on the Pond' and then on the album *Miles in the Sky*. Both of these recordings would also herald the first appearance of electric guitar, with the line-up expanding within the space of a year to include two additional keyboard roles, most notably on the 1968 album release *In a Silent Way*. By 1969–70 and the recording of Davis's most successful album of the period, *Bitches' Brew*, the line-up had expanded further to include even more keyboard contributions, as well as sitar, electric bass, bass clarinet, two drummers, and Latin percussion.[6] It was on this album also that the wah-wah pedal would make its first marked appearance on a Davis recording, warping and transforming his signature sound as never before.[7]

During the 1970s, things continued to change and expand even further, with the addition of new band members and new instruments: the EMS Synthi A, the Yamaha drum machine and YC45 electric organ, as well as traditional African percussion. By this stage, Davis had started dividing his time between his wah-enhanced trumpet and the Yamaha organ, used to generate chordal swells, percussive or ambient effects. In short, the music of this period featured more of everything: more musicians, more guitars, more electronic devices, more percussion, expanded rhythm sections. It is the work of this later phase of the electric period that is of most interest here, when – at its most intense and its least restrained – the music somehow became indelibly bound up with a number of esoteric associations, stretching from the centre of the Earth out into the reaches of the Cosmos.

Evening, 1 February 1975:
Pangaea, or The Geology of Miles

On 1 February 1975 at the Royal Festival Hall in Osaka, Japan, Davis and his band of the time performed two landmark concerts. The music in these concerts would be abridged and released as two separate and lengthy albums, the first entitled *Agharta* and the second entitled *Pangaea*. These remain to this day the last available musical documents attributed to the name of Miles Davis between 1975 and 1980 as illness, drug abuse and the exhaustion born of constant touring caused him to have a break-down. Although it is not entirely clear how the albums acquired these names, what is beyond question is that each name has a strange, ambivalent history. Their naming symptomatises a number of key aspects of the music of the mid-1970s and the ways in which we might characterise this period.

A number of interesting things have been written on the history of these names, from a variety of different perspectives. David Toop's account of Davis's electric experiments in *Ocean of Sound* points us in the direction of 'a bizarre collection of authorities on the unprovable' (Toop 1995: 94), in particular the work of Joscelyn Godwin in his considered and often tremendously alarming document entitled, *Arktos: The Polar Myth in Science, Symbolism and Nazi Survival* (1996). In this work, he describes the uses and abuses of these names within the writings of a variety of nineteenth- and twentieth-century myth-makers, esotericists and (pseudo-) scientists, one of whom – Saint-Yves d' Alveydre – we shall return to when looking at the first of the two concerts performed on 1 February 1975. In the interests of intelligibility, however, it will be necessary for us to suspend chronology and begin with the second of the two concerts performed on that day.

Beginning with the name of *Pangaea*, and the first of two relatively lengthy quotes from the same source, Godwin provides the following description of the term's emergence into credibility during the early twentieth century, with the idea of 'continental drift' as expounded by Alfred Wegener:

> When Alfred Wegener (1880–1930) proposed the theory of Continental Drift in 1915, he was regarded as something of a crank, especially by American geologists. Wegener conceived of the continents as plates floating on the softer body of the earth, rather like pieces of shell on a hard-boiled egg . . . Wegener's ideas were so out of line with contemporary geological theory that he was long dismissed . . . Thirty years after his death on an expedition in Greenland, the accepted wisdom had

changed, and the earth was again considered fluid enough, beneath its crust, for Wegener's ideas to be reconsidered. Today every student of geology is familiar with plate tectonics and with the map of 'Pangaea', the primordial continent into which all the present ones are ingeniously fitted in jigsaw fashion, its shores washed by the waves of 'Panthalassa', the one primordial ocean. Later the land masses are believed to have fragmented, first into super-continents with names like Gondwana and Laurentia, then eventually into the six or seven continents of today.[8] (Godwin 1996: 216)

'Pangaea' was therefore initially held by geologists to be a term without much credibility, but by the 1960s, geologists had accepted the theory of the primordial continent and indeed, if one does browse a geology textbook nowadays one will find myriad references to the land of Pangaea.

The Miles Davis concert which would inherit the same name is believed by some commentators to embody certain traits indicated by the concept of continental drift. Toop, by way of Godwin, claims the following:

The music on *Pangaea* is divided, probably as an afterthought reflecting Davis's preoccupations of the time, into two titles: 'Zimbabwe' and 'Gondwana'. So in his mind this music was inspired by lost civilizations, united land masses, utopias of the mythical future and, as Kevin White-head suggests, continental drift. (Toop 1995: 100)

Toop's claims here – as elsewhere in his book – are quite subjective and without solid foundation, an aspect of the book that Toop himself would likely not apologise for, given its personal and oftentimes anecdotal orientation. We might turn to Kevin Whitehead, the person cited by Toop, and his own account of the concert:

As the titles here imply, Miles is mindful of the big picture. The site of the South African nation of Zimbabwe (still white-ruled Rhodesia when this music was recorded) was a nexus of African civilization before the year 1000. The names 'Pangaea' and 'Gondwana' take you a lot further than that – they have to do with continental drift. Some five hundred million years ago, Gondwana was the original super-continent, which eventually split up into Africa, South America, India, Australia and Antarctica. More recently – a mere three hundred million years ago or so – Gondwana rammed up against another super-continent to form Pangaea which contained all of the world's land mass, the future North America and Europe included. Then Gondwana broke off again before seismic uphea-vals split into the smaller continents that exist today.[9]

On the face of it, Whitehead's account is more politically prescient than Toop's, observing as it does the parallels between the titles of the two huge monolithic tracks into which the concert divides – Zimbabwe and Gondwana – and their supposed geological origins, with the latter incorporating the former in the clash with 'the future North America and Europe' with the eventual breaking off of Gondwana.

Potentially then, we have an allegory of the clash during the early 1970s between Africa and African America, and the dominant ideology of (white) North America and Western Europe. Whitehead's observations are both intriguing and revealing with regard to the music and politics of Miles Davis, but one must remember that the music in question is *instrumental* music, and furthermore, music that defies the canonical conventions of (Western) musicological analysis, so to discern the political force of the music one must consider how it implies materiality.

To cite Whitehead again, Those titles are clues to the way the music works: these performances draw on a dizzying array of cultures, and are constructed with massive slabs of sound. The shifts in the rhythmic foundation are seismic.'[10]

It is indeed the case that the music works with huge washes of processed sound alongside its polyrhythmic complexity, underpinned by the dense, heavy motor-force of the rhythm section, and the unrehearsed, heavily improvised nature of the music all combining to provide the most pliable structural support, a complex musical temporality transforming the more heavily structured, metred, harmonically and melodically-oriented music of both Western European and North American popular and classical musical idioms. Spatially, the music oscillates between extremely dense and utterly sparse deployments of the auditory field, continuing to embody the spatial economy of Davis's earlier music but pushing it to new extremes.

The task therefore cannot and should not be to penetrate the elusive mind of Miles Davis, or to provide a definitive interpretation of his music, but rather to situate this proper name in relation to those others under consideration here in more Deleuzian and Deleuze-Guattarian terms, which might enable us to bring the esoteric and ethereal preoccupations of the likes of Godwin, Toop and Whitehead down to earth.

On Semiotic and Musical Matters: The Spinozism of Deleuze and Guattari

In '10,000 BC: The Geology of Morals (Who Does the Earth Think It Is?)',[11] Deleuze and Guattari appeal to the language of geology to develop a complex and dense materialist account of social and cultural formations. The date, as with all of the plateaus making up *A Thousand*

Plateaus, marks a profound instance of 'deterritorialization', a term whose function will shortly become clearer. The plateau begins with a reference to Professor Challenger, a fictional figure lifted from the science fiction writings of Sir Arthur Conan Doyle, whose short story 'The Day the World Screamed' describes Challenger's megalomaniacal project of penetrating the core of the Earth (it is perhaps no coincidence then that Conan Doyle was himself connected – albeit posthumously – with the early twentieth-century spiritualist *Polaires*, a movement with allegiances to the Agharta myth, to which we shall return (Godwin 1996: 90).

Deleuze and Guattari begin their plateau as follows:

> The same Professor Challenger who made the Earth scream with his pain machine, as described by Arthur Conan Doyle, gave a lecture after mixing several textbooks on geology and biology in a fashion befitting his simian disposition. He explained that the Earth – the Deterritorialized, the Glacial, the giant Molecule – is a body without organs. This body without organs is permeated by unformed, unstable matters, by flows in all directions. (Deleuze and Guattari 1987: 40)

To the uninitiated, Deleuze and Guattari might seem themselves to be dabbling in esoteric rituals with their combination of science fiction, geology and biology, and their references to 'bodies without organs' and the 'giant Molecule'. Such apparent disregard for disciplinary integrity is often the thing that divides their detractors from their advocates. What is ultimately at stake here is an attempt to produce a thoroughgoing materialist approach to cultural-historical formations which situates their development very firmly in the movements of matter itself. This aim is underpinned by the philosophical effort to remove the vestiges of transcendence from our understanding of how the world functions, and to substitute an immanent, open, process-based account. Deleuze and Guattari maintain that it is possible to explore an array of processes ranging from the formation of organisms and subjects to linguistic and semiotic processes (to which we shall return) without reducing them to transcendent or final causes. Inspired by Nietzsche's *Genealogy of Morality*, as implied in the plateau's subtitle, Deleuze and Guattari resituate the formation of 'morals' within the geological time of the Earth and what combines the various processes marking this temporality are two connected tendencies: stratification and destratificaton:

> Challenger quoted a sentence he said he came across in a geology text-book. He said we need to learn it by heart because we would only be in a position to understand it later on: 'A surface of stratification is a more

compact plane of consistency lying between two layers'. The layers are the strata. (Deleuze and Guattari 1987: 40)

Deriving the method from the geological technique of stratigraphy, or the visual observation and analysis of changes inscribed in the layers of the Earth's crust over vastly extended periods of time, Deleuze and Guattari suggest that we can view the movements of the Earth according to the way in which an unformed 'plane of consistency' either coalesces into strata or tends towards drift, or fluidity, marked by the 'body without organs'. Here is a characteristic disciplinary sleight of hand by Deleuze and Guattari as they combine geology with Antonin Artaud's performance piece, 'To Have Done with the Judgment of God', linking these via the common idea of fluid, dynamic modes of self-organisation deemed to affect both human bodies and the body of the Earth). 'The organism is . . . the judgment of God . . . The organism is not at all the body, the BwO; rather, it is a stratum on the BwO, in other words, a phenomenon of accumulation, coagulation, and sedimentation . . .' (Deleuze and Guattari 1987: 159).

However, it is not just the movements of the Earth that they suggest we can view in this way. Arguing through and beyond geology they claim that '[S]ubstances are nothing other than formed matters . . . Substances as formed matters refer to territorialities and degrees of territorialization and deterritorialization' (Deleuze and Guattari 1987: 40).

By abstracting from the geological to speak of substance more generally, Deleuze and Guattari open up the *processual* dimension of geology to embrace many other formations and deformations that we might seek to analyse, as characterised by Challenger's pedagogic whimsicality: 'He skipped over the immense diversity of the energetic, physico-chemical, and geological strata. He went straight to the organic strata, or the existence of a great organic stratification' (Deleuze and Guattari 1987: 40).

Are Deleuze and Guattari committing their own more serious version of pedagogic whimsicality in making Challenger the spokesperson for their philosophical ideas? Manuel DeLanda's account of Deleuze and Guattari's appeal to geology provides one of the most pragmatic and accessible descriptions of how they use the ideas derived from this discipline to produce a 'diagram' of different structure-generating processes: 'These common processes cannot be fully captured through linguistic representations alone; we need to employ something along the lines of *engineering diagrams* to specify them (DeLanda 1997: 58).

DeLanda here emphasises the limitations of 'linguistic representations' and in so doing reiterates the point made with regard to an interpretation of the music and myth of Miles Davis. The alternative he posits is the use of diagrams to map processes without forever fixing them as impermeable structures, but rather producing a kind of 'motion-capture' which explores the very machinations of these processes as they occur in the rifts of material interactions, agglomerations, and liquefactions.[12] To quote DeLanda once again:

> I wish to argue here that there are also abstract machines (as Deleuze and Guattari call these engineering diagrams) behind the *structure-generating processes* that yield as historical products specific meshworks and hierarchies. Particularly instructive among hierarchical structures are social strata (classes, castes). The term 'social stratum' is itself clearly a metaphor, involving the idea that, just as geological strata are layers of rocky materials stacked on top of each other, so classes and castes are layers . . . of human materials. (DeLanda 1997: 59)

He then asks the following question: 'Is it possible to go beyond metaphor and show that the genesis of both geological and social strata involves the same engineering diagram?' (DeLanda 1997: 59). Ultimately, for DeLanda, Deleuze and Guattari, the answer is yes. Rather than stay with DeLanda's account, let us return to that of Deleuze and Guattari, and their idea of the 'machinic assemblage'.

They argue that the relationship between the tendencies towards relative fixity or stasis, in the movement towards stratification and the movement towards more fluidity or de-stratification are negotiated by 'machinic assemblages'. They don't give much in the way of a description of these machinic assemblages here, but do elaborate in more detail elsewhere in *A Thousand Plateaus*, as we shall see later. We might provide a brief description of these assemblages as combinations of bodies in the loosest sense: organic, human and/or non-human, technological bodies in various admixtures whose variation itself changes according to which process is being analysed (geological, linguistic, organic). The combination of these bodies is more or less restricted in the ways in which their interactions occur. In the case of more restricted combinations we describe the process as one of stratification, and in less restricted ones, destratification. Where there are organic instances, such as human bodies, we might describe their de-stratification as a movement towards the body without organs, a literal dis-organisation of the body facilitated by exploring its connections to non-human bodies rather than treating it as a self-contained, pre-ordained entity.

In the case of Miles Davis's *Pangaea* it is possible to view the use of technical machines (which, on this account of 'machines' would include more 'conventional' instruments as well) – to quote Kodwo Eshun – as so many 'acoustic prosthetics' or 'sonic de-stratifiers'; and the combinations of trumpet, microphone, wah-wah pedal, Synthi, echoplex, and so on, along with the expanded rhythm section, open up a wider set of connections, enabling the production of effects and sounds that hitherto had not existed or been possible. The combinations therefore tend towards a process of destratification, a deterritorialisation of the territorial relationships pertaining to the human components: band members, audiences and listeners, in directly proportional relation to the proliferation of new technological devices, or the non-human bodies of keyboards, synthesisers, and so on. One might also consider the recording equipment used by Teo Macero to manipulate the recordings of this period, making his own contributions to the processual transformation of the concert material, keeping the whole thing relatively fluid, non-linear and spatio-temporally indeterminate. To this list we might also add the records, tapes, sleeves (which are actually very interesting and replete with analytic potential in their own right, but for which there is sadly insufficient space available here), stereos, loudspeakers, and so on.

So if the task of ethics and politics is, as Deleuze and Guattari state, to 'gently tip the assemblage' towards the 'plane of consistency' (Deleuze and Guattari 1987: 161), it would seem that this is how we could provide an account of the ethical and political force of the music of electric Miles Davis without having to revert to exclusively linguistic representation, or to the diagnosis of intention. *Pangaea*, and its sonorous blocks, shift in relation to one another in ways that de-stratify musical conventions – harmonic, melodic, rhythmic, textural – and open up new ways of connecting bodies together. The name 'Pangaea' marks the destratification of the organic level of the human, making for a more intense listening experience. Of course not everybody likes this music, and even those who do might not readily position themselves in such a relation to the music, but there is no denying the proliferation of styles – musical and more generally cultural – that the electric music of Miles Davis profoundly influenced, for example the urban culture of hiphop and – in Britain – jungle and drum'n'bass, which found an astonishing precursor in Davis's 1974 *Dark Magus* concert recording, its innovative use of drumming to create a precursor to the 'breakbeat'. To destratify then, is perhaps to accede to the ethical in the Spinozist sense of bodies increasing their capacity to act. We might then read both *Anti-Oedipus* and *A Thousand Plateaus* as ethical in the Spinozist sense, because they both seek to produce 'common notions', thus also potentially contesting the role of Nietzsche as the philosophical *Ur*-figure of the former work. That said,

Nietzsche, or at least *Deleuze's* Nietzsche (on this score, Badiou is on more solid ground), does provide us with a means of thinking how we might interpret the instrumental works in question, if interpret we must. 'A phenomenon is not an appearance or even an apparition but a sign, a symptom which finds its meaning in an existing force' (Deleuze 1983: 3).

This quote from *Nietzsche and Philosophy* is taken up by Brian Massumi in what remains to this day one of the most pragmatic descriptions of materialist semiotics:

> Take wood. A woodworker who sets out to make a table does not pick just any piece of wood. She chooses the right piece for the application. When she works it, she does not indiscriminately plough it with a plane. She is conscious of the grain and is directed by it. She reads it and interprets it. (Massumi 1992: 10)

This is the beginning of Massumi's embodied account of Deleuze and Guattari's adapted version of the 'glossematics' of the Danish linguist Louis Hjelmslev. the work of the latter is key to the semiotic dimension of *A Thousand Plateaus* which underpins 'The Geology of Morals' via the idea of 'double articulation' (Deleuze and Guattari 1987: 45) and which Massumi's rendering illustrates well. The difference between the Hjelmslevian glossematics as used by Deleuze and Guattari and the more established linguistics and semiotics of the Saussurean sign is essentially a difference based on a particular materialist approach to the sign founded on a complex interplay of matter, substance, content and expression. Returning to the woodworker example:

> What she reads are signs. Signs are qualities (color, texture, durability, and so on). And qualities are much more than simply logical properties or sense perceptions. They envelop a potential – the capacity to be affected, or to submit to a force (the action of the plane; later, the pressure of salt shakers and discourteous elbows), and the capacity to affect, or to release a force (resistance to gravity; or in a nontable application, releasing heat when burned). (Massumi 1992: 10)

The reference to 'salt shakers and discourteous elbows' anticipates the process of transformation whereby the wood of the woodworker crosses a threshold, from the wood of the tree as the 'content' of the woodworker's expressive 'interpretation'. 'Expression' here is not to be taken in any sense, but in the strict sense of the formation of material 'substance' into more-or-less stable aggregates. Such a formation in this case yields crafted pieces of wood which can then be used to construct an 'object', such as a table, and in doing so the 'expression' of the woodworker's plane – at the level of substance, that is, the material aggregate that is the tree from which it was taken – transforms the substance according to a new function: the 'resistance to gravity', or the ability to support objects such as salt-shakers. Hereby, the interpretation of the wood that was previously an expression of its material and substantial content has itself become the content of another, *social* form of expression. 'His [the woodworker's, and the shift in gender position is here to be read strategically] interpretation is a creation, not just of a physical object, but of a use-value, a cultural object, a table for steak and potatoes' (Massumi 1992: 11). As a result, '[T]he distinction between content and expression is not only functional, it is relative and reversible' (Massumi 1992: 12). This reversibility of relation between forms of content and of expression is Guattari's innovation, and it is ultimately what latently or implicitly distinguishes the Hjelmslevian approach to semiotics from that of Saussure. As such, it is also what makes a more material approach, and moreover, one that is capable of *diagramming process.*

There is another very important aspect to Massumi's embodiment of Hjelmslev's glossematics, and it is the reference to 'the capacity to be affected . . . and to affect', and here one can locate the fundamental role of Spinoza in Deleuze and Guattari's work. In taking up the Spinozist concept of the 'common notion', Deleuze shows very clearly that the whole approach to philosophy such as the one elaborated in 'The Geology of Morals', the eliding of diverse disciplines, is entirely bound up with the endeavour to establish common notions:

> The common notions . . . are so named not because they are common to all minds, but primarily because they represent something common to bodies, either to all bodies (extension, motion and rest) or to some bodies (at least two, mine and another). (Deleuze 1988: 54)

To seek what connects such seemingly different and unconnected ideas as the material make-up of Earth, language and semiotics, is effectively to produce 'common notions', and – following Spinoza – the production of such ideas has parallel effects on the (human) body. As such, to engage in this kind of thought, from a Spinozist perspective, is also to increase a body's capacity to affect and be affected, to change the relations of motion and rest that connect different bodies together in the very process of thinking such relations *qua process itself.*

This is how one might more clearly understand 'The Geology of Morals' and more generally the philosophical approach of Deleuze and Guattari from an *ethical* perspective, as the production of an ethical ontology or 'ethology'. The univocity of Spinoza's thought – whether or not it connects to multiplicity – implies such an ethical orientation, which is arguably what makes Spinoza a more important precursor to Deleuze and Guattari than either Nietzsche or – as Badiou argues – Bergson. Where it concerns the present case, the very materiality of music and sound and their direct manipulation on *Pangaea*, explores the relations between musical bodies – their extension, motion and rest – and the geological associations implied in the name 'Pangaea' both emphasise this, but also emphasise the role played by drift, or by *process qua process*. It is perhaps this that connects the various bodies composing the assemblage – via the common notion of material drift – that lends the music an ethical potential whereby the subjectivities of those human bodies connected as part of the assemblage are in a position to increase their capacity to affect and be affected. To the extent that electronically processed instrumental music of this kind can be read or interpreted it is through the adapted use of Hjelmslev elaborated by Deleuze and Guattari that this may best be achieved, whereby the strata occupied by the music, musicians, instruments, listeners, and so on, are doubly articulated through the play of content and expression – 'Content and expression are two variables of a function of stratification' (Deleuze and Guattari 1987: 44) – and it is through the extensions and expansions: technological, cultural and musical that the variables are set in motion. All of this may amount at one and the same time to a material 'interpretation' of *Pangaea*, whereby the music expresses its material and substantial content and these expressions themselves form the content of more social and political forms of expression.

Nevertheless, there remains the question of exactly how we might deem the music political from a more specifically Deleuzian or Deleuze-Guattarian perspective. In order to deal with this aspect, we must skip to another plateau, '1837: Of the Refrain'. Proceeding according to the aim outlined in the introduction, it is only fitting that we do so by recourse to the case, which takes us back a few hours in time to the first concert of the day, released on record as *Agharta*.

Afternoon, 1 February 1975:
Agharta and the Cosmic Refrain

As promised, we shall proceed via another lengthy quote from Godwin, only this time we shall briefly reference his account of the Agharta myth, in particular the work of Saint-Yves d'Alveydre, the nineteenth-century Christian 'hermeticist' and his description of the 'subterranean city':

Thousands, even millions of students have never penetrated beyond the first suburban circles; few succeed in mounting the steps of this formidable Jacob's ladder which lead through initiatic trials and examinations to the central cupola.

The latter, a work of magical architecture like all of Agarttha [sic], is lit from above with reflecting panels that only allow the light to enter after it has passed through the entire enharmonic scale of colors, in comparison to which the solar spectrum of our physics treatises is merely the diatonic scale.

[Agharta] appears iridized like a view from beyond the Earth, confounding the celestial forms and bodily appearances of the two worlds, and drowning in celestial radiances all the visible distinctions between race in a single chromatic of light and sound, singularly removed from the usual notions of perspective and acoustics. (Godwin 1996: 85)

Here one is given a very clear sense of the highly disturbing character of such esoteric ideas as expounded by Saint-Yves, and as Godwin demonstrates, these ideas did not need much in the way of propagandist revisionism to turn them towards the Aryan aims of National Socialism. Hence it seems strange that Miles Davis, in the immediate aftermath of the seismic upheavals affecting the United States from the late 1960s, both domestically and internationally, would revert to such an ostensibly reactionary or even dangerous set of associations. One possible key might be the idea of a post-tonal, non-diatonic form of auditory perception, which Davis was certainly promoting during these concert recordings from 1975. Also, the idea of the 'hidden land' or 'subterranean city' does itself have a rich history in African-American music and its accompanying mythical associations. For examples of this, one might consider the prolific musical and mythico-poietic output of Sun Ra and his various 'arkestras', indebted as it was to nineteenth-century ideas of 'solar' myth; or else, the more recent examples of Cybotron's 'Techno City', which as Simon Reynolds explains was:

inspired by Fritz Lang's vision in *Metropolis* of a future megalopolis divided into privileged sectors high up in the sky and subterranean prole zones. According to [Rick] Davis, Techno City was equivalent to Detroit's Woodward Avenue ghetto; the dream of its denizens to work their way up to the cybodome, where the artist and intellectuals lived. (Reynolds 1995: 10)

This latter example points at once to the utopic/dystopic ambivalence of new technology, beholden to techno music outfits such as Cybotron, and to the idea of the subterranean city (although here, unlike Agharta, the enlightened city is above rather than below the Earth). One final instance of such an assemblage is that of DJ Spooky the Subliminal Kid, who – according to a recent book by Patricia Pisters – calls himself 'a spatial engineer of the invisible city: "Gimme two records and I'll make you a universe",[13] he says in an interview' (Pisters 2003: 210).[14]

One has to imagine that a positive political deployment of this myth is based less on the idea of effacing the distinctions between races (certainly given the ostensible militancy of Miles Davis's group on these recordings within the more general climate of radical black politics in the late 1960s and early 1970s), and more on the ways in which the music, the sound and the mythological associations of Agharta coincide in terms of the production, performance and reception of the music. It is here that the role of colour and the difficult relationship between the visual and the sonorous is brought to the fore, the 'single chromatic of light and sound, singularly removed from the usual notions of perspective and acoustics' (Godwin 1996: 85).

This relationship is explored in part in 'Of the Refrain' along the following lines:

> Color clings more, not necessarily to the object, but to territoriality. When it deterritorializes, it tends to dissolve, to let itself be steered by other components. This is evident in the phenomena of synesthesia, which are not reducible to a simple color-sound correspondence; sounds have a piloting role and induce colors that are superposed upon the colors we see, lending them a properly sonorous rhythm and movement. (Deleuze and Guattari 1987: 348)[15]

The Cosmic Refrain

In '1833: Of the Refrain', Deleuze and Guattari return, as they do at numerous junctures, to some of the key terms that we encountered earlier from 'The Geology of Morals': territory, deterritorialisation, and assemblage. As is characteristic of the book one has to skip between plateaus in order to draw out the wider connections and implications between these terms. In this plateau, the emphasis is more on territory and deterritorialisation than on strata and destratification. The terms are not equivalent, but they do overlap. The inscription of the Earth's surface is initially what is at stake here, rather than the stratigraphic divisions lying beneath the surface. By recourse to a number of other disciplines, in particular ethology, musicology and literature, they provide a very rich and detailed account of how one might conceive the relationship between bodies and their environments. Amongst the examples they give is the child who sings in the dark to ward off the threat of chaos, whose singing, through an interplay of rhythm and movement takes various milieu components (the space of a room, the walls that delineate its boundaries, its voice) and combines these to stake out a territory that allows it to retain a relationship to itself and its environment:

I. A child in the dark, gripped with fear, comforts himself by singing under his breath. He walks and halts to his song. Lost, he takes shelter, or orients himself with his little song as best he can. The song is like a rough sketch of a calming and stabilizing, calm and stable, center in the heart of chaos . . . Now we are at home. But home does not pre-exist: it was necessary to draw a circle around that uncertain and fragile center, to organize a limited space. Many, very diverse components have a part in this, landmarks and marks of all kinds. This was already true of the previous case. But now the components are used for organizing a space . . . (Deleuze and Guattari 1987: 311)

Returning briefly to the problematic of colour introduced briefly before, it is worth noting that the primary illustration of the milieu-territory-refrain relation in 'Of the Refrain' is an ethological one, at once ethological in the sense outlined earlier of an ontological ethics, and in terms of the discipline of ethology as developed in the work of Konrad Lorenz and Irenäus Eibl-Eiblsfeldt, among others:

What defines territory is the emergence of matters of expression (qualities). Take the example of color in birds or fish: color is a membrane state associated with interior hormonal states . . . It becomes expressive . . . when it acquires a temporal constancy and a spatial range that make it a territorial, or rather territorializing, mark: a signature . . .' (Deleuze and Guattari 1987: 315)

Here one finds the idea of colour as a matter formed into expression that in the case of certain animal species constitutes a 'block of space-time', where milieu components such as colour and/or sound (for example, in the behaviour of certain bird species) constitute a territory.[16] The 'signature', or the proper name, hereby marks a movement of territorialisation rather than deterritorialisation.

Inevitably, the milieu components and the territory marked across them are insufficient, as one always has to move beyond that immediate space, opening up to different roles and functions. This marks a movement towards 'the World' a moment of uncertainty and improvisation where the territory opens itself up to a potential deterritorialisation which can increase the level of connection between bodies.

III. Finally, one opens the circle a crack, opens it all the way, lets someone in, calls someone, or else goes out oneself, launches forth . . . hazards an improvisation. But to improvise is to join with the World, or meld with it. One ventures home on the thread of a tune. (Deleuze and Guattari 1987: 311)

The consolidation of milieu components, the marking of a territory and the movement towards 'the World' collectively constitute the 'refrain', an idea taken from music to describe a moment or a motif that returns in a piece of music. The refrain here, as with the strata, stratification and destratification of the earlier plateau are raised to a higher power by being taken beyond the confines of their founding discipline to describe a wider array of interactions. Hence it is possible to talk about a child singing in the dark as being a refrain, not simply in terms of the content of his song, but the very way in which the song functions in its territorialisation of the child and its environment. Deleuze and Guattari analyse the function of the refrain from a more properly musical perspective throughout the course of the plateau by delineating different refrains in the history of Western classical music, although there is insufficient space here to go into any detail. There is only scope to focus on the last stage, which is the one most relevant to the case in question. The most recent moment in this tradition, the 'Modern' moment, primarily concerns the music of the twentieth century, and as such remains the problem of more recent examples from within this tradition. One might cite, as Deleuze and Guattari do themselves, the work of the composer Edgard Varèse, and his method of sound 'ionisation':[17]

> Varèse's procedure, at the dawn of this age, is exemplary: a musical machine of consistency, a sound machine (not a machine for reproducing sounds), which molecularizes and atomizes, ionizes sound matter, and harnesses a cosmic energy. (Deleuze and Guattari 1987: 343)

The problem of this particular stage in the development of music is how maximally to deterritorialise the refrain, which is to say that it is a case of moving away from territorial relationships and individual assemblages of bodies (sonorous and musical *but also* organic, or human) towards what they describe as the 'cosmic', a freeing up of sound at the very level of its material constitution. In so doing, successful examples of music from this 'Modern' moment harness the very forces that make up the cosmos, the elementary combination of matter and force that goes into each territorial inscription and each assemblage of bodies.

Deleuze and Guattari state that each moment in the development of Western European music is marked by a particular relationship to social modes of organisation and interaction, and this is constituted by a relationship to a 'people', yet it is not an already-existing people so much as one that is 'missing'. Correlative to a cosmicisation of the world by liberating it from a fixed relationship to territories or limited deterritorialisations towards much more extensive or even 'absolute' deterritorialisations, at the level of the Earth, is a 'depopulation of the people' that opens up the possibility for new, and eminently more mobile subjectivities to develop:

> Instead of being bombarded from all sides by a limiting cosmos, the people and the earth must be like the vectors of a cosmos that carries them off; then the cosmos itself will be art. From depopulation make a cosmic people; from deterritorialization, a cosmic earth – that is the wish of the artisan-artist . . . (Deleuze and Guattari 1987: 346)

Miles Davis can be seen as an 'artisan-artist' who taps into the flows of matter (consider the inclusion on these recordings of a water drum),[18] and if this is the case then it becomes much clearer what the value of his preoccupation with mythology might be: the relationship between sound, music and a 'people' characterising the *Agharta* myth.[19]

Conclusion: Some Minor Observations

The names of Agharta and Pangaea hereby take on a deterritorialising function, rather than a territorialising one, marking a 'collective assemblage of enunciation' that exists alongside the machinic assemblage of bodies, whereby the names take on a political force. Of course, when one is dealing with instrumental music, what is enunciated is not strictly speaking linguistic. This applies in the case of Agharta and Pangaea, but also Miles Davis, and also Teo Macero. The proper name would then come to mark a deterritorialising function such as the one Deleuze and Guattari attribute to the work of Franz Kafka, such that the relations of movement and rest affecting the strata (social, political, economic, cultural) mark shifts in intensity (Deleuze and Guattari 1986: 88).

In conclusion, we might add to the strategic, diagrammatic and enunciative roles of the names Agharta, Pangaea and Miles Davis the function of 'fabulation' as being quintessentially political, and this returns us to the question of why electric Miles Davis proves a worthwhile 'mediator', both for Deleuze and Guattari's own concepts, but also for their philosophical approach to the relationship between art and politics.

> When a people is created, it's through its own resources, but in a way that links up with something in art . . . Utopia isn't the right concept: it's more

a question of 'fabulation' in which people and art both share. We ought to take up Bergson's notion of fabulation and give it a political meaning. (Daniel W. Smith, in Deleuze 1998: 174)

And what might this task amount to? 'A mythmaking or fabulating function that brings *real* parties together to produce collective utterances or speech acts as the germ of a people to come.'

References

Badiou, A. (2000), *Deleuze: The Clamor of Being*, trans. L. Burchill, Minneapolis: University of Minnesota Press.

Bogue, R. (2003), *Deleuze on Music, Painting and the Arts*, New York and London: Routledge.

Caygill, H. (1998), *Walter Benjamin: The Colour of Experience*, New York and London: Routledge.

DeLanda, M. (1997), *A Thousand Years of Non-Linear History*, New York: Zone Books.

Deleuze, G. (1983), *Nietzsche and Philosophy*, trans. H. Tomlinson, London: Athlone Press.

Deleuze, G. (1986), *Cinema 1: The Movement-Image*, trans. H. Tomlinson and B. Habberjam, London: Athlone.

Deleuze, G. (1990), *Expressionism in Philosophy: Spinoza*, trans. M. Joughin, New York: Zone Books.

Deleuze, G. (1989), *Cinema 2: The Time-Image*, trans. H. Tomlinson and R. Galeta, London: Athlone.

Deleuze, G. (1988), *Spinoza: Practical Philosophy*, trans. R. Hurley, New York: City Lights.

Deleuze, G. (1993), *The Fold: Leibniz and the Baroque*, trans. T. Conley, New York: Columbia University Press.

Deleuze, G. (1995), *Negotiations 1972–1990*, trans. M. Joughin, New York: Columbia University Press.

Deleuze, G. (1998), *Essays Critical and Clinical*, trans. D. W. Smith and M. A. Greco, London: Verso.

Deleuze, G. and Guattari, F. (1986), *Kafka: Towards a Minor Literature*, trans. D. Polan, Minneapolis: University of Minnesota Press.

Deleuze, G. and Guattari, F. (1987), *A Thousand Plateaus*, trans. B. Massumi, Minneapolis: University of Minnesota Press.

Deleuze, G. and Guattari, F (1994), *What is Philosophy?*, trans. G. Burchell and H. Tomlinson, New York and London: Verso.

Eshun, K. (1998), *More Brilliant than the Sun: Adventures in Sonic Fiction*, London: Quartet Books.

Genosko, G. (1998), *Undisciplined Theory*, London: Sage.

Godwin, J. (1996), *Arktos: The Polar Myth in Science, Symbolism and Nazi Survival*, Gardena, CA: Scb Distributors.

Guattari, F. (1995), *Chaosmosis: An Ethico-Aesthetic Paradigm*, trans. P. Bains and J. Pefanis, Sydney: Power Press.

Massumi, B. (1992), *A User's Guide to Capitalism and Schizophrenia*, New York: Zone Books.

Nietzsche, F. (1993), *On the Genealogy of Morality and Other Texts*, Cambridge: Cambridge University Press.

Pisters, P. (2003), *The Matrix of Visual Culture: Working with Deleuze in Film Theory*, Palo-Alto: Stanford University Press.

Reynolds, S. (1995), *Energy Flash: Journey through Rave Music and Dance Culture*, London: Picador.

Tingen, P. (2001), *Miles Beyond: The Electric Experiments of Miles Davis*, New York: Billboard Books.

Toop, D. (1995), *Ocean of Sound: Aether-Talk, Ambient Sound and Imaginary Worlds*, London: Serpent's Tail.

Discography

Davis, M. (1993), *Pangaea*, Columbia.

Davis, M. (1994), *Agharta*, Columbia.

Davis, M. (1997), *Dark Magus*, Columbia.

Davis, M. (1998), *Miles in the Sky*, Columbia.

Davis, M. (1998), *Panthalassa: The Music of Miles Davis 1969–74*, 'mix translation' by B. Laswell, Columbia.

Davis, M. (1998), *The Complete Bitches' Brew Sessions*, Columbia.

Davis, M. (2001), *The Complete In A Silent Way Sessions*, Columbia.

Notes

1. Printed in the sleevenotes to Miles Davis, *The Complete In a Silent Way Sessions* (Columbia, 2001).
2. The term 'plateau' is used instead of 'chapter' after Gregory Bateson's use of the term in his own work on Balinese culture, where the orientation is toward sustained or prolonged instances of intensity rather than instantaneous expenditures of energy ending in satiation or resolution (Deleuze and Guattari 1987: 158).
3. The idea of 'folding' as it is used here is derived from that of Leibniz, in his late work on the philosopher (Deleuze 1993).
4. Commentators generally agree that this period encompasses the years 1967 to 1975 and it has been argued, though not unequivocally, that this period continued after his five-year 'silence' between 1975 and 1980 up until his death in 1991 (Tingen 2001: 8).
5. On the idea of 'mediators', see Deleuze 1995: 125.
6. For the role of the sitar in the recording of *Bitches Brew*, see *The Complete Bitches' Brew Sessions* (1998).
7. The 'wah-wah' pedal creates a nasal sound which in some ways replicates the sound of the human voice, a phenomenon not without its relevance in thinking of the 'voice' of Miles Davis and its transmutations but also of the machinic status of musical instruments and their technological extensions.
8. It is interesting to note that the now-established science of geology is connected to the ideas of nineteenth- and early twentieth-century esoteric ideas, a fact that will take on further significance by the end of the chapter. Furthermore, the name of 'Panthalassa' was taken up in more recent times in a 'mix translation' of Miles Davis's electric period by the contemporary producer, composer and bassist, Bill Laswell (*Panthalassa: The Music of Miles Davis 1969–74*, 1998).
9. Printed in the sleevenotes to *Pangaea* (1975).
10. Ibid.
11. It is worth mentioning here that the fact that each of the 'plateaus' has a date serves to indicate that they all mark a moment of intense deterritorialisation,

where a major shift – geological, cultural, economic, social, or artistic – has taken place, or else a combination of these. One might endeavour to think of the date and times of Miles Davis's two concerts in Osaka as potentially marking such an intensive transformation.

12. cf. Eshun 1998: 166.
13. See Note 18 below.
14. For Spinoza, the city is a space that – in principle – is suited to the pursuit of 'reason' which for Spinoza is bound up with the affirmation of one's being as part of a 'multitude'; 'Thus Spinoza describes the City as a collective person with common body and soul, "a multitude which is guided, as it were, by one mind". That the process of its formation is very different from that of reason, that it is prerational, does not prevent the City from imitating and preparing the way for reason' (Deleuze 1990: 266).
15 Whilst Deleuze and Guattari do provide a useful inroad into the much-needed philosophical reconsideration of the relationship between musical or auditory and pictorial or visual conceptions of colour, there remains a lot of work to be done in this area. A very valuable source for commencing such a reconsideration is the early work of Walter Benjamin, as brought to light by Howard Caygill (Caygill 1998: Chapter 1 and throughout).
16 For a more detailed account of the role of animals in the refrain, see Genosko 1998: Chapter 3. See also Bogue 2003: Chapter 1, and Chapter 5 of this volume.
17 Once again it is perhaps no coincidence that Miles Davis's producer Teo Macero was a former pupil of Varèse and whose cut-and-paste techniques owe much to the early tape experiments of the French composer.
18 In discussing the concept of the matter-flow or 'phylum' in direct relation to music, Guattari very interestingly elaborates his own approach based on the much-undervalued idea of the 'incorporeal universe of reference', his name for the semiotic dimension that accompanies territories. The myths of Agharta and Pangaea might in this instance be viewed themselves as such universes of reference; see Guattari 1995: 48–9.
19 Again, perhaps the two most detailed accounts to date of this entire aspect of Deleuze and Guattari's work are Genosko (1997) and Bogue (2003).

Notes on Contributors

Jean-Godefroy Bidima
was born in Mfoumassi (South Cameroon) and studied at the Universities of Yaoundé (Cameroon). He obtained his Ph.D. at the Sorbonne (1991) on the work of the Frankfurt School. His major publications include *Théorie Critique et Modernité Negro-Africaine. De l'Ecole de Francfort à la Docta Spes Africana* (1993, Paris: Publications de la Sorbonne), *La Philosophie Négro-Africaine* (1995, Presses Universitaires de France), *L'art Négro-Africain* (1997, Paris: Presses Universitaires de France) and *La Palabre, une Juridiction de la Parole* (1997, Edition Michalon). He teaches as Directeur de Programme in the Collège International de Philosophie in Paris.

Ronald Bogue
is Professor of Comparative Literature at the University of Georgia. He is the author of *Deleuze and Guattari* (1989, Routledge), *Deleuze on Literature* (2003, Routledge), *Deleuze on Cinema* (2003, Routledge), *Deleuze on Music, Painting, and the Arts* (2003, Routledge), and *Deleuze's Wake* (2004, SUNY Press).

Ian Buchanan
is Professor of Communication and Cultural Studies at Charles Darwin University Australia. He is the author of *Deleuzism: A Metacommentary* (2000, Edinburgh University Press) and *Michel de Certeau: Cultural Theorist* (2000, Sage). He is also the editor of *A Deleuzian Century?* (Duke University Press), *Deleuze and Literature* (Edinburgh University Press) and *Deleuze and Feminism* (Edinburgh University Press).

Jeremy Gilbert
teaches Cultural Studies at the University of East London. He is co-author of *Discographies: Dance Music, Culture and the Politics of Sound* (1999,

Routledge) and co-editor of *Cultural Capitalism: Politics after New Labour* (2001, Lawrence and Wishart).

Greg Hainge
is currently a lecturer in French at the University of Adelaide, Australia. He received his Ph.D. in French Literature and Critical Theory from the University of Nottingham. He is the author of *Capitalism and Schizophrenia in the Later Novels of Louis-Ferdinand Céline: D'un . . . l'Autre* (2001, Peter Lang) and has published numerous articles and chapters on French literature, theory, film, noise and other unrelated subjects.

Drew Hemment
is an AHRB Research Fellow in Creative Technologies at the University of Salford, UK and founder and director of the futuresonic festival of electronic music held annually in Manchester, UK. He is also a freelance writer, curator and producer. He is currently working on a new inter-disciplinary art project, LOCA: Location Oriented Critical Arts, a well as curating the Mobile Connections and Turntable Re:mix programmes at futuresonic, 2004.

Eugene W. Holland
is currently working on books on nomad citizenship and capitalist perversion. He has published extensively on Deleuze in anthologies and journals including the *South Atlantic Quarterly, Strategies* and *Substance*. He teaches in Comparative Studies, and French and Italian at Ohio State University.

Timothy S. Murphy
is the author of *Wising Up the Marks: The Amodern William Burroughs* (1997), General Editor of the journal *Genre: Forms of Discourse and Culture*, and translator of works by Gilles Deleuze and Antonio Negri. He is currently Associate Professor of English at the University of Oklahoma.

Nick Nesbitt
is an assistant professor of French at Miami University, Ohio. He has published articles on Adornian musical aesthetics, jazz, African musical modernity, and postcolonial francophone literature and culture. He is the author of *Voicing Memory: History and Subjectivity in French Caribbean Literature* (2003, University of Virginia Press).

Phil Turetsky
is a lecturer in the Department of Philosophy at Colorado State University. He is the author of the book *Time*, published as part of Routledge's 'Problems of Philosophy' series.

Marcel Swiboda
received his Ph.D. from the University of Leeds in February 2003, where he also spent two years as Co-Editor of the journal *Parallax*. He is currently working as a lecturer in Cultural Studies at the University of Leeds.

Index

Abstract Machine, 3, 14
Actualisation, 151
Adorno, 18n2, 54, 160, 167, 176, 183
Aeon v Chronos, 39, 85
Affect, 39, 63, 77, 104
Allonnes, d', 176–94
Amusicality, 49
Arendt, 191
Artaud, 12
Assemblage, 3, 11, 14, 77, 132–5, 143
  Assemblage Converter, 12
Attali, 26, 127
Axiomatic, 43

Babbitt, 168
Badiou, 5, 62, 192, 197
Baroque, 178
Beethoven, 63, 129, 183
Benjamin, 64
Berg, 61
Bergson, 55, 85, 148, 161
Berio, 168
Björk, 48
Bloch, 187
Body, 7, 72, 140
Body without Organs, 3, 5, 12, 110, 119, 136, 203
Bogue, 121
Boulez, 65, 76, 84, 103, 176
Braudel, 31
Bricolage, 41, 88, 160
Buchanan, 40, 42, 51

Butler, 7

Cage, 77, 80, 162
Cale, 133
Can, 120, 133
Canetti, 26, 128, 140
Capitalism, 30, 51, 125
Chaos, 4, 154, 192
Chopin, 59
Cinema, 76
Cohen-Levinas, 176
Colebrook, 37
Coleman, 133
Coltrane, 68, 133
Concrete Rules, 3
Consistency, 12, 54
Content and Expression, 15, 22
Corbett, 41, 119
Cosmos, 98, 123, 198

Davis, 69, 120, 133, 197
Debussy, 60, 136
De-Composition, 89
DeLanda, 203
Democracy, 190–1
Deterritorialise, 14, 38, 96, 166, 202
Dialectics, 4, 18n4, 54, 189
Difference, 5
Difference Engine, 87
Disco, 125–6
Double Articulation, 6, 16, 143

Eastern Music, 41, 130
Edison Effect, 79

Electronic Music, 76
Ethics, 5, 64, 71, 115, 140, 205
Ethology, 110, 207
Event, 36, 78
Evolution, 12, 23

Face, 14
Freud, 2–3

Glass, 105, 164

Habit, 145
Haecceity, 36, 44, 77, 106, 141
Haka, 140
Haptic, 179
Hegel, 13, 18n8, 55, 189
Hennion, 43
Hjelmslev, 22, 206
Holey Space, 47

Immanence, 4
Improvisation, 118
Incorporeal Transformation, 108
Internal Difference, 54
Itineration, 25, 88

Jazz, 25, 68, 134

Kafka, 10, 76, 101, 213
Kant, 57
Kinecepts, 145
Kleist, 104

Labour, 24, 128
Lacan, 2–3, 14
Leibniz, 1, 161
Ligeti, 168
Line of Flight, 15, 79, 120, 180
Logos, 21
Love, 9, 15
Lyotard, 136, 177

Macero, 205
Mahler, 190
Massumi, 18n2, 207
Memory, 147, 187
Messiaen, 66, 96
Metal Music, 95

Micropolitics, 79
Milieu, 9
Minor Music, 76, 101, 188
Modernism, 68, 71, 79, 121, 212
Multiplicity, 9, 148, 163
Murphy, 40
Music
   and becoming, 16, 36, 96, 178
   concept of, 15, 39, 76, 96
   and death, 15, 101
   and fascism, 17, 66, 111
   and ontology, 36
Musique concrete, 164, 167
Muzack, 28, 50

Negri, 71
Nietzsche, 60, 177, 190, 202
Nomad Science, 23, 112
Nomadism, 20, 112
Nomos, 21
Nono, 66
Non-sonorous, 99

Performance, 79, 149
Pinhas, 170, 177
Plane
   of Composition, 38
   of Consistency, 3, 12
   of Immanence, 37
   of Organisation, 38
Platonism, 37
Polis, 21
Pop Music, 40, 76, 165
Postmodern, 136
Proust, 180
Psychoanalysis, 165

Raga, 129
Rancière, 176, 193
Rebitiko, 182
Refrain, 16–17, 39, 48, 95, 100, 114, 131, 178, 210
Repetition, 20, 87, 140
Reterritorialise, 14, 38, 96, 166
Rhizome, 3, 12, 118, 160
Riemann, 57
Royal Science, 22, 112

Schaeffer, 77, 164
Schoenberg, 58, 162, 187
Schubert, 110
Sensation, 113, 161
Serialism, 66
Singularity, 22
Smith, 40, 214
Smooth and Striated, 25, 47, 112, 163
Sonic Machine, 78
Spinoza, 4–5, 55, 71, 141, 205
Stockhausen, 77, 123
Stratification, 3, 6–12
Synthesiser, 130

Territory, 51, 165
Twelve Tone, 58

Uexküll, von, 10

Utopia, 20, 184

Varèse, 77, 89, 212
Variation, 20, 149
Virtual, 61, 96, 151, 163
Voice, 165, 167

Wagner, 57
War Machine, 112
Webern, 61
Western Music, 39, 96, 101, 121

Xenakis, 185

Young, 119

Žižek, 2–3, 18n2, 18n7
Zouk, 189